Highly Favored

of the Lord

Volume II

Mike Stroud

cimprint@live.com

This book is designed to provide accurate and authoritative information with regard to the subject matter covered.

This is not an official publication of The Church of Jesus Christ of Latter-day Saints.

 Second Edition.
ISBN-13:978-1546336754
ISBN-10:1546336753

DEDICATION

To the Lord Jesus Christ for His grace and loving kindness.

Highly Favored

of the Lord

CONTENTS

	Introduction	3
12	The Comforter	8
13	Unbelief	32
14	Unbelief Revisited	50
15	Priesthood	72
16	Priesthood II	94
17	Devils and Unclean Spirits	116
18	Devils and Unclean Spirits II	135
19	The Spirit of Prophecy and the Spirit of Revelation	164
20	Made Sure	180
21	Neutralized	188
22	The Remnant	207
23	The Terrestrial World	230
24	The Terrestrial World II	254

ACKNOWLEDGMENTS

Thank you to Shelle McDermott for her help in encouraging, organizing, and bringing this all to fruition. Nothing would have happened without her.

Editors
Phillis Ann Postak
Elizabeth Postak

Transcribers
Carol Crisp
Pat Crisp
Robert Briscoe

Introduction

Funeral Sermon was given June 25, 2016, by Mike Stroud

For Fay

Well, I want to talk to Fay for just a minute because she is here. That's one of the gospel truths we know. Those who've departed are allowed to view family and friends for up to few days after the spirit leaves the body. So, Fay, this is for you: "That wasn't that bad, now was it?" [Audience laughs] I say that because I had a chance to be with Fay as she was struggling with this transition. And sometimes she was ok with it, and other times she said, "I'm not going to do this!"

I like Fay's faith. She reminded me of me. She was a **"seeker of truth."** That made people uncomfortable. I've known her for twenty-five years. I've sat in classes with her as a student, and I've sat in classes with her as her teacher, and she made some people uncomfortable because she was always questioning. Some people thought that her questioning was a lack of faith, and I even know people who have accused her of that. They would say of her inquiries, "Just be faithful Fay. It doesn't matter." I always appreciated the fact that she was not satisfied with that, and would push it, and push it, always looking for something more. In 2000, Fay and I had a chance to go to Israel together. I'd been there before, and this time I went as a tour guide, and she was on the tour. Now, the Israeli government requires that there be two tour guides; one an Israeli and another, in our case, an American. So, when we got there, there were several times when the Israeli guide would take over the group, and I would say, "Fay, let's go!" And we would pull away and go look at things that weren't on the agenda. We just had a good ol' time doing that. We were reminiscing about that the other day and she pulled out a photo album and there was a picture of myself and her, looking much younger! [Audience laughs] But it was a great experience, one I've never forgotten and one that I know she cherished. Being able to go to the Holy Land, not because it was with me, but because once she went there and saw things with her own eyes; her personal study and personal understanding of Jesus Christ and His life and ministry were forever-ever changed.

Now, as she was struggling, I want to share with you the last conversations I had with Fay. There was never a time that we didn't meet together, not once, where we didn't discuss doctrine. She wanted to know, and so the scriptures were always handy, and I would ask her, "What have you learned? Share with me what you've learned." And she would share some things, but it would always be accompanied by something like this, "But I have a question about that?" And I think of when the Savior was brought before Pilate, the Roman Procurator, and you can read about this at the end of the gospel of John. He was turned over to Pilate, and Pilate asked Him a question,

> *Art thou the King of the Jews?*

And Jesus answered him,

> *Sayest thou this thing of thyself, or did others tell it thee of me?*

And Pilate yelled out,

> *Am I a Jew? Thine own nation and the chief priest have delivered thee unto me* [to be crucified]*: Art thou a king then?*

And Jesus said,

> *To this end was I born, and for this cause came I into the world, that I should bear witness unto the truth.*

And then Pilate asked this question, and this is the sum and total of it,

> *What is truth?*

And that's a question you and I should ask. That's a question that Fay asked all of the time and sought to find an answer for. **What is truth?**

You are living in a world, my friends, that's filled with half truths; things that the scriptures call *the precepts of men, the philosophies of men mingled with scripture, the traditions of the fathers* that have been passed down and *inherited lies*, and passed them on to their children. The scriptures say this is *the very mainspring of all corruption [in the world] and the earth groans under the weight of its iniquity*. That's a big problem in this world! And it's part of the plan of our Heavenly Father for it to be so! None of what we experience in this life is outside of the plan of God for His children. Nothing! Even the worst experiences are designed to do something for each one of us, to bring us to a higher level, to lift us up. But the question still comes, what is truth? And in the modern scripture, the Lord defined it. He said:

> *And truth is knowledge of things as they are, and as they were, and as they are to come;*

There is such a thing, my friends, as absolute truth; unadulterated, straight from heaven, unchanged, powerful, and filled with light. Fay sought for those things. It is a challenge to find that in this world. And yet, all of us have been given a source of light and truth that never fails, is never deceptive, never altered, never adulterated, and can be relied upon one hundred percent. But, it requires us to exercise choice to tap into that source of perfect, absolute, never-ending truth. And that's through something called the Holy Ghost. The Holy Ghost is a personage, and He's here in this world, and His purpose is to bear testimony of the truth, not mixed with error, not adulterated with *the philosophies of men* and *the traditions of the fathers*. One of the worst things that can happen to us in this life is for us to feel that we are in possession of truth and zealously act after that, only to find out that what we held as truth was adulterated and only partial truth. It's like a friend of mine said, "You spend your whole life putting the ladder against the wall and climbing the ladder only to find out at the end, that the ladder was on the wrong wall." Why do we settle for something less than what Father in Heaven wants us to have? Fay didn't want to do that?

As she was struggling, one of the last conversations we had was her asking, "Why is this happening to me?" I'd say, "Are you in pain?" and she would say, "No." But the fact that she was losing her independence really got to her. Susie told me that when she finally got to a point where she couldn't be mobile anymore, from that point on, things went down quickly. I was amazed at how quickly things went down, and she transitioned from here to there. It was amazing to me and what a great blessing. In talking about these things, she would ask, "What's the purpose of all of this? Why do any of us have to suffer and struggle at this point in transitioning from here to there?" There is a great reason for that. This is a schoolroom—it's a one room schoolhouse. You, young people, don't know what that was, but you older folks do. It was a one-room building where you have all different grades of people attending in the same room. That's what this life is. You have people here that have advantages, and there are people who don't have such great advantages.

Let me quote you a scripture in the *Doctrine and Covenants*, a book of revelation given to a prophet in our day:

> *Whatever principle of intelligence we attain unto in this life, it will rise with us in the resurrection. And if a person gains more knowledge and intelligence in this life through his diligence and obedience than another, he will have so much the advantage in the world to come.*

And that, my friends, is the sum total of what we are trying to do. That one scripture explains the purpose of this life. It's for us to have experiences that we can't have in any other way, which gives us an advantage that will take us into the next world. You want to leave here and go there, advantaged, not disadvantaged. There was a world before this, and when that world ended, because of agency and choice, there was a whole group of people that found themselves in a disadvantaged position. All of you in this room came from that world and came here with an advantage over those who were judged and had a disadvantage. You have a physical body. Not only that, you were allowed to come into this world and experience things that they can't. That group who is disadvantaged is here as evil spirits. They provide the opposition necessary for you and me to gain the experience and knowledge that leads to the wisdom necessary to give us the advantage in the world to come. It's all a plan. It's so beautiful. There's nothing wasted here. There's no experience wasted unless you ***choose*** *to allow that experience to be a wasted experience. Whatever happens to us in this life—I don't care how bitter, I don't care how brutal—it can make you better or bitter, every experience. We talked about that. I'd say, "Fay, you're having these experiences, these last hours, these last days that are absolutely necessary for you, that you can't get in any other way but this, so that when you come into that next world, you go there with an advantage. And it's in the wisdom of Him who knoweth all things." That's beautiful doctrine. It gives meaning and purpose to what we're doing here and allows you to look at adversity, difficulty, and trials and look at it with a different eye and a different view. So, loving Father in Heaven knows. I counseled with Him before I came here to this life, about these various experiences and agreed to them because I knew the end result. I knew what it would be, and I was able to see it. Before she came here, Fay also saw what kind of a person she would be after she left here and had experienced all of these things. I saw peace settle upon her once she understood that. It's an advantage in the world to come. And there's another world after that. And another one after that. I testify to you that Fay understood these things. Sometimes she wasn't always lucid, but when she was lucid, she grasped the idea that, "I need this now and it was foreordained for me by a loving Father. This is His signature that He loves me, that He hasn't forgotten me, and that I'm a part of a plan, much bigger and more glorious that I ever thought before." In the name of Jesus Christ, amen.*

References:
St John 18:33-38
D&C 93:24
D&C 130:18-19 principle of intelligence

Chapter Twelve
Podcast 012 The Second Comforter

Tonight, I want to talk about the greatest crowning achievement we can obtain while in mortality. According to the Prophet Joseph and others, the greatest achievement that we can obtain in this life, is to have a personal audience with the Lord Jesus Christ. It has a name, and it's called the *Second Comforter*. There's actually been quite a bit written about it. It's not something we talk a lot about in the Church anymore, but there is still plenty of information on it. So, hopefully, tonight this lesson will give us a foundation that will pique our interest, and cause us to seek a little more into this great opportunity that we have ahead of us as members of The Church of Jesus Christ of Latter-day Saints. The scriptures are full of it, and I want to start out with the one the Prophet Joseph Smith uses to introduce this concept. It's in the *New Testament* Gospel of John. This will be our take-off scripture. We want to start in John 14:16. First, I'll read this to you, and then I'll tell you what the Prophet Joseph Smith said and also a comment by Elder Bruce R McConkie. Verse 16:

> *And I will pray the Father, and he shall give you another Comforter, that he may abide with you forever;*
> *[17]Even the Spirit of truth; whom the world cannot receive, because it seeth him not, neither*

knoweth him: but ye know him; for he dwelleth ***with*** *you, and shall be* ***in*** *you.*

Now, this *First Comforter* is the Holy Ghost. There are two *Comforters* that are spoken of by the prophets and in the scriptures. There is a reason why they are called *Comforters*. Until we obtain these *Comforters*, we remain in a state of unrest. These *Comforters* are designed to move you from a state of agitation, or unrest, into a condition, or a state of rest and peace. We'll come back to that in just a moment. The Lord said to His Twelve:

[18] I will not leave you comfortless: ***I*** *will come to you.*

Now, we're moving into something else. Notice in verse 17, it says that the *First Comforter*, *"Even the Spirit of truth;"* He will dwell *"with you, and shall be in you."* Then in verse 18, we are introduced to a whole new concept, *"I will not leave you comfortless,* ***I will come to you****."*

Student 1: So, is verse 17 the Holy Ghost and 18 Christ?

Mike: 16 and 17 are talking about the Holy Ghost and in 18, we are now moving into something else. Notice that in verse 17 he said that the *First Comforter* will be, *"****with*** *you" and "****in*** *you,"* and then verse 18 says, *"****I*** *will come to you."* It's interesting that these verses show a sequence. You have to become experienced with the *First Comforter* and have an interaction with Him before you can obtain the *Second Comforter*. The *First Comforter* prepares you to receive the *Second Comforter*. The *Second Comforter* is the personal ministration of the Lord Jesus Christ. Let's go to verse 19:

[19] Yet a little while, and the world seeth me no more; but ye see me: because I live, ye shall live also.

[20] At that day ye shall know that I am ***in*** *my Father, and ye* ***in*** *me, and I* ***in*** *you.*

We talked a lot about that last week. Now, verse 21 is the verse that is a mystery to the Christian world:

[21 He that hath my commandments, and keepeth them, he it is that loveth me: and he that loveth me shall be loved of my Father, and I [this is Jesus

speaking] *will love him,* ***and will manifest myself to him***.

Now, there's the promise. If you keep the commandments, and you love the Lord, He will come and manifest Himself to you. The Christian world reading this thinks that this is a symbolic representation of Jesus dwelling in the heart of man. In the Christian world, He can do that because they have Jesus being a spirit, the Father being a spirit, the Holy Ghost being a spirit, and all three are one, and one is three, etc. But, Joseph Smith said that this is an old sectarian notion and is not true. This has reference to a personal manifestation of the Lord Himself, where you can have a personal audience with Jesus Christ, and I want to emphasize, IN THIS LIFE. The part I want to emphasize in tonight's lesson is this: Whenever we think about this high and lofty doctrine of having a personal encounter with the resurrected Christ, we always want to push that into some future, non-mortal period of time. We want to push that into the spirit world after we die, or we want to push it into the Millennium when Christ reigns personally upon the earth, or we want to push it on into eternity after the resurrection in the celestial world. But none of these appearances that I'm going to talk to you about tonight are referring to anything further than mortality. This is designed to happen **now**! That's why we started the lesson out tonight by saying that the crowning experience of mortality is to have a personal audience with the resurrected Christ. So, I want you to know that everything that we're talking about here, tonight, has to do with what the scriptures call, *"While yet in the flesh."* That means while you are still mortal. This is before your physical death. This is before your resurrection. This is before the spirit world. This is **now**. You can tell that we're talking about **now** because there are all kinds of conditions that are necessary in order for you to experience an encounter with the Lord. In other words, if you're in the Millennium, there's no condition, other than the fact that you are qualified to get to the Millennium. But, there are conditions here. Notice verse 21, *"He that hath my commandments, and keepeth them* [see, there's a condition], *he it is that loveth me: and he that loveth me shall be loved of my Father, and I will love him, and will manifest myself to him."*

Now, in the other scriptural places, you're going to see all kinds of conditions that must be met by mortal men and women, in order to have this experience. When we see the Savior after mortality, for example, all eyes will see Him together in the Millennium. You'll see Him after the resurrection of the dead. Everyone will be brought forth from the dead, resurrected, and stand before the judgment bar of God, to be judged of their works. Everybody is going to see Him. That is a default encounter. That means everybody is going to do that at some future time. The scriptures say that *"Every knee shall bow and every tongue confess that Jesus is the Christ."* See, that's a default. There are no conditions there. Everyone will be brought forth. So, whenever we see any conditions, stipulations, or qualifications that must be met before this encounter, it's always pertaining to mortal life. Does that make sense?

So, the big stumbling block of this is, whenever anyone talks about seeing the Lord, they always want to push it into some other realm other than mortal life, and that's not what the scriptures are talking about. Now, go back to John 14 and look at verse 22:

> *Judas saith unto him, not Iscariot, Lord, how is it that thou wilt manifest thyself unto us, and not unto the world?*

See, Judas has a question there. "Are you talking about a personal experience where we see You at some future time, while we're still in this world?" See, he has a question. "Or, is this referring to when everyone in the world is going to see You at some future time that You've talked about?" Now, look at what the Lord says here in verse 23:

> *Jesus answered and said unto him, If a man love me, he will keep my words:*

Now, here's a stipulation again; you have to keep the commandments, you have to live the words of Christ:

> *and my Father will love him, and* ***we*** *will come unto him* [meaning the Father and the Son], *and make our abode with him.*

Abode means what? It means they'll take up a residence with you. They are going to come to where you live and visit you and see you, and there are many men and women who have had this experience throughout the history of the world.

Student 1: Well, we pierce the veil, but it's not always in the temple, then?

Mike: No, most of the times it takes place are **not** in the temple. Now, keep in mind what we've talked about in the past and that this encounter can take place in a vision, or it could be a visitation. Remember the difference between a vision and a visitation and what Joseph Smith saw when he encountered the Father and the Son. That's a *Second Comforter* experience. He talked to Them, They talked to him, there was a free discussion back and forth, but it was a vision; meaning that Joseph and others who have had this will say, *"whether in the flesh or out of the flesh, I know not."* So, he's saying, "I don't know if I was on Earth or some other place. I don't know where I was. But, I saw Them, They saw me, I talked to Them, and They talked back to me." That's a *Second Comforter* experience. A visitation is where you see and hear and **touch** something, and in this case, you not only touch Him, but He touches you. There's an ordination that takes place, and we'll talk a little bit about that. You actually receive a higher order of the priesthood and some ordinances along with this audience. So, there's the take-off on that.

In the *Teachings of the Prophet Joseph Smith* page 150, the Prophet Joseph Smith said this could also be experienced by the Saints in the last dispensation as well. And, that's a promise we have. Here's what he said:

> *When the Lord has thoroughly proved him* [meaning a Latter-day Saint man or woman] *and finds that the man is determined to serve Him at all hazards, then the man will find his calling and election made sure, then it will be his privilege to receive the* ***other comforter****, which the Lord has promised the Saints.*

The *"other comforter"* is the Lord Jesus Christ Himself, who will come to you.

Now, when you're going through the temple, everything in the temple, the whole temple allegory, is teaching you how to come up in this life and obtain this personal audience with the

Lord. The whole temple endowment, the whole ceremony, the allegory, is pointing you towards receiving the *Second Comforter, which* you do at the veil. The purpose of the *Second Comforter*, the Lord Jesus Christ, is to prepare you in all things, to be received into the presence, and have an audience with the Father. So, here we have three Gods. We have God, the Holy Ghost, we have God, the Son, Jesus Christ, and we have God, the Holy Father. You can see that one of the main purposes of the Holy Ghost, if not **the** main purpose, is to prepare you in all things, to have a personal audience with the Lord Jesus Christ, and enter into His presence. That's the purpose of the Holy Ghost, the *First Comforter*; to prepare you to receive the *Second Comforter*. The God of the telestial world that we are in is the Holy Ghost. His purpose is to prepare you to meet the God of the terrestrial world, which is the Lord, Jesus Christ. The purpose of the Lord, Jesus Christ, the *Second Comforter*, is to prepare you in all things to enter into the presence of the God of the celestial world, which is The Holy Father. Each one of these three Beings has a main purpose, and that's to prepare you in all things to enter into the presence and receive from that Person, at a higher level, what's reserved for you, and what you need to complete your journey back to the Father. The temple allegory is showing us step by step, how to do that. When you enter the terrestrial room in the temple, it is symbolic of a third estate. The third estate is a millennial, terrestrial world. That is the world of the Lord, Jesus Christ. The Son of God presides over that terrestrial/ millennial world. The Holy Ghost's purpose is to sanctify, cleanse, purify and transform men and women in the telestial world, and to prepare them to physically, emotionally and spiritually be able to encounter the God of the terrestrial world and survive the encounter. If you are taken into the presence of the Son of God, the God of the terrestrial world, and you are not prepared to enter His presence, you would die in the attempt because the glory of the terrestrial is greater than the glory of the telestial. Telestial beings, without being transformed, transfigured, translated, changed, and taken into the presence of a terrestrial being, will die in the encounter. They have to be changed. The same is true of entering a terrestrial world. A person entering a terrestrial/millennial world has to be changed again and brought up to a level where they can go into the celestial world and be able to abide the presence and glory of God, the Father. Does that make sense?

Student 1: Yes, because you have been teaching us that everything is step by step by step; always preparing for something bigger.

Mike: Yes, always! That is a great concept if we can grab hold of it. It gives us a wonderful view and insight into the purpose of mortality and what we're doing here and what we're trying to accomplish before our time here ends.

Let's go to the first scripture in the *Doctrine and Covenants* that the Lord reveals to us this doctrine of the *Second Comforter*. It's in section 67. This is eighteen months after the official restoration and organization of the Church. It's only been eighteen months since they had that little meeting at the Peter Whitmer farm, where the Church was officially organized. That's not much time. But, even this early in the history of the Church, look at what the Lord says:

> *[10] And again, verily I say unto you that it is your **privilege**, and a **promise** I give unto you that have been ordained unto this ministry,*

I've underlined the words privilege and promise. Now, we've got something here. The Lord says I'm giving you a privilege and a promise to do something and here are the conditions. If this were something in the future, something after death, he wouldn't need to have these conditions:

> *that inasmuch as you* [1] *strip yourselves from jealousies and* [2] *fears, and* [3] *humble yourselves before me, for ye are not sufficiently humble,*

Do you see those three conditions? Now here's the promise:

> *the veil shall be rent and you shall see me and know that I am—*

That is the first reference in this dispensation and in modern scripture, which tells us about a personal encounter with the Lord, Jesus Christ.

> *not with the carnal neither natural mind, but with the spiritual* [mind].

Now, notice verse 11. We talked about how in order for this to happen, you have to be changed. This can't happen yet to these people. They're eighteen months into the history of the Church, and they're not ready to obtain this privilege and promise:

> *[11] For no man has seen God at any time in the flesh, except quickened by the Spirit of God.*

That tells you that there have to be some changes made from the state that we're in right now, in our natural man, fallen state. There have to be some changes made. You just can't survive this encounter:

> *[12] Neither can any natural man abide the presence of God, neither after the carnal mind.*

And then he tells them:

> *[13] Ye are not able to abide the presence of God now, neither the ministering of angels; wherefore, continue in patience until ye are perfected.*

We talked about that last week, in fact, that's one of the scriptures we used. That's your first promise in modern, latter-day, revealed, restoration scripture that you have a privilege and a promise that God gives you, that you can have a personal audience with the Lord, Jesus Christ. Isn't that exciting?

I'd like to read you a comment by Elder Bruce R McConkie. This is from *The Mortal Messiah,* page 575:

> *After the* ***true saints***

And I underlined *"true saints."* If you have true saints, then you have to have false saints, or "Latter-day aint's," instead of Latter-day Saints. This Friday, I'm going with a friend up to Utah. A friend's wife passed away two days ago, and he asked me to speak at her funeral. I was talking to him last night, and this man has been a temple president and a mission president and is very well experienced in the doctrines of the Church. I asked him, "What do you want me to talk about?"

And he said, "Well, the room is going to be filled with social Latter-day Saints." That was the comment he used, and he invited me to speak on a subject that would help **them**. So, back to Elder McConkie's quote. Now, you're going to see a sequence here. Here is a list:

> *After the true saints* [1] *receive and enjoy the gift of the Holy Ghost;* [2] *after they know how to attune themselves to the voice of the Spirit;* [3] *after they mature spiritually so that they see visions, work miracles, and entertain angels;* [4] *after they make their calling and election sure and prove themselves worthy of every trust—after all this and more—it becomes their right and privilege to see the Lord and commune with him face to face. Revelations, visions, angelic visitations, the rending of the heavens, and appearances among men of the Lord himself—all these things are for all of the faithful. They are not reserved for apostles and prophets only. God is no respecter of persons. They are not reserved for one age only, or for a select lineage of people. We are all our Father's children. All men are welcome. And he inviteth them all to come unto him and partake of his goodness; and he denieth none that come unto him, black and white, bond and free, male and female; and he remembereth the heathen; and all are alike unto God, both Jew and Gentile. (2 Ne. 26:33)*

Let's go to the next one and look at some scriptures in the *Doctrine and Covenants* that allude to this. In the history of the Church, section 76 is known as "The Vision." Let's go to verse 22, where Joseph Smith and Sidney Rigdon are at the John Johnson home in Hiram, Ohio. They are working on the revision of the *Bible*, what we call the Joseph Smith Translation. This was in February 1832, and the Church is just over two and a half years old. While they were translating in the 5th chapter of the Gospel of John, they had a question about the resurrection of the dead and a whole vision opened up that was 119 verses long. Joseph Smith said that these 119 verses of scriptures only represented 1/100th of what they saw. So, they only wrote down 1/100th of these things they saw:

> *[22] And now, after the many testimonies which have been given of him* [Christ], *this is the*

> *testimony, last of all, which we give of him: That he lives!*
> *[23] For we saw him* [This is a Second Comforter experience], *even on the right hand of God; and we heard the voice bearing record that he is the Only Begotten of the Father—*

Now, let's go to the end of section 76, and there are some marvelous promises involved at the very end. Let's start at verse 113:

> *This is the end of the vision which we saw, which we were commanded to write while we were yet in the Spirit.*
> *[114] But great and marvelous are the works of the Lord, and the mysteries of his kingdom which he showed unto us, which surpass all understanding in glory, and in might, and in dominion;*
> *[115] Which he commanded us we should not write while we were yet in the Spirit, and are not lawful for man to utter;*

Remember, he said that this was only 1/100th of what they saw and that he wrote down. There were other things that he wanted to write down, but they were commanded **not** to write them down. Now, go to verse 116. Think of the *Second Comforter*. Think about our privilege and promise:

> *[116] Neither is man capable to make them known, for they are only to be seen and understood by the power of the Holy Spirit, which God bestows on those* [Here are your conditions. Remember that to have this encounter, there are conditions] *who love him, and purify themselves before him;*
> *[117] To whom he grants this privilege of seeing and knowing for themselves;*
> *[118] That through the power and manifestation of the Spirit,* ***while in the flesh****, they may be able to* ***bear his presence*** *in the world of glory.*

Looking at that, and you can see that if we meet certain conditions, and the Lord lays them out for us, we have the privilege of seeing and knowing for ourselves, **while in the flesh**, to be able to bear His presence. In other words, you're in the presence of Christ, and to bear means to survive it! It means that you go into His presence in the world of glory. Either He comes here and changes you, or you are taken there. Either you see it in vision, or you have a personal visitation. This is why those who have had these experiences will say, like Paul and like Joseph, *"Whether in the flesh or out of the flesh, I know not...* I don't know where I was, I don't know if I was mortal, I don't know if I was translated, I don't know if my body was transfigured, but I do know that I saw Him and spoke to Him and He spoke to me *face to face as one man speaks with another."* They may not understand the environment and the exact circumstances of the encounter, but there is no question about the encounter. They speak with God, face to face, as one man speaks to another.

Let's go to another one. So, what the Lord is doing is that He is preparing the saints, step by step, piece by piece, to have this experience. You know it's a commandment of God that you do this? Let's go to section 101 for a minute. Let's throw one in here real quick.

The Lord says this in *Doctrine and Covenants* 101:38:

> *And seek the face of the Lord always* [that's the Second Comforter], *that in patience ye may possess your souls, and ye shall have eternal life.*

Now, let's go to section 88. When you obtain this encounter with the Lord, there are a number of sequences for blessings that are inherent in this personal administration. You can't have this experience and not obtain certain things. Certain things go along with this. One of the things that go along with this is the promise of eternal life. When you stand in the presence of Christ and have the *Second Comforter* experience, one of the things you have obtained from Him is His promise to you that you **will** have eternal life. There are no conditions set to it at this point. All through the scriptures, it says:

> *And* ***if*** *you keep my commandments and endure to the end,* [then] *ye shall have eternal life, which gift is the greatest gift of God.*

Notice that it starts with the word ***"if."*** Well, when you have the *Second Comforter,* the "***if***" is removed. Everything up to this point is conditional. It's like a patriarchal blessing. There are blessings mentioned in the patriarchal blessing, but at the end of the blessing, it will say, these things are all conditioned upon your faithfulness. It's the same in every temple ordinance we enter into. The marriage ordinance talks about the blessings of Abraham, Isaac, and Jacob; the blessings of kingdoms, thrones, principalities, powers, and dominions, and all of these blessings. And then it says, "According to your faithfulness." Do you see that condition? So, all of these blessings are yours conditioned on your faithfulness. When you have this *Second Comforter* experience, the condition is removed. When you enter into the presence of the Lord, you obtain the promise of *eternal life*. He may lay his hands upon your head and ordain you a king and a priest, and if you're a woman, a queen, and a priestess, and seal upon you *eternal life* in the celestial world, that *"Where I am, you may be also, that you have obtained part and portion with Me in My Kingdom."* These are words that have been spoken to mortals from the mouth of God Himself as they stood in His presence.

Section 88:3 starts out:

> *Wherefore, I now send upon you another Comforter, even upon you my friends, that it may abide in your hearts, even the Holy Spirit of promise; which other Comforter is the same that I promised unto my disciples, as is recorded in the testimony of John.*
>
> *[4] This Comforter* ***is the promise which I give unto you of eternal life, even the glory of the celestial kingdom****;*

Now, that's what you obtain, that promise. Who gives you that promise? Where does it take place? It takes place as you stand in the presence of the resurrected Christ and obtain that promise. Can you see why it's called the *Second Comforter*? In this world, we are always in a state of questioning or quandary. What's my status before God? Am I pleasing to him? Is the course of my life that I'm pursuing acceptable to him? We always have this unrest. We'd like to know. Maybe we have a feeling that we're okay, but we don't have a sure witness. When God, with His own mouth, calls you by your name and you obtain from Him this promise, you enter into *His Rest*. This means that all of these concerns that you have had are resolved, and you are **comforted** and obtain what the scriptures call, *"The rest of the Lord."* Your concerns pertaining to your standing in mortality and your future in eternity are once and for all laid to rest. This is something that is obtained as you have *this Second Comforter* experience with the Lord Jesus Christ. The Holy Ghost is preparing you all along the way to have this encounter.

In the temple, we have people called *presenters*. We have temple workers that follow us all the way through the endowment allegory. The *presenter* is to prepare you in all things to have this encounter with the Lord. The *presenter* is very symbolically the Holy Ghost, or angels, or the *spirits of just men made perfect*, who work under the direction of the Holy Ghost, who works under the direction of the Son of God. There's a hierarchy here, you can see it in the temple. You see one "exalted being" speak to another "exalted being" of a lower station, and say, *"Go down and do this...and then come back and report to me."* So, you have various stations of people, gods (with a small ***g***) if you will, who are in various stages of their own personal progression, and acting as ministers and servants and messengers for Gods of a higher station, to help bring those up to a higher level to where They (the Gods) are. That's what that's all about. Let's go to section 88:62 and look at something else here. There are times in eternity when Christ is nearer than other times. There are times when Christ is nearer to His brothers and sisters, the children of the Father, and there are times when He is not near. So, look what he says in verse 62:

> *And again, verily I say unto you, my friends, I leave these sayings with you to ponder in your hearts,*

Think about the things we have talked about tonight. These are things which the Lord wants us to ponder:

> *with this commandment which I give unto you,*
> ***that ye shall call upon me while I am near—***

Now, this revelation in section 88 was given December 27, 1832. The Lord is near at times of restoration of lost truth. The Lord is not near in times of apostasy. So, when we have a restoration following an apostasy, the *Restorer of Truth* is near, and He's near now. Now, look what He says in verse 63:

> *Draw near unto me and I will draw near unto you;*

See the conditions? You have to do something here. This encounter is not going to be something that is just bestowed upon us with no effort on our own:

> *seek me diligently and ye shall find me;*

All through the scriptures, we have this scriptural formula: ask, and you shall receive, seek and ye shall find, knock and it shall be opened unto you. It's all through the scriptures, but here in 88 is the only place where it says, *"seek **me** diligently and ye shall find **me.**"* That's an injunction to obtain the *Second Comforter*:

> *ask, and ye shall receive; knock, and it shall be opened unto you.*

You knock at the veil. There is a way to knock.

Now, let's go to verse 67, and here are more conditions:

> *And if your eye be single to my glory, your whole bodies shall be filled with light, and there shall be no darkness in you; and that body which is filled with light comprehendeth all things.*

This is the important one, think of the *Second Comforter*:

> *[68] Therefore, sanctify yourselves that your minds become single to God, and the **days*** [not day] *will come that you shall see him; for he will **unveil his face unto you*** [that's the Second Comforter], *and it shall be in his own time, and in his own way, and according to his own will.*
>
> *[69] Remember **the great and last promise** which I have made unto you; cast away your idle thoughts and your excess of laughter far from you.*

He refers to this appearance in verse 68 as *"the great and last promise."* There are a lot of marvelous promises that God has in store for His children, but this one is *"the great and last promise"* that "*the days will come that you shall see him, for he will unveil His face unto you.*"

Student 1: So, let me ask you something. *"The great and last promise"* is what He is going to promise you when you have this experience?

Mike: Yes. In other words, this is available to you. This is the crowning achievement of mortality. There is nothing greater that can happen in the second estate, than to be brought into the presence of Christ and have a face to face, one on one encounter with Him.

Student 1: THAT is *"the great and last promise."*

Mike: That's *"the great and last promise."* Go over to verses 74-75:

> *[74] And I give unto you, who are the first laborers in this last kingdom, a commandment* [now remember, here are some conditions] *that you assemble yourselves together, and organize yourselves, and prepare yourselves, and* ***sanctify*** *yourselves; yea,* ***purify*** *your hearts, and cleanse your hands and your feet before me, that I may make you clean;*

Why does He want you to be clean?

> *[75] That I may testify unto your Father, and your God, and my God, that you are clean from the blood of this wicked generation; that I may fulfil this promise,* ***this great and last promise****, which I have made unto you, when I will.*

Which is what? That, "I will come to you. I will come and take up My abode with you. I will introduce you to the Father and He will come to you." See, the scriptures are loaded with this stuff if we are tuned into it, and we realize that it is not referring us to some distant, eternal time. It's the HERE AND NOW! It's desirable to have this experience now because the advantage it gives you while you're still alive in this world, and the advantage that you obtain in the next world from having this experience here, are unspeakable. Let's go to section 93, the last one from *Doctrine and Covenants*, and then I'll take you to the *Book of Mormon*. Now, here is a list of five things. See, the Lord has been teaching us, starting from section 67 to 76 to 88, and now to section 93. The purpose of the *Doctrine and Covenants* is to teach us doctrine step by step by step on how to obtain a personal audience with the resurrected Savior. 93:1:

> *Verily, thus saith the Lord: It shall come to pass that* ***every soul***

So, this is now showing us that this is available to every man and woman. Women can obtain the *Second Comforter* with or without their husband. It's not required for you to be equally yoked to a husband or a wife, in order to have this. This is an individual, personal, one on one. This is Christ speaking:

> *Verily, thus saith the Lord: It shall come to pass that every soul* [1] *who forsaketh his sins and* [2] *cometh unto me, and* [3] *calleth on my name, and* [4] *obeyeth my voice, and* [5] *keepeth my commandments,* [here it is] ***shall see my face and know that I am;***

I have an acquaintance that has had this experience. He has a website and breaks down those five things in section 93 into individual commentaries. This is a man who has stood in the presence of Christ. He has had his *"calling and election made sure."*

Student 1: Why did he tell you that? They're not supposed to do that, right?

Mike: Well, we're *told* that we aren't supposed to do that. But actually, when you have these experiences, you're under an obligation to tell others about it, it's just the timing and who you tell. If we were not to speak of these things, then you would not have a record of this anywhere in the *Doctrine and Covenants*, because somebody somewhere is telling us these things and we're reading about it. If the brother of Jared had not written down and talked about his experience with the Lord on the mountaintop, you and I would never know about it. The key is, you don't *cast your pearls before swine*. It doesn't say that you don't cast them. It just says you don't cast them before swine; otherwise, they will *turn and rend you*. So, when you have a sacred experience, the Lord wants you to testify of that. You **must** testify of that. The key is who, and when, and how. That has to be Spirit directed. Does that make sense? Otherwise, if we don't testify of these experiences, then we can't be in a position to help others rise up through our testimony, and obtain the same experience. Let me give you an example of that, and then we'll come back to this.

Go to Moroni 7. If you have the visitation of an angel, should you talk about it? If an angel comes and talks to you, should you talk about it? This is Moroni talking about faith, hope, and charity, and if the gifts of the Spirit have ceased, it's because faith has ceased. Verse 29:

> *And because he hath done this, my beloved brethren, have miracles ceased? Behold I say unto you, Nay; neither have angels ceased to minister unto the children of men.*

Now, for the next four verses, you have the most intense description of how to obtain the visitation and ministry of angels of anything found anywhere in the scriptures.

> *[30] For behold, they* [the angels] *are subject unto him* [Christ], *to minister according to the word of his* [Christ's] *command, showing themselves* [the angels] *unto them of* ***strong faith and a firm mind in every form of godliness.***

Do you want to have angels visit you? Those are the conditions that are required before you have the visitation of angels. Now, why do they come? Watch:

> *[31] And the office of their* [angels] *ministry is to call men unto repentance, and to fulfil and to do the work of the covenants of the Father* [that's their job], *which he hath made unto the children of men, to prepare the way among the children of men,* ***by declaring the word of Christ unto the chosen vessels of the Lord,***

In other words, those who are *of strong faith and a firm mind in every form of godliness*, the Lord refers to them as *"chosen vessels of the Lord."* And they appear to them:

> *that they may* ***bear testimony*** *of him.*

What are they supposed to do after they obtain these visitations and ministrations? They are to testify of it. They are to tell people about it. Why are they to testify of these sacred experiences?

> *[32] And by so doing* [testifying of it], *the Lord God prepareth the way that* ***the residue*** *of men...*

That's the rest of us, the ones who are **not** the chosen vessels. That's those of us who are not having these experiences. We are to hear from someone who does and bears testimony of it:

that the residue of men may have faith in Christ,

The purpose of talking about and testifying of these things is to help those who are not having these experiences to have faith in Christ:

that the Holy Ghost may have place in their hearts, according to the power thereof; and after this manner bringeth to pass the Father, the covenants which he hath made unto the children of men.

So, you are to testify of these things, **but** you're only to testify as directed by the Spirit, at a time and place and in a way, and to the person that the Spirit directs. That way you don't cast your pearls before swine.

Let me read a comment to you. In *A New Witness for the Articles of Faith*, page 492, under the heading "The Crowning Revelation of Life," Elder McConkie speaks about receiving a personal visitation of Christ. Remember the difference between vision and visitation:

There is a true doctrine on these points [a doctrine unknown to many, and unbelieved by more], *a doctrine that is spelled out as specifically and extensively in the revealed word as are any of the other great revealed truths. There is no need for uncertainty or misunderstanding, and surely, if the Lord reveals a doctrine, we should seek to learn its principles and strive to apply them in our lives.*

Now, we've spent an hour showing, from the scriptures, that this is something the Lord wants us to do:

This doctrine is that mortal man [and woman], *while in the flesh, has it in his power to see the Lord, to stand in His presence, to feel the nail marks in His hands and feet, and to receive from Him such blessings as are reserved for those only* [here's your criteria/conditions] *who keep all His commandments and who are qualified for that*

> *eternal life which includes being in His presence forever.*

His last statement is this:

> *Let us at least sample the holy word and see what the Lord has promised as to seeing His face and being in His presence while we are yet pilgrims far removed from our heavenly home.*

Isn't that a marvelous quote?

Here's another one by Elder McConkie from *The Promised Messiah*, pg. 582. This is a wonderful thing for those of us who go to the temple:

> *The purpose of the endowment in the house of the Lord is to prepare and sanctify His saints so that they will be able to see His face, here and now, as well as bear the glory of His presence in the eternal worlds.*

That's the purpose of the endowment. I have one more statement. Joseph Smith said:

> *The other Comforter spoken of is a subject of great interest, and perhaps understood by few of this generation. After a person has faith in Christ, repents of his sins, and is baptized for the remission of his sins and receives the Holy Ghost* [by the laying on of hands], *which is the first Comforter, then let him continue to humble himself before God, hungering and thirsting after righteousness, and living by every word of God, and the Lord will soon say unto him, son, thou shalt be exalted. When the Lord has thoroughly proved him, and finds that the man is determined to serve Him at all hazards, then the man will find his calling and his election made sure, then it will be his privilege to receive the other Comforter, which the Lord hath promised the Saints, as is recorded in the testimony of St. John, in the 14th chapter, from the 12th to the 27th verses.*

There's much more on this. Let me give you my friend's website that I was telling you about. His blog is called *"The Perfect Day"* (ldsperfectday.blogspot.com). You will find a wealth of information from a man who is a Latter-day Saint, and who doesn't hold any high position of authority. He's not an apostle, a Seventy, or a stake president. He's a faithful Latter-day Saint man, and he's obtained these things we're talking about. What he does is, he anonymously shares with those who read his blog posts, how he was able to accomplish those things and what the Lord has taught him in the process. If you are interested in this subject, it is well worth your consideration to study the things he has written.

Satan is in the wings all the time to influence priestcraft and pride and to do things to get a "following" and for "the pride of man," to be lifted up in the praise of man. It's a continual trap. You have to be able to do things with an eye single to the glory of God, and with no thought of what's in it for you.

Student 1: You don't have to have permission from the Brethren, right?

Mike: No, in fact, if you have to have permission on everything, you're being *"acted upon"* instead of *"acting."* You want to be able to *step-out*, but you have to be careful. There is a safety net within the Church, and there is great information, but ***the mysteries of godliness* are not going to be revealed to you in a general conference address. The *mysteries of godliness* are going to come to you through personal revelation** and through the power of the Holy Ghost. On your path, the Lord will place mentors, messengers, and you will receive people, that will help you along the way. You need to be familiar enough with the Spirit and mature enough in your spirituality, that when you hear something that doesn't feel right, it just bothers you. It leaves you upset and disquieted, rather than resonate or *distil upon you as the dews of heaven*. You have to be able to discern what to embrace and what to discard. Whatever you listen to or read, whether it's this podcast or **anything**, you need to be able to discern by the power of the Holy Ghost, whether it's true of false. You can't wait for the Brethren to okay everything. If you're going to wait for the Brethren to okay everything that comes into your pathway, you are going to miss much of what God has in reserve for you. I watch very carefully what I say. I try to stay in the scriptures and the words of the prophets. I try to do that which edifies and builds faith, while at the same time, encouraging us to look into things that we ordinarily, as members of the Church, are reluctant to look into, or don't know about, because those are where great treasures are that the Lord has reserved. For example, the doctrine of the *Second Comforter* was taught openly in the early days of the Church. It's not something that's taught right now. Yet, the Brethren will refer to it periodically, but it's not something that's taught. So, if you want to know about this, you're going to have to go back into the Restoration statements that were made in the early history of the Church.

I invite anyone who is listening to this podcast, if you have any questions, feel free to call me, and I'll be glad to text with you, or talk with you on the phone, or email you back and forth. We do quite a bit of that during the week. My podcasts open up information that people haven't considered, but they don't answer all the questions, so many questions come throughout the week, and I'm happy to be able to answer those. My whole purpose is to help people understand the restoration doctrines that were revealed through the Prophet Joseph Smith, and to get a better feel for them, and to seek for personal revelation and become more experienced in discerning truth from error, through the power of the Holy Ghost. Ultimately, brothers and sisters, the only hope we have of making it back to the presence of our Father, and successfully completing this estate, is to take Holy Spirit for our guide. Everything else—general conference, the Brethren, the prophets, the writings of the apostles—is designed to move us towards that point where we become experienced and expert in receiving and recognizing the promptings of the Holy Ghost.

References:
John 14:16-23
Teachings of the Prophet Joseph Smith page 150
D&C 67:10-13
Elder Bruce R McConkie, *The Mortal Messiah,* page 575:
D&C 76:22-23
D&C 76:113-118
D&C 101:38
D&C 88:3-4
D&C 88:62-63

D&C 88:67-69
D&C *88:74-75*
D&C 93:1
Moroni 7:29-32
Bruce R McConkie *A New Witness for the Articles of Faith*, page 492
Elder McConkie from *The Promised Messiah*, pg. 582

The Perfect Day
ldsperfectday.blogspot.com
http://ldsperfectday.blogspot.com/

"Seek the Face of the Lord Always"

Elder Bruce R. McConkie
of the Quorum of the Twelve
(Excerpts from The Promised Messiah, Chapter 31, p.575-595)

After the true saints receive and enjoy the gift of the Holy Ghost; after they know how to attune themselves to the voice of the Spirit; after they mature spiritually so that they see visions, work miracles, and entertain angels; after they make their calling and election sure and prove themselves worthy of every trust—after all this and more—it becomes their right and privilege to see the Lord and commune with him face to face. Revelations, visions, angelic visitations, the rending of the heavens, and appearances among men of the Lord himself—all these things are for all of the faithful. They are not reserved for apostles and prophets only. God is no respecter of persons. They are not reserved for one age only, or for a select lineage or people. We are all our Father's children. All men are welcome. "*And he inviteth them all to come unto him and partake of his goodness, and he denieth none that come unto him, black and white, bond and free, male and female; and he remembereth the heathen; and all are alike unto God, both Jew and Gentile.*" (2 Ne. 26:33.)

Seeing the Lord is not a matter of lineage or rank or position or place of precedence. Joseph Smith said: "*God hath not revealed anything to Joseph, but what he will make known unto the Twelve, and even the least saint may know all things as fast as he is able to bear them, for the day must come when no man need say to his neighbor, Know ye the Lord; for all shall know him. . . from the least to the greatest.*" (Teachings, p. 149.) The fact is that the day of personal visitations from the Lord to faithful men on Earth has no more ceased than has the day of miracles. God is an unchangeable Being; otherwise, he would not be God. The sole issue is finding people who have faith and who work righteousness.

"For if there be no faith among the children of men God can do no miracle among
them; wherefore, he showeth not himself until after their faith." (Ether 12:12.)

Elder Bruce R. McConkie elaborates (B. R. McConkie, New Witness, p. 492):

What greater personal revelation could anyone receive than to see the face of his Maker?

...And is it an unseemly or unrighteous desire on man's part to hope and live and pray, all in such a way as to qualify for so great a manifestation? There is a true doctrine on these points, a doctrine that is spelled out as specifically and extensively in the revealed word as are any of the other great revealed truths. There is no need for uncertainty or misunderstanding and surely, if the Lord reveals a doctrine, we should seek to learn its principles and strive to apply them in our lives. This doctrine is that mortal man, while in the flesh, has it in his power to see the Lord, to stand in His presence, to feel the nail marks in His hands and feet, and to receive from Him such blessings as are reserved for those only who keep all His commandments and who are qualified for that eternal life which includes being in His presence forever.

Elder McConkie wrote (B. R. McConkie, Promised Messiah, pp. 582-584):

"Therefore, sanctify yourselves that your minds become single to God" -and now we come to the crowning promise of the Gospel- *"and the days will come that you shall see him; for he will unveil his face unto you, and it shall be in his own time, and in his own way, and according to his own will"* (D&C 88:68). That is the Lord's promise, His great promise, His crowning promise, His last promise. What is there that can excel in importance the obtaining of that spiritual stature which enables one to see the Lord? And so the next words spoken by the Lord to His friends were: *"Remember the great and last promise which I have made unto you"* (D&C 88:69).

Elder McConkie wrote (B. R. McConkie, Promised Messiah, pp. 594-595):

Few faithful people will stumble or feel disbelief at the doctrine here presented that the Lord's apostolic witnesses are entitled and expected to see his face and that each one individually is obligated to "call upon Him in faith in mighty prayer" until he prevails. But the Twelve are only a dozen in number. There are seldom more than fifteen men on Earth at a time who have been ordained to the holy apostleship, which brings us to another statement made by Elder Cowdery in his apostolic charge (J. Smith, Jr., Documentary History, 2:196): *"God does not love you better or more than others."* That is, apostles and prophets do not gain precedence with the Lord unless they earn it by personal righteousness. The Lord loves people, not office holders. Every elder is entitled to the same blessings and privileges offered the apostles. Indeed, *"an apostle is an elder"*

(D&C 20:38); such is the title by which he is proud to be addressed. The priesthood is greater than any of its offices. No office adds any power, dignity, or authority to the priesthood. All offices derive their rights, virtues, authorities, and prerogatives from the priesthood. It is greater to hold the Melchizedek Priesthood than it is to hold the office of an elder or of an apostle in that priesthood. The Lord loves his priesthood holders, all of whom are given the same opportunity to do good and work righteousness and keep the commandments. All of the elders in the kingdom are expected to live the law as strictly as do the members of the Council of the Twelve, and if they do so live, the same blessings will come to them that flow to apostles and prophets. Apostles and prophets are named as examples and patterns of what others should be. The Quorum of the Twelve should be a model quorum after which every elders quorum in the Church might pattern its course... I repeat: apostles and prophets simply serve as patterns and examples to show all men what they may receive if they are true and faithful. There is nothing an apostle can receive that is not available to every elder in the kingdom. As we have heretofore quoted, from the Prophet's sermon on the Second Comforter (J. Smith, Jr., Teachings, 27 June 1839, p.149): *"God has not revealed anything to Joseph, but what He will make known unto the Twelve, and even the least saint may know all things as fast as he is able to bear them."* It follows that everything stated by Elder Oliver Cowdery in his charge to the apostles could also be given as a charge to all elders. Every elder is entitled and expected to seek and obtain all the spiritual blessings of the Gospel, including the crowning blessing of seeing the Lord face to face.

Chapter Thirteen
Podcast 013 Unbelief

First of all, I'd like to do a little follow-up on last week's lesson on the *Second Comforter*. I had some good feedback, and a lot of people enjoyed that information. I gave you two or three examples of the *Second Comforter* from the *Doctrine and Covenants*, and I'd like to give you one from the *Book of Mormon*. The words *"Second Comforter"* aren't used, but if you could learn to recognize these encounters with Jesus Christ, you can see them all through the scriptures. Let's go to 2 Nephi 31. In verse 2, Nephi is giving his final address. These are the last writings of Nephi. He's in his seventies; he's closing out his book, and he's about to deliver up the records to his brother Jacob:

> *Wherefore, the things which I have written sufficeth me, save it be a few words which I must speak concerning the doctrine of Christ;*

And then he continues on all the way through the 31st chapter, and into the 32nd chapter, and then in verse 6 he says:

> *Behold, this is the doctrine of Christ,*

So, from 2 Nephi 31:2 all the way to 2 Nephi 32:6, you have *"**the doctrine of Christ.**"* The *doctrine of Christ* is the system or plan, designed to bring man from his natural, fallen, unredeemed state in a telestial world, all the way up into the presence of Jesus Christ—while in the flesh, while still in mortality—to be redeemed from the Fall. So, the *Book of Mormon* description of being *redeemed from the Fall* is to be brought back into the presence of Christ, and have a personal encounter with him. That is the *Book of Mormon* definition of being *redeemed from the Fall*. Now, I want to go back to verse 6, and we're looking for that time when you're at the veil, and you're invited through the veil into the presence of Christ. Nephi has had this experience. He says:

> *Behold, this is the doctrine of Christ, and there will be no more doctrine given until after he* [Christ] *shall manifest himself* ***unto you in the flesh***.

That is so bold and so clear and so plain. Just as we talked about last week with the *Second Comforter*, a lot of people would interpret this as the time of the Second Coming, or that it's going to be in the Millennium. No, it isn't because all of the conditions for Him to manifest Himself unto you *in the flesh* are found in the *"doctrine of Christ."* The *doctrine of Christ* is the condition necessary to have this encounter. That plan is laid out now, from 2 Nephi 31:2 to 32:6, and is the systematic, organized plan on how to be *redeemed from the Fall*, enter into the presence of Christ, and have that personal encounter *in the flesh*. I've read and taught these verses hundreds of times, over thirty years in the Church Education System, and until you're ready and the Spirit shows it to you, these things remain hidden. They are truly hidden in plain sight. Once you see them, you wonder how you have always missed them. Look at the rest of verse 6:

> *And when he shall manifest himself* ***unto you in the flesh****, the things which he shall say unto you shall ye observe to do.*

You see that? It's a personal encounter. He has an agenda for the personal encounter. There is a uniquely personal experience reserved for you when you reach this point and stand in His presence. Section 50 gives you a little bit of a hint on what that is, but let's look a bit further in 2 Nephi 32. Look at verse 7:

> *And now I, Nephi, cannot say more;*

He wanted to tell us more; he has much more to tell us. He's had this encounter; he's had this ordination; he's had the Savior lay his hands on his head; he's seen the prints of the nails in His hands and His feet; he's been invited to thrust his hand into the Savior's side. He is an apostolic witness of the resurrected body of Jesus Christ. He wants to tell us more about it, but he says:

> *the Spirit stoppeth mine utterance,*

Now, don't you wish he had been allowed to tell us more? Why do you think he was stopped? Why do you think the Spirit allowed him to go this far and no further?

Student 2: It would condemn us.

Mike: Why would it condemn us?

Student 2: We would be accountable for something that we weren't prepared for.

Mike: Very good comment. It ends up being so personal, and it was for Nephi only, right? So, if you want to know what it is that Nephi found out, you have to seek the same experience.

Student 5: I also think it's because he wants us to exercise faith. In other words, we need to work to get this blessing and have this personal encounter given to us. It's kind of like He gives us everything free up to this point, but after this, we have to pay the price in order to get it.

Mike: Very good! Good comment. Now, look at what he says:

> *and I am left to mourn because of the* ***unbelief****,*
> *and the* ***wickedness****, and the* ***ignorance****, and the*
> ***stiffneckedness of men****;*

There are the reasons why he couldn't go further, and I want to say tonight, brothers and sisters, those are the reasons that will keep us from having this experience that Nephi is talking about. So, let's look at those things again; what is he saying? Here it is again, *"unbelief, and the wickedness, and the ignorance, and the stiffneckedness of men;"* and look at how he ends it:

> *for they will not* ***search knowledge****,*

Now, think of the scripture over in John 17:3. It says:

> *And this is life eternal, that they might* ***know*** *thee*
> *the only true God, and Jesus Christ, whom thou*
> *hast sent.*

That verse is talking about *knowledge*, and that *knowledge* is *"perfect knowledge."* When you stand in His presence and obtain this *Second Comforter*, your faith, at least in that experience, is finished. That's why, in another place, Jesus is referred to as *"the author and the* ***finisher*** *of our faith."* When I read that a while back, I thought, "What does it mean to have your faith finished?" Well, *faith finished*, is replaced by knowledge, "*perfect knowledge*." Notice the condemnation there at the very end of 2 Nephi 32:7:

> *for they will not search knowledge, nor understand great knowledge, when it is given unto them in plainness, even as plain as word can be.*

I would ask you, what greater knowledge can there be in mortality than to stand in the presence of Christ, and have your faith in that thing finished, and have *perfect knowledge* that He is; even *"when it is given unto them in plainness, even as plain as word can be."*

Nephi cannot give this to us any more clearly and in any more plainness than he has done there. If we want to take this message of what the *doctrine of Christ* is all about and where it is leading us, and if we want to twist that around and wrest that, and make it mean something more than what the literal words portray, then we do so to our own condemnation. Here the *doctrine of Christ* is the same as the temple allegory. The temple allegory, from initiatory on through to the veil, is the *doctrine of Christ*. It's how Christ, through His plan, His atonement, brings us up through a step-by-step process, redeems us from our fallen state, changes our very nature, sanctifies us, introduces us at the veil, and the veil is parted, and we're invited in. Well, that's the *doctrine of Christ*. In another place, it's referred to as the *"mystery of godliness"* because, when you enter into His presence and obtain from Him what He has, you obtain promises that have to do with immortality and eternal life. For you, the mortal probation (the second estate), even while you're still living in it, you graduate from it, you pass it. The judgment day is advanced as far as you're concerned, and you have passed the second estate, even though you're still living and breathing in it. It's a passed estate. You have kept your second estate. Isn't that marvelous? Comments or thoughts on that?

Student 2: I want that.

Mike: We all want that. And, by the way, as I said last week about the *Second Comforter*, it is not limited to men, nor to married couples. Single women and men can have this experience. In fact, I think that a husband and wife, who have this, have it individually before they experience it together because this *Second Comforter* is so intimate, and so personal, and so individual. You know that it is because the example in the *Book of Mormon* was that 2,500 people were there and he invited them to come forward **one by one**. He didn't invite them to come up in two's, three's, five's, or dozens, but one by one. That gives us the indicator of how we can experience it. When it happens, it will be you and the Savior.

Yesterday, I spoke at a funeral down in St. George, UT. My friend's wife died, and he requested that I speak about how his wife wanted to be a *daughter of Zion*, and how to obtain that status. When we would get together, we would talk and have study time together. Whether in St. George or Arizona, there was always one to two hours of in-depth study time; just the 4 of us. It always centered on the topic of Zion. I might mention that when you enter into the presence of the Lord and obtain the *Second Comforter*, you have obtained a "Zion status." You can't have that experience and come out of that, and not be a Zion man or a Zion woman.

Student 1: Wouldn't it be the other way around? Wouldn't becoming a Zion person come first?

Mike: It does. In fact, the other thing we talk a lot about is a society and also about building a city. We also talked about real estate in Jackson County, Missouri. We talked about the city called New Jerusalem. But, all of that is a moot point until you have men and women who have, on an individual basis, risen up and obtained personal Zion. The definition that ties in with all of this is that Zion is a terrestrial principle. Zion is not telestial. So, when you obtain these great blessings and have these experiences that we've been talking about the last two weeks, you become a terrestrial man or woman, still living in a telestial world. There are so many things that happen. When you have this encounter with the Lord, you're also ushered into a new organization, a new church, called *The Church of the Firstborn*. All of these things are tied in with this. That doesn't mean that you cease your membership in The Church of Jesus Christ of Latter-day Saints; you just now hold dual membership. One membership is what the Brethren have referred to as "the outward church below," which is The Church of Jesus Christ of

Latter-day Saints. "Below" means the telestial world and "outward" means it's a physical organization, maintained and led by physical, mortal people. Its purpose is to prepare you for all things to enter into membership in *the inner church. The inner church* is terrestrial, and it's Zion.

Let's go on over to Section 107:18, and let me give you a definition from the scriptures of this transition from one place to another. The Melchizedek Priesthood that we have in the "outer church below," The Church of Jesus Christ of Latter-day Saints, is to train you and tutor you in its ordinances, rights, and laws, so you can rise up and obtain a higher order of the priesthood. That higher order of the priesthood cannot be conferred by mortal men. It's not something you obtain by priesthood ordination by other priesthood bearers, mortal men. This higher ordination comes under the hands of God. You are called into that by His own voice.

Student 5: When you say that it comes under the hand of God, do you mean Heavenly Father, or do you mean an angel that is representing the Lord or God? I know when we talk about the Lord we are talking about Jesus Christ—

Mike: Right.

Student 5: And when we say, God, we are talking about Heavenly Father. I'm not sure if this is a doctrine, but I heard that sometimes the Lord will send an angel and when the angel speaks, he is speaking on behalf of God, and he would be referred to as God.

Mike: That's an excellent question, and the answer is, yes. This can come under the hands of the Savior Himself, or He can authorize what He calls in the scriptures, "the angel of His presence." There are angels that have the authority to act in the name of Christ. For example, there was an angel that went before the *children of Israel* when they rejected the invitation on Sinai to come into the presence of the Lord. The Lord said this of His angel, *"for my name is in him,"* which is an interesting statement. He is called *the angel of the presence of the Lord.* "He has My name," which means, "he speaks in My name as though he were Me." This principle is called *divine investiture of authority.* In the telestial world, we call it *power of attorney.* In other words, they have an agent who is authorized to act in their behalf, as though they were that person. When we went on our mission, we had a legal document drawn up so that my niece could be my power of attorney. She can sign documents in my name, and she can act as though she's my agent in every way. So, whether it comes from the hand of Christ himself, or whether He authorizes a heavenly messenger to bestow these promises and these ordinations on you, it's still eternal and binding in nature. It's the same.

Student 5: Yeah, I would think so because when the Lord mentions in the *Doctrine and Covenants*, that His word is binding whether it's spoken by Him or by his prophets, it is the same.

Mike: Right. It's the same kind of principle, isn't it? Now, let's look at Section 107:18:

> *The power and authority of the higher, or Melchizedek Priesthood, is to hold the keys of all the spiritual blessings of the church—*

Notice the dash; now we're going to list those blessings. Here they are:

> *[19] To have the privilege of* [1] *receiving the mysteries of the kingdom of heaven,*

Don't you find it interesting that the first thing listed is to receive the mysteries? I think of what Joseph Smith said, *"I advise all to go on to perfection, and seek deeper and deeper into the mysteries of Godliness."* That's coming from the Prophet Joseph. Not so much anymore, but periodically, we'll have well-meaning members of the Church come up and say, "Leave the mysteries alone. They're not important to our salvation." That is a counter statement to everything scriptural and prophetic that comes from God and His spokesmen. I spoke about the mysteries yesterday a little bit at that funeral because these people that we've been studying with were like sponges. We're talking about mysteries right here. These are the mysteries. And, the very first verse of the first book in the *Book of Mormon*, 1 Nephi 1:1, *"I, Nephi, having been born of goodly parents."* You know that one? Go down a few lines, and it says:

> *Yea, having had a great knowledge of the goodness and the mysteries of God,*

See? Right in the very first verse, Nephi is telling us, "I have something here, and I'm going to teach you how to get it." The whole purpose of the *Book of Mormon* is for us to obtain what Nephi obtained. So, going back to verse 19:

> [2] *to have the heavens opened unto them,* [3] *to commune with the general assembly and church of the Firstborn, and* [4] *to enjoy the communion and presence of God the Father, and Jesus the mediator of the new covenant.*

That's what you get. All of those privileges are yours as you stand in the presence of Christ, obtain and receive the *Second Comforter*, and the promises and ordinations that are associated with that. You keep hearing me say *ordination.* There is an *ordination* involved here. Let's go to *Doctrine and Covenants*, section 50. It talks about men and women who come up to this level of godliness. Verse 17:

> *Verily I say unto you,* ***he that is ordained of me***...

Who is the "*me*" that it's speaking of here? Look at verse 1:

> *Hearken, O ye elders of my church, and give ear to the voice of the living God;*

So, who's speaking here? This isn't Joseph Smith speaking. This is God speaking. And, in verse 17 he says, *"he that is ordained of me."* I take that literally. I don't take that symbolically, meaning, "Well, my father ordained me and we traced his priesthood genealogy back to Peter, James, and John, through seven different levels." I don't take it that way. That's my ordination to the Melchizedek Priesthood in the Church of Jesus Christ of Latter-day Saints. We're not talking about that one. That one has to precede this one. What we've had happen to us as men in the Church is preparatory and anticipatory of **this** that we're talking about. Remember the *mysteries of God* are hidden in plain sight. How many times have we read that in verse 17, and tied that into some physical ordination that takes place under the hands of a mortal man? Why do we change that? Why don't we take that literally? Now, go over to verse 26. Here it is again:

> *He that is* ***ordained of God***...

Now, we want to say, "Well, that takes place when my high priest group leader, or the stake president, or someone ordains me to be a high priest." No, it doesn't! Take it literally, because look at what follows after it says, *"ordained of God,"* and ask yourself if this happened to you when you were ordained by your stake president, father, elders quorum president, or someone else? Did this happen to you when you were ordained an elder?

> *[26] He that is* ***ordained of God*** *and sent forth, the same is appointed to be the greatest, notwithstanding he is the least and the servant of all.*
>
> *[27] Wherefore,* **he is possessor of all things**; *for* ***all things are subject unto him, both in heaven and on the earth, the life and the light, the Spirit and the power, sent forth by the will of the Father through Jesus Christ, his Son.***

Think about that, *"all things."* Think of everything that you can think of, and you are in control of that, and it obeys you. Do you think that's something you get through a physical ordination to the priesthood in the Church? I don't think so! Now, it gets better:

> *[28] But no man is possessor of all things except he be purified and cleansed from all sin.*

Do you see the "condition?"

When I was ordained an elder, I wasn't purified and cleansed from all sin. I didn't even know anything about it. I was just 19 yrs old, and someone said, "Get over here and sit down and we're going to lay hands on your head and ordain you an elder." Now look at the next verse:

> *[29] And if ye are purified and cleansed from all sin, ye shall ask whatsoever you will in the name of Jesus and it shall be done.*

We are talking here about a priesthood ordination that is something more profound than what we are talking about in the Church.

Student 5: From the beginning, I realized this and shared it often with my sister: In the Book of Helaman, when the sign was given of the birth of Jesus Christ, around that time was when Nephi obtained this ordination from Him.

Mike: He did. Nephi received this ordination, and you can read about it in the Book of Helaman, chapter 10. Here, Nephi, the son of Nephi, the son of Helaman, the son of Helaman, the son of Alma, the son of Alma, obtains what section 50 is talking about. So, you're right [student 5]. Now, brothers and sisters, something is happening in the Church. Something magnificent is taking place. I caught a feel for it this last general conference. We, as men and women, priesthood bearers and sisters, and husbands and wives, are being asked to *step-up*. Basically, what we are being told by the Brethren is that our past activity level in the Church will not be enough to sustain us in the future. If we don't do something different from this point forward, we're not going to survive the day that's coming.
Student 5: I think a general authority said that when a prophet speaks, try to focus on the timeframe for when his prophecies will come to pass; it will be about ten years. So, I tried to put that to the test. I listened to the 2006 General Conference, and it was a little bit shocking, but it was surprising that everything that they were counseling us about as members, we are going through today (in 2016), as a society and across the whole world.
Mike: Interesting! I would invite you to go back and read President Russell M. Nelson's opening address from the last general priesthood meeting. He did something very significant this time around. He built on something that Boyd K. Packer had said five to ten years ago in a general conference. Brother Packer said this:

> *We have done very well at distributing the authority of the priesthood. We have priesthood authority planted nearly everywhere. We have quorums of elders and high priests worldwide. But distributing the* ***authority*** *of the priesthood has raced, I think, ahead of distributing the* ***power*** *of the priesthood. The priesthood does not have the strength that it should have and will not have until the power of the priesthood is firmly fixed in the families as it should be.*

That was Brother Packer's lamentation; that we've done well in ordaining them, but our ordained men don't have "power." Now let me read to you what President Nelson said; listen to this statement. This is from this last conference:

> *I urgently plead with each one of us to live up to our privileges as bearers of the priesthood. In a coming day, only those men who have taken their priesthood seriously, by diligently seeking to be taught by the Lord Himself, will be able to bless, guide, protect, strengthen, and heal others. Only a man who has paid the price for priesthood power will be able to bring miracles to those he loves and keep his marriage and family safe, now and throughout eternity.*

Then he goes on to talk about how we obtain *power **in** the priesthood.* Now, pay attention to that terminology; not power **of** the priesthood, but *power **in** the priesthood.* That terminology is only used in one place that I know of on the earth. It's not in the scriptures anywhere, and it's only used at the most sacred place at the veil, just prior to entering into the presence of the Lord. It's only used there. Then he goes on to talk about how we can obtain that. I was just thrilled. I said to Margie, "That was a historic speech! This is a mile marker in the progress of the Church in preparing a people for the *Second Coming* of the Lord. This is a call to rise up and do something more."

Then, President Monson closed that priesthood address, and he only spoke for about six minutes. He used an example of a friend he knew who was shot down during World War II:

> *During World War II, a friend of mine was serving in the South Pacific when his plane was shot down over the ocean. He and the other crew members successfully parachuted from the burning plane, inflated their life rafts, and clung to those rafts for three days.*
>
> *On the third day, they spotted what they knew to be a rescue vessel. It passed them by. The next morning it passed them by again. They began to despair as they realized that this was the last day the rescue vessel would be in the area.*

> *Then the Holy Spirit spoke to my friend: "You have the priesthood. Command the rescuers to pick you up."*
> *He did as prompted: "In the name of Jesus Christ and by the power of the priesthood, turn about and pick us up."*
> *Within a few minutes, the vessel was beside them, helping them on deck. A faithful and worthy bearer of the priesthood, in his extremity, had exercised that priesthood, blessing his life and the lives of others.*

I think that what we're doing now is moving into a phase where we've got to access these powers. **If we always do what we've always done, we'll always get what we've always got.** As a Church, we're not accessing the gifts and powers of the priesthood like we need to in order to be prepared for what's coming.

Now, what **is** coming, brothers and sisters? I don't know if you follow the earthquakes and the volcanoes and the "ring of fire," but everything is getting very interesting. The whole earth is in turmoil, and men's hearts are failing them. So, all of the signs of the *Second Coming* are being fulfilled in a major way all around us. What's happening is that the earth is being prepared to move from a telestial to a terrestrial place. The earth is going to make this transition. It's going to go. And all the shaking and moving and everything that is happening right now is preparatory to this planet moving out of its place in this nine-planet solar system, lighted by a sun, and moving somewhere closer in the Milky Way system toward the center, where God and the Elohim dwell. It's going to move a third of the way back. Right now, we are two-thirds removed from the center of our system. The Mothers and Fathers, the Elohim, dwell in the galactic bulges of these huge galaxies; in those big light bulges, you see in the center of a galaxy. You know why there is light there? It's because the Men and Women who live there in the center of these galaxies are Beings of Light and light originates independently from them. They become light sources because of the gospel plan of Jesus Christ. Now, we're two-thirds of the way out. We're so far out from the center that we need a planet that we call the sun, to give us light. We're behind a veil of darkness of cosmic dust and at such a far distance that we need a planet that's on fire to provide light for us. When the earth leaves this solar system, it will move back a third closer to the center. At that point, there will be no need for a SUN because you now enter a terrestrial world, and the God of the terrestrial world is the SON. He will provide the light for the terrestrial millennial reign. After a thousand years, those of us who have been transformed and can make the transition will now go back to the Father of Lights. That's what the Hebrew calls the "Holy Father." He's the Father of Lights. Not light—light**s**—that's plural. It's something to ponder! We are living in a time in the history of the world when the earth is now in its preparatory stage to make the transition. All the cataclysmic events (the tidal waves, the earthquakes, the tornados, the whirlwinds, the famine, etc.) are part of the transformation process that the earth will go through to go from a telestial world to a terrestrial world. We, as God's children, need to have those same transforming events take place in order for us to abide the change. **Most of God's children on the earth won't make that transition.** Most of the population of the earth will **not** make this coming transition. Their bodies will die in a fire. Their spirits will go into a holding place, and they will be there for one thousand years, in a continuing education situation because they did not graduate from the telestial classroom. So, they now need to have a continuing education experience in a holding place where Satan still has power, and the righteous will minister to them from a sacred place. Those who qualify to make this transition will enjoy a millennial reign for a thousand years where they'll be in the presence of the Lord in a terrestrial world, **the third estate**. Questions or comments?

Student 5: On what do you base these teachings and ideas that we will move closer to the center of the galaxy?

Mike: That was taught by Joseph Smith, Brigham Young, Heber C. Kimball, John Taylor, Wilford Woodruff, and Parley P. Pratt. You can read about it in many sources. One is called, *Key to the Science of Theology* by Parley P. Pratt. It's spoken about extensively in the *Journal of Discourses* and Brigham Young just said, "Yes, this planet moves back." Interesting that the place it moves back to is the place that it originally was. The Garden of Eden planet, the planet Earth in its Garden of Eden state, was where this planet is returning back to for the Millennium. If you want to run a pattern, look at what it was like in the Garden of Eden, and you can almost see an exact pattern of what it will be like in the Millennium. The millennial third estate, the terrestrial world is an Edenic (Eden) paradisiacal (paradise) state. That's why the tenth Article of Faith says, *"the earth will be renewed and receive its paradisiacal glory,"* and that is a terrestrial world. Jesus Christ is the God of the terrestrial world. So, when you obtain these blessings, all of these things that we've been talking about now, they accompany the experience of the *Second Comforter*. It's even possible for you at that time to make a request, because as you stand in His presence and as the interview ends, God will say, "My daughter; is there anything you request of Me before I go back to the Father?" Before you get to that point, you will have been inspired by the Holy Ghost, and you will have already had the request given to you by personal revelation. So, when He asks you that question, you can answer with an inspired request, and **your request shall be granted**. Does that sound familiar? Does this wording sound familiar? How about this one, "What is wanted?" Does that sound familiar? You are invited to make an inspired request. At that point, when you're in His presence, there have been some people who have said this, "I want to remain on the earth, as long as the earth stands, and bring souls unto You until You come in glory." So, their request was what? To be translated. Others have said, "I want to come into Your presence as soon as my ministry on the earth is completed." So, you go down, and you see that every one of these great prophets in the scriptures has had this experience. They've stood in the presence of God, God asked them what they wanted, they made an inspired request, and He grants it. And then you can see the fulfillment of that request later on in their ministry.

Student 5: When the Three Nephites asked that question of the Lord, it said they felt a little bit shy. What does that mean?

Mike: People who have shared this experience say that when you stand in the presence of God, your first feeling is one of seeing where He is, and where you are, and the great distance between you is intimidating. You stand in His glory and behold where you are on the path, and the feeling is intimidating. But, every one of the people who has shared this has said that this feeling quickly disappears and is replaced with an overflowing spirit of love and familiarity. But, your first feeling is, "Oh, my!" Do you remember what Isaiah said when he was brought into the presence of the Lord? He said, *"I am undone."* Do you remember what the brother of Jared did? He dropped to the ground on his face, and the Savior said, *"Why hast thou fallen?"* You see, it's just overwhelming, but quickly followed by a spirit of love and familiar intimacy, and then you're embraced and held in His arms.

Student 5: As if He's your friend.

Mike: He is your best friend. He is, and He knows you so well, so perfectly, so intimately. One man I know, when he had this encounter, said, "It's You!" That's what came out of his mouth! Think about that. "It's You!" Another person said, "Do you know what the first thing is that the Savior says to you? Do you know what the first words out of His mouth are as you stand in His presence and the immediate shock of this encounter wears off? Do you know what the Savior's first words are to you after He calls you by name?" He calls you by your familiar name, not a formal name. He said, "The first words he says are, 'Thank you.' And then He lists some things that He's grateful you've accomplished." Think about it, brothers and sisters. It's no small thing for you to rise up in a stature of faith and confidence with the Lord that you can enter into His presence.

I think of when Nephi was interviewed by the Holy Ghost in 1 Nephi 11:4. The Holy Ghost asked him a question:

> *Believest thou that thy father saw the tree of which he hath spoken?*

That's the question, see? And, Nephi says,

> *[5] Yea, thou knowest that I believe all the words of my father.*

Then, for the whole next verse, the Holy Ghost is just ecstatic and rejoices, and says, *"Hosanna to the Lord, the most high God;"* And you sit back and wonder why the Holy Ghost is so excited about Nephi when he said, *"I believe all the words of my father."* Did you ever wonder about that? I've thought about it, and here's my opinion. It is so rare for a human being, a man or a woman, to come up to that level of faith and confidence, that when heaven and the angels finally find one, there is tremendous rejoicing in heaven! It's tremendous because the whole world is in darkness and unbelief. So, if they can find one man or one woman somewhere, who says, "I believe it all," and they are not just words, but have it in their heart, even if it's just the grain of a mustard seed, these angels and spirits know that and they rejoice because it's rare, but it's not impossible.

Now, in closing tonight, just let me say that this wasn't the lesson I had prepared to give tonight, but that's all right. The one thing that keeps us from all of this is not a lack of faith. It's not faithlessness that bars the path and shuts the gate to all of these blessings. It's *unbelief.* Do you want to try a little interesting scriptural study this week? Go to lds.org to *scriptures* and put in the word *unbelief.* Then, just read all of the scriptures, knowing that the *Book of Mormon* calls *unbelief* the iniquity of the gentiles and the curse of the House of Israel. All of the visions, all of the dreams, all of the manifestations and visitations, the miracles, signs, everything that you read about in the scriptures, are withheld because of *unbelief.* Not faithlessness. You're probably saying, "What are you talking about, Brother Stroud? Isn't faithlessness the same as unbelief?" It's not. So, let me share my thoughts about these two, and we'll end the lesson tonight.

To give us a launch pad on where we can begin to build, let's talk about how to obtain these promises and these blessings. Faithlessness is where you just don't believe anything that is Godly. You don't believe that there is a God. You believe that if there is a God, that He's powerless. You believe that maybe God worked at one time in history, but He doesn't work anymore. That's a great belief in the Christian world. You don't believe that there is anything like the *ministration of angels* or the *gifts of the Spirit*. That's faithlessness. Now, let's bring it up to a different level. Let's say that you DO believe in all of those things. So, you have faith, and you believe that these things that are written in the scriptures actually did happen. You have no doubt in your mind that when you read about these things in the *Holy Word* that they really did happen to men and women, then and there. You have faith in that. You have no problem with that. Now, let's bring it a little closer to us. Let's leave all the dead prophets and let's come among the living. So, do you believe that the First Presidency and the Quorum of the Twelve have access to all the things that are mentioned in the scriptures and the sacred experiences that we've been talking about for weeks? We would say, "Sure, I believe that. I have faith in that." You have faith that Thomas Monson, Hal Eyring, Jeffrey Holland, and those brethren have had a *Second Comforter* experience? I believe that. I don't know that all of them have, but I believe that some of them have. I don't have any problem with that. How about the Seventies? Yes, I don't have any question about that at all. How about your stake president? Now you're looking a little closer, aren't you? You might say, "My stake president is a great spiritual giant, and I don't have any problem with seeing my stake president in possession of these wonderful blessings and experiences." How about your bishop? "Ahhh, well, you know, maybe. Sure, why not?" How about **you**? And you bring it down now to **you**. You bring it on down, and you look in the mirror. You read about all these experiences in the *Holy Word* and you know they happen to others, but you just can't see it happening to **you**. That, my friends, is *UNBELIEF.*

So, as the Lord says, *"I leave these sayings with you to ponder in your hearts."* It is for all of us to ponder, and see if we can come to a point where somehow, we can begin to entertain the idea that Mike Stroud could actually have a brother of Jared experience; that in this life we can each have an encounter with the resurrected Christ, one on one, face to face. You see, it has to be available, brothers and sisters. It has to be, or God is a liar because He says, "I am no respecter of persons and in Me, there is no shadow of changing. I am the same yesterday, today and forever." You might not be able to see this yet, but the question is, "Is it available to you? Can it happen to you?" The answer is a resounding, "Yes!" I believe God is a God of truth and cannot lie. So, the problem isn't with Him. The problem is with me. I'm so distracted in the telestial world. I am so frustrated with my weaknesses that I, like Nephi, look at myself and say, "Oh, wretched man that I am." I see that, and I just cannot overcome the obstacle that's there, and that says, "This is your right and your privilege, Mike, to have the veil opened and know that I Am." And, every time that I go to the temple, from the beginning initiatory, to where I pass through the veil, the whole allegory is teaching me how to do this, **in this life**. Nothing in the temple, brothers and sisters, is pointing to after physical death. Have you ever noticed that physical death is not mentioned anywhere in the temple allegory? We are the ones that put it after death. It's not there. Everything in the temple ceremony has to do with the system in the telestial world, to redeem us from the Fall, and bring us back into the presence of God, while we're still in the flesh. Everything. When you see that and start to grasp that, it changes your view; it increases your confidence that you can now begin to *"call upon me while I am near— Draw near unto me and I will draw near unto you; seek me diligently and ye shall find me."*

References:
2 Nephi 31:2
2 Nephi 32:6-7
John 17:3
D&C 84:23-25 *children of Israel* rejected the invitation to see Lord on Sinai
Exodus 23:20-23 Angel of the Lord
Ensign, Apr. 2002, 17–18 The authority to speak on behalf of Heavenly Father is referred to as divine investiture of authority
D&C 107:18-19
D&C 50:17, 26-29
April 2010 General Conference Priesthood Session, Boyd K. Packer
April 2016 General Conference Priesthood Session, Russell M. Nelson
April 2016 General Conference Priesthood Session, Thomas S. Monson
D&C 88:62-63

Chapter Fourteen

Podcast 014 Unbelief Revisited / Priesthood Introduction

Last week's lesson was on unbelief. I want to add just a couple of little postscripts on that. Let's go to *Doctrine and Covenants* section 84. You may remember, as I do, that when Ezra Taft Benson became the president of the Church, the theme of his presidency, and I think it must be the main theme of his ministry, was the *Book of Mormon*. And to get the Saints into the *Book of Mormon*, he quoted section 84, verse 54. Section 84 was given in 1832, so the organization of the Church was only two years old, and yet a startling thing is mentioned beginning in verse 54. The Lord says this to the Latter-day Saints:

> *And your minds in times past have been darkened because of* ***unbelief****, and because you have treated lightly the things that you have received—*
> *[55] Which vanity and* ***unbelief*** *have brought the whole church under condemnation.*

That was in 1832, two years after the organization of the Church. The Lord says the whole Church is under condemnation. Then going on to verse 56:

> *And this condemnation resteth upon the children of Zion, even all.*

[57] And they [the children of Zion] shall remain under this condemnation until they repent and remember the new covenant,

Another word for covenant is testament. So, whenever we read in the *Bible* where it says the *New Testament* or the *Old Testament* you can replace the word testament with covenant; the old covenant and the new covenant. And here He is talking about even a newer covenant than the *New Testament* new covenant:

even the book of Mormon and the former commandments which I have given them, not only to say, but to do according to that which I have written—

In verse 57, it leads us to believe that the way we treat things lightly that we receive from Him, *"which **vanity** and **unbelief** have brought the whole church under condemnation,"* is that we talk about it, but we don't **do** it. Notice at the bottom of verse 57, *"not only **to say** but **to do** according to that which I have written."* You can talk the talk, but you can't walk the walk. It has always been a form of hypocrisy throughout the world to say one thing and do something else. That's the definition of hypocrisy, a hypocrite. According to the definition the Lord gives, the whole Church is under condemnation because they have received something from Him and they treated it lightly, which means they talk about it, but they don't **do** it. And one of the things that they treated lightly was the *Book of Mormon.*

You might find this interesting. It's a historical fact that for several years after the organization of the of the Church, the Brethren and the elders taught the gospel and the restoration out of the *Bible*, and hardly touched the *Book of Mormon* in their missionary endeavors. Did you know that? And at one time there was a big rally, I can't remember where it was, but it seems to me it was in Pennsylvania somewhere. I'd have to look it up. But, Parley P. Pratt said that Brother Rigdon spoke and used exclusively the *Bible* to prove the Restoration:

When he was through, brother Joseph arose like a lion about to roar; and being full of the Holy Ghost, spoke in great power, bearing testimony of the visions he had seen, the ministering of angels which he had enjoyed; and how he had found the

> *plates of the Book of Mormon, and translated them by the gift and power of God. He commenced by saying: "If nobody else had the courage to testify of so glorious a message from Heaven, and of the finding of so glorious a record, he felt to do it in justice to the people, and leave the event with God." The entire congregation were astounded; electrified, as it were, and overwhelmed with the sense of the truth and power by which he spoke, and the wonders which he related.*

So, it was a real problem that the early members of the Church were not using the *Book of Mormon* to move forward the cause of the Church, and ultimately the cause of Zion.

Now, go back to verse 58. If they talk about it but don't **do** it then they can't:

> *...bring forth the fruit meet for their Father's kingdom; otherwise [if we remain just talkers or hearers of the Word and not doers] there remaineth a scourge and judgment to be poured out upon the children of Zion.*

Then he asks the question:

> *[59] For shall the children of the kingdom pollute my holy land? Verily, I say unto you, Nay.*

President Benson quoted that many times during his presidency in the early to mid-1980's and said that the Church was still under condemnation because we still haven't learned the lesson to not treat lightly the things the Lord has given us, which He calls vanity and unbelief. So, we have to ask ourselves a question. President Benson gave a talk in 1988 called *I Testify*. He got up and bore his testimony, and it was powerful. The question is: Have we done any better in 2016 than we were doing in 1988? That's the question we have to ask ourselves. And does the Lord still consider the Church organization under any kind of condemnation that's mentioned here in section 84? If so, the good news about that is that individually you don't have to be. We can each individually stand approved of the Lord by learning the lessons that He's talking about here in the scriptures, and not treating lightly with unbelief and vanity, the things the Lord gives us. Does that make sense?

Student 1: Sure.

Mike: It's a sobering thought to consider that less than two years after the organization of the Church the Lord said that His Church was under condemnation. I hope that we come out from underneath that. I hope that in 2016 we are not still found under condemnation. I will mention that I have not heard any leader since President Benson, in any general conference refer to section 84, verses 54 through 58 like President Benson did. So, I guess we're left on our own to judge as to where we stand as an institution and move forward accordingly because one thing you want to do is to move forward.

Now, last week we talked about unbelief. We mentioned that there is a difference between faithlessness and unbelief. You can have faith and unbelief at the same time. I know that sounds contradictory, but unbelief is how you personally view what you can accomplish according to the promises of the Lord; not what others can do and have done, but unbelief brings it home to you. That's where you start by looking in the mirror, and you start asking yourself the questions like, "Is it possible for me to entertain angels? Is it possible for me to have the kind of faith where I can call down the powers of heaven and command and control the elements of nature?" We read about all these things throughout the scriptures. We know that they are true and we have the faith that they are true. I have no doubt that in my mind that what I read about in the scriptures that others have done, actually took place. There's no question. But, when I think about **me** doing some of those same things, then I start to waver. A verse the Lord uses is James 1:5:

> *If any of you lack wisdom, let him ask of God, that giveth to all men liberally, and upbraideth not; and it shall be given him.*
>
> *[6] But let him ask in faith,* ***nothing wavering****. For he that wavereth is like a wave of the sea driven with the wind and tossed.*

So, where the wavering from Mike Stroud comes in, is when I start to consider what I'm able to do according to my faith and my priesthood power. What am I able to accomplish and do I have the faith that what I read about in the scriptures can be duplicated in my own life? If I don't, I'm suffering from unbelief. Does that make sense, brothers and sisters? Do you have any questions or comments on that concept before we look at a couple of other scriptures? Unbelief is the great stumbling block to progress for the Latter-day Saints; the great stumbling block! Now, in President Benson's talk, *Beware of Pride*, he said that pride was the universal sin and a great stumbling block to the establishment of Zion.

Let's look at another scripture over in Mormon chapter 9. This is one that Margie and I were reading this week and saw it in a different light than we've seen it before. This is Moroni, who was reading an epistle of his father that was given in a synagogue. It mentions the fact that if miracles cease, then it's because of unbelief. Now, you can read that whole thing. If you look at verse 15, he asked the question:

> *And now, O all ye that have imagined up unto yourselves a god that can do no miracles, I would ask of you, have all of these things passed, of which I have spoken?*

See, he's looking at all of the scriptures; he's got the brass plates, he's got all the writings from Adam up to Jeremiah, plus their own experiences. So, can you imagine yourselves a God that can do no miracles?

> *Has the end come yet? Behold I say unto you, Nay; and God has not ceased to be a God miracles.*

So, that's the theme that runs through the whole 9th chapter. Now, go to verse 20. This is a great self-evaluation for us, brothers and sisters. This is what we would call *"an hard saying."* So, you look at yourself and ask yourself the question: Do you see miracles in your life? Are you observing, are you participating in, and are you witnessing miracles in your life? Ask yourself that question. He says:

> *And the reason why he ceaseth to do miracles among the children of men is because that they* ***dwindle*** *in unbelief.*

And I think that word **dwindle** is a classic *Book of Mormon* word. It's a word we find used a lot in the *Book of Mormon*. I would have to do a word search, but I don't know if that word is even used in the *Bible* anywhere. But, it is used over and over in the *Book of Mormon*; **dwindle**. So, I looked it up. In the *1828 Merriam Webster dictionary*, which is the dictionary that Joseph Smith had, it says, "to diminish gradually, to decrease, and become smaller from the original." You get that feeling of going backward; **dwindle** in unbelief. That seems to tell me that this problem of unbelief doesn't come upon you all at once; very few things do, but it begins slowly and subtly. You have to have the gift of discernment, some of the gifts of the Spirit, to even know that it's overtaking you. I know people who've said to me, "I just don't feel about these things the way I used to." Did you ever have anybody say that to you when you are talking about spiritual things, or about the Church, or the programs of the Church, or testimony? "I just don't feel the way I used to." They recognize that at some past time, they were in a place where they are not now. And they are surprised when they look at their lives, to see where they are now, still being able to remember what they once enjoyed. That's the feeling of dwindling. So, back to verse 20. If there are no miracles among the children of men it is because they **dwindle** in unbelief:

> *and depart from* ***the right way****, and know not the God in whom they should trust.*

Now, another name for *the right way* is righteousness. The word righteousness starts out with the word *right*. There's no such thing as *leftousness*. It is righteousness and righteousness means you are traversing *the right way*. When you start to dwindle in unbelief, the next step is that you *"depart from the right way, and know not the God in whom they should trust."* If they ever did know him, they've lost that knowledge and have gone backward, and that's *"dwindling in unbelief."* It's a process of going backward, diminishing, and decreasing from something greater. Now, here are some keys that tie into this. Look at the next verse, Mormon 9:21:

> *Behold, I say unto you that whosoever believeth in Christ,* ***doubting nothing****,*

> *whatsoever he shall ask the Father in the name of Christ it shall be granted him; and this promise is given unto all, even unto the ends of the earth.*

You ought to triple underline this one, *"doubting nothing."* And your big criterion is, *"Believe in Christ, doubting nothing."* There are no other criteria. If you ask something of Christ and you doubt nothing, if it's not asked amiss and it's a righteous desire, then you should be able to realize that. Now, go to verse 25 and let's see what Moroni is trying to teach us:

> *And whosoever shall believe in my name, **doubting nothing**, unto him I will confirm all my words, even the ends of the earth.*

There's that *doubting nothing* again. Down to verse 27:

> *O then despise not, and wonder not, but hearken unto the words of the Lord, and ask the Father in the name of Jesus for what things soever ye shall stand in need. **Doubt not,***

So, three times in seven verses, the Lord says ***doubt not***. Now, He says the reason miracles cease is because of unbelief. So, doubting is an indicator that you are suffering from unbelief. Of course, that makes sense, doesn't it? These two terms are tied together. Now, back to verse 27:

> *but be believing, and begin as in times of old, and come unto the Lord with all your heart, and work out your own salvation with fear and trembling before him.*
>
> *[28] Be wise in the days of your probation;*

Unbelief; this is a huge problem. And again, most people believe that unbelief is the same thing as having no faith. It is not. It's different. These are two different terms.

Let's go to Ether chapter 4 and let me show you where, again, Moroni addresses this. Now, the cure for unbelief is to pray for the gifts of the Spirit. When the gifts of the Spirit start to be realized in your life, you bring forth fruit. I want to share some of the fruits of doing away with unbelief. Look at Ether 4, verse 15. It's a marvelous scripture:

> *Behold, when ye shall rend that veil of unbelief...*

Boy, here Moroni calls unbelief a veil. Think about that for a minute. There are several different veils. There's not just one veil. There are several different veils. The physical body is a veil. God dwells by His Spirit, His mind, power, and intelligence inside you. But your physical body veils that. This is why when a person dies and lays the physical body down, they immediately come into contact with the spiritual realm that's invisible as long as you're in the body. That body is a veil. So, back to Moroni:

> *[15] Behold, when ye shall rend that veil of unbelief which doth cause you to remain in that awful state of wickedness, and hardness of heart, and blindness of mind,*

Look at that. Those are some synonyms to unbelief: wickedness, hardness of heart, and blindness of mind. If we can break through the veil, if we can rend that veil of unbelief, look at what is on the other side:

> *then shall the great and marvelous things which have been hid up from the foundation of the world from you—yea, when ye shall call upon the Father in my name, with a broken heart and a contrite spirit, then shall ye know that the Father hath remembered the covenant which he made unto your fathers, O house of Israel.*

Now, if I want to *rend the veil of unbelief*, then I need to come into a state of grace, having a *broken heart and a contrite spirit*. Now, grace is a power. Grace is strength and power. Whenever Nephi talks about the strength of the Lord, he's referring to the grace of Jesus Christ. Grace or strength is an enabling power and a divine help. So, if you come into this state of grace called a broken heart and a contrite spirit, you cannot at the same time be in a state of unbelief. You can't do it. If we want to *rend the veil of unbelief*, we should seek to find ourselves in a state of grace that the scriptures call *a broken heart and a contrite spirit.* There are two or three other terms that tie into that: meekness, humility, lowliness of heart. When you put all of those things together, you rend the veil of unbelief, and what's on the other side of that are the *"great and marvelous things which have been hid up from the foundations of the world."* What do we call those? The *mysteries*. Brothers and sisters, when you start to have *the mysteries of God* unfolded to your view, you are not behind the veil of unbelief. The very fact that they are being unfolded to your view, by revelation, by the power of the Spirit, and by the Holy Ghost, is an indicator and is proof that you are not found behind that veil of unbelief.

Well, let's leave that for now. I can't think of anything else I want to add onto the concept of unbelief, other than that it's a great stumbling block and literally keeps us from the higher things of the gospel of Jesus Christ. It blocks you out from *the mysteries of godliness* and all of the powers of the priesthood. I'd like to share with you, in the last few minutes, the last half of the class, some thoughts on priesthood. So, I will end last week's class on unbelief and open the door a little bit for some thoughts on priesthood.

My patriarchal blessing admonishes me to search, study, and understand the priesthood. Today at church, in the Gospel Essentials class, the lesson was on the priesthood. The teacher asked the question, "What is the priesthood?" A sister missionary that was there raised her hand and said, "It's the power and authority of God." And that's true. That's pretty much the standard answer that we give whenever we want to define the term *priesthood.* We recognize the power and authority to act in the name of God. *Given to man*, we should add that in there; the power and authority of God, *given to man*, to act in His name. Those are good definitions, and they are true. But, like all things in the gospel, there are different levels of understanding of truth. And when you understand a greater level of truth, it doesn't diminish the lesser level of truth because all truth can be circumcised into one great whole. There's not one truth sitting out here in the periphery, that's not a part of another truth that's right before your eyes. All truth is circumscribed into a whole. We hear that in the temple. Let's chat a little bit about priesthood for just a minute. Let me throw some ideas out for you to think about. The scriptures talk about *the **right** of the priesthood* and *the **rights** of the priesthood.* It talks about the ***doctrines** of the priesthood* and *the **doctrine** of the priesthood*—singular and plural. It talks about *the keys of the priesthood.* And so, all of these different terms are tied in with the priesthood, but we only have one little basic definition. So, let's see if we can open this up a little bit further.

This is just my own experience. One day while I was pondering this, I took the word priesthood, and breaking it up I noticed the word *hood* at the end. I had never paid any attention to that before. Then my mind started to go from there to other places, and I thought about other words that have the word *hood* attached to them: brotherhood, sisterhood, neighborhood, knighthood, motherhood, fatherhood. Suddenly, a picture started to evolve as I thought about all these words in my mind that end with the word *hood.* What they all have in common with each other is that they are each a group or a community of like-minded things or people. So, you have a knighthood, and a knight is a person that belongs to a group of other knights, and they belong to this society where knighthood is experienced. Fatherhood is a group of fathers; motherhood is a group of mothers; a neighborhood is a group of neighbors. So, with that in mind, I took the word priesthood, and it is a group of priests! Instead of talking about a thing or a power, which it is, we are now talking about a group of individuals. If we go into heaven, we would talk about the society of priests. It starts to open up some interesting thoughts as to things we hear in the temple, in the initiatory, in the scriptures, and Joseph Smith talked about receiving ordinances that make men priests and women priestesses. When we start talking about that group of people we start talking about a society of exalted men and women that exist in heaven on the other side of the veil. So, the priesthood is now not only a power, but I believe you can look at it as a power that comes from a society of priests and priestesses. And if you tap into that power, you enjoy some of the privileges that they enjoy.

Let me present another thought to you, and just kind of consider these things a little bit. In *A New Witness for the Articles of Faith,* Brother McConkie comes out and lists priesthood, faith, and the Holy Spirit (not the Holy Ghost), and says that those three things are the same thing. So, Brother McConkie (and we quoted this in another class) comes out and says that that the Holy Spirit also may well be faith and priesthood, and then he mentions one other thing, the Omniscience of God. The Omniscience of God means that He knows all things. Go to section 121, verse 34 and let's look at this. We have all heard this quoted so many times that most of us can quote it from memory:

> *Behold, there are many called, but few are chosen. And why are they not chosen?*
> *[35] Because their hearts are set so much upon the things of this world, and aspire to the honors of men, that they do not learn this one lesson—*

Now, here's the lesson to learn. If you learn this lesson, you move from called to chosen, and from chosen to elected, and from elected to an *election made sure*. This is known as *calling and election made sure*. The two things that keep that from you are that you aspire to the honors of men, and your hearts are set upon the things of this world. Now, here's the lesson. Here is what we should learn in order to move forward:

> *[36] That the* ***rights*** *of the priesthood...*

And we ought to ask ourselves a question: what are those rights? What does that mean? I guess at this point most of us would say, "Well, the rights are for me to be able to kneel and bless the sacrament. The rights are for me to give blessings to the sick. The rights are for me to bless and name babies on Fast Sunday in Church." And those certainly are rights of the priesthood, but look at what he says:

> *That the rights of the priesthood are inseparably connected with the* ***powers of heaven****,*

We ought to ask ourselves another question. What is that? All of this is talking about the priesthood. If we were to take and capitalize the words *Powers and Heaven,* instead of *powers* with a small **p** and *heavens* with a small **h**; if we put a capital there you now make those proper nouns, and they become names of people, not some ambiguous thing. Now you are referring to individuals that are where? In heaven. So, the rights of the priesthood are inseparably connected with this society of priests and priestesses that dwell behind the veil in an exalted state. If you want to enjoy those rights, you have to tap into this society of men and women who live in heaven. And look at the rest of verse 36:

> *and that the powers of heaven cannot be controlled nor handled only upon the principles of righteousness.*
> *[37] That they* [meaning the rights of the priesthood] *may be conferred upon us, it is true;*

Then he talks about when you use unrighteous dominion, etc. and ends with:

> *Amen to the priesthood or the authority of that man.*

Now, last week, President Nelson had some comments on priesthood power, and I read you that statement last week, from general conference by President Packer. The whole Church is being asked to rise up now and access something greater. We've got ordinations done well. We've got that figured out in the Church: ordained. But we do not have the **power** in the priesthood that should accompany or follow an ordination. There is no power that automatically follows an ordination for the ordination's sake. There is no power in the ordination, nothing. It's an ordinance that is supposed to open the door and give you a right to obtain and achieve something greater. The lamentation of Boyd K. Packer and President Nelson is that we receive the ordination and become stuck as priesthood bearers. So, we're not enjoying the rights of the priesthood. Now, if we are saying that the rights of the priesthood are to perform ordinances and go to the temple and do that, then I guess you could say we are enjoying the rights.

But, I want you to go with me over to the *Joseph Smith Translation.* Let me show you some rights of the priesthood that are available to us. The *Joseph Smith Translation* is just before the maps and after the *Bible dictionary.* So, in our priesthood class today, the teacher asked, "Would any of you like to share with us some of the experiences you've had with the priesthood, and how the Lord has blessed you with the priesthood?" We heard some great stories. A young man who had been inactive for seven years had a baby that was very sick and in the hospital. The baby was going to be air-vacked out and was turning blue. The doctor said, "We've got to get him out of here!" A bishopric that wasn't from his ward walked in, they laid hands on the baby and gave a priesthood blessing. And as they were running the baby down the hall, his color started to change, and the baby started to look differently. They stopped and said, "Gee, there is no need to air-vac him out." And that definitely was the priesthood blessing. You and I have seen things like that. But, go with me to Genesis chapter 14 in the *Joseph Smith Translation*, and let me give you some of the rights of the priesthood. Do you see Genesis 14:25- 40? Verse 30 says:

> *For God having sworn unto Enoch and unto his seed with an oath by himself; that* ***every one*** *being ordained after this order and calling should have* ***power****, by faith, to break mountains, to divide the seas, to dry up waters, to turn them out of their course;*

I want to emphasize something, and I want you to mark where it says, ***"every one."*** Everyone who's ordained after this order and calling has the right to do these things. It gets better in verse 31 and gives you more:

> *To put at defiance the armies of nations,*

You're going to see that in a coming day. You're going to see individuals, single men, or small groups of men—priesthood bearers—that will raise their arms in sacred signs and will stop armies, call down fire from heaven, speak and the earth will open up and swallow their enemies, will have a fire coming at them and cause it to go around them and leave them unscathed. We're going to see that. Brothers and sisters, you're going to see miracles in a coming day, that will take the greatest miracles that you read about in the scriptures, and make them look like child's play; because if we don't have those miracles in the coming day, there will be nobody on Earth left to meet the Savior when He comes. So, some things have got to change, and I feel that this last conference was a historical turning point on what the priesthood needs to do. Go back to verse 31:

To put at defiance of the armies of nations, to divide the earth, to break every band, to stand in the presence of God; to do all things according to his will, according to his command, subdue principalities and powers; and this by the will of the son of God which was from before the foundation of the world.

Now, that priesthood power is available to every man in the Church today. It's available. And, if you don't believe that as a man you can do that, and if a wife doesn't believe her husband could do that, then you're suffering from what? ***Unbelief!*** Now, let me leave that for just a minute.

Those are some of the great powers of the priesthood that are going to be manifested in a coming day. I don't believe those powers are manifested very much today because I think that we think that our ordinations are all that's necessary to give us that power, and they're not. The ordination, again, in and of itself, has no power. No ordination, no ordinance has power within itself. You just don't go in and have an ordinance, or ordination and think that because of that ritual, somehow, you're going to receive power. All that ordinations and ordinances do are to open the door and make available to you something you could not have had before the ordinance or the ordination took place. It is the same thing as receiving the *gift of the Holy Ghost*. As Brother David A. Bednar said that it's an invitation; it's a priesthood injunction (which means a command) for you now to go out and obtain the constant companionship of the Holy Ghost. So, when you are ordained an elder, a seventy, or a high priest, inherent within that are certain miracles that can be performed that belong to that priesthood, but you have to go out and claim those things. The only way that they can be claimed is based *"upon the principles of righteousness." Doctrine and Covenants* 121:36 says:

> *That the rights of the priesthood are inseparably connected with the powers of heaven, and that the powers of heaven cannot be controlled nor handled only upon the principles of righteousness.*

Questions or comments on that. Does that sound right?

Student 1: I sometimes feel, with unbelief, maybe we don't want to be that way, but we don't want to be prideful either. You know, we think maybe when we have more confidence we are becoming prideful. Do you know what I'm saying?

Mike: Yes. You hit a word there, and the word is *confidence*. Every time that you tap into this power that resides in heaven and can be called down upon yourself through exact ways, every time you have success in that, what does it do to your *confidence* in the Lord? What does it do to your *faith*? You have enough of these experiences in your life, and your *faith* becomes **unshaken**. So, *confidence* is a key. There in section 121 verse 45, it says:

> *Let thy bowels also be full of charity toward all men, and to the household of faith, and let virtue garnish thy thoughts and unceasingly; then shall thy* ***confidence*** *wax strong in the presence of God;*

If you want to see that in action, go to Ether 3:4-13, where the brother of Jared sees the finger of the Lord. At least the hand of the Lord comes through the veil, and Mohanri Moriancomer sees it and falls to the earth. And the Lord asked, *"Sawest thou more than this?"* And the brother of Jared says, *"Nay; Lord, show thyself unto me."* You talk about *confidence*! This man's confidence/faith was so strong that in Ether 12:21, Moroni says that the Lord could not *"be kept without the veil."* He couldn't do it. It was impossible for the Lord to hide Himself from the brother of Jared because of his *confidence* and *faith. Confidence* doesn't come overnight. It comes a little bit at a time. The point is that we need to be about **doing.** It goes back to section 84, where the Lord condemns us when He says, you talk a lot, but you don't **do**. You say, but you don't **do**, and so we are condemned with what He calls vanity and unbelief. Until we start **doing**, we can never have the experiences that increase our *confidences* to the point of the brother of Jared. And then we start to obtain these great blessings that Moroni said had *"been hid up from the foundation of the world"* because of unbelief. They are *hid*. See, I think we talk in our classes about some of these things, and as we talk about them, we start to have more and more experiences. And as you have these experiences you are under an obligation to share these experiences with others, but you have to be careful. Margie and I were talking about how everyone says, "Don't cast your pearls before swine." You've heard that, right? So, when people have these sacred experiences, we all quote that scripture. That's the scripture everyone always uses when they want to say, "You shouldn't talk about these things." But, let's stop and look at the rest of that scripture in Matthew 7:6 for just a minute:

> *Give not that which is holy unto the dogs, neither cast ye your pearls* ***before swine,*** *lest they trample them under their feet, and turn again and rend you.*

Notice it doesn't say, "**Don't** cast your pearls." It says not to cast them "***before swine.***" You **are supposed** to *cast your pearls*, brothers and sisters. You are supposed to share your spiritual experiences with others. Here's one of the false doctrines that come up in the Church. It's a lot like the one that says, "Leave the mysteries alone." That's damning doctrine. Here's another one, "Those that have these experiences don't talk about them and those that don't have these experiences do." That's false doctrine. You are under a commandment to testify of these things.

I think that we talked a little bit about that last week, and I shared with you the experience over there in Moroni chapter 7, where it talks about receiving angels. We talked about two groups who received these sacred experiences, and one is called the *chosen vessels* of the Lord. And then it says that they are commanded to testify of these things to "others" so that they might have faith and come up and obtain the same thing. Moroni calls these "others" *the residue of men*. This week Margie and I were talking about that in our private scripture reading, and we found another one in 3 Nephi 12:1. This is the beginning of what we call *The Sermon at the Temple*. It's a reiteration of *The Sermon on the Mount*, but let's read it carefully:

> *And it came to pass that when Jesus had spoken these words unto Nephi, and to those who had been called, (now the number of them had been called, and received power and authority to baptize, was twelve) and behold, he stretched forth his hand unto the multitude, and cried unto them, saying:*

This is the **first** *Beatitude*:

> *Blessed are ye if ye shall give heed unto the words of these twelve whom I have chosen from among you to minister unto you, and to be your servants; and unto them I have given power that they may baptize you with water; and after that ye...*

"Ye" is everybody. This is the congregation. This is the several thousand people there that are going to be ministered to by the Twelve:

> *and after that ye are baptized with water, behold, I will baptize you with fire and with the Holy Ghost; therefore blessed are ye if ye shall believe in me and be baptized, after that ye have seen me and know that I am.*

Now, watch. This is the congregation that has been baptized by fire:

> *[2] And again, more blessed are they who shall believe in your words because*
> *that* ***ye shall testify*** *that ye have seen me, and that ye know that I am.*

Did you see that? Notice that He's not talking to all these people and saying, "Now that you have seen Me and know that I am, I want you to keep your mouth shut and don't tell anybody about it at all. It's too sacred to talk about." If these people had not gone out and testified about what they had seen, you would not have the 200 years of millennial peace that follows the ministry of Christ in America. You would not have it. Do you think all the Nephites that survived those three days of terrible tempest were here at this point, in 3 Nephi 12? Do you think that every surviving Nephite was there? They were not. There were 2,500 people on that first day, which goes from chapter 12 all the way to chapter 19. Then they went out that night and *noised it abroad* (3 Nephi 19:2) so that the next day others could also witness. So, there are many people that were not witnesses to what Christ personally taught on the first day, the second day, or on the last day that He was there. Although, I'm sure they continued to come in. The point is, those who saw, and heard, and touched, were commanded to go out and *testify to others* what they had seen, and heard, and touched. For what purpose? So that *the residue* that was not there could have faith and be taught and brought up to a point where they could see, and hear, and touch at some later date. So, when it *says don't cast your pearls before swine,* yeah, you better not; because if you cast your pearls before those who are not ready for it, who the Spirit tells you not to, they're going to turn and rend you. They're going to persecute you. They're going to revile you. They're going to make fun of sacred things. But, you **do** cast your pearls. This is the same thing as the Lord saying, *"Beware of false prophets, for inwardly they are ravening wolves."* And so, all of the anti-Mormons and the anti-Joseph Smith people quote that scripture in Matthew 7, saying that we shouldn't believe Joseph Smith; beware of false prophets! Well, the point of this is that He doesn't say, "Beware of all prophets." He says, *"Beware of false prophets."* Now, if you've got false prophets, then you have to have what? True prophets, because there's the opposition. So, when it says, *"Don't you cast your pearls before swine,"* it's not saying, "Don't ever *cast your pearls.*" It is just saying to be selective, be inspired by the Spirit of revelation as to who you share these things with. Otherwise if [student] shares with me a sacred experience that she had, what's that going to do to me? If she's inspired to share it with me, what's that going to do to me? I'm going to look at her and say, "You know, if [student] can have an experience like that, I know I can too!" And I'm going to start seeking for that. Whereas, if I think those things have ceased with the death of the apostles and we can only read about them in scripture, or if they're reserved only for the First Presidency and the Quorum of the Twelve and assorted general authorities; then I'm never going to get them because I'm not an apostle and I don't sit in those quorums; therefore, it is not available to me. So, I need to have somebody share with me their pearls, as inspired because what that does is, it starts me on the path of asking, seeking, and knocking.

In closing, I'll share with you an experience that shows you how that works. I knew about the *Second Comforter* doctrine that we've been talking about for the last three weeks. I knew about the doctrine, I understood it, and I knew that Joseph had taught it. And I knew that some of the early Brethren in the Church had taught it. But, everybody that I knew of that had obtained the *Second Comforter* was a leader in the early Church, or were apostles in the *New Testament*, or were prophets, etc. So, even though I knew the doctrine, I didn't really understand that Mike Stroud could do this. If I don't believe that I can accomplish this, there is no need to seek after it. And then I was in Hong Kong, China and we were attending the Hong Kong temple, and I was reading a book called *The Second Comforter*. I had a singular experience. This book was written by a man who is an ordinary member of the Church. He's never been a general authority. I think the highest position that he's ever had in the Church was a High Councilor and a Sunday School President. He's a convert to the Church, joining the Church when he was 19 years old while in the military. He wrote a book called *The Second Comforter*, and the whole book talks about this doctrine. I understood all the doctrine and what he was writing was a good refresher course for me: "This is what Joseph said, this is what the *Book of Mormon* said, etc." I got to the end of that book, in the last chapter, and I can tell you where I was; I was in the patron housing of the Hong Kong temple. They had bunk beds, and I was lying on the lower bunk, reading the last chapter. The last chapter started out like this, "Brothers and sisters, I have seen Jesus Christ. He has ministered to me and commanded that I should write this book." And I remember that when I read that, the Holy Ghost revealed to me and gave me the knowledge that this could happen to me. That was in 2006, that was ten years ago, and that began my quest for all of these things. That doctrine opened up other doctrines; the things that lead up to it. There are certain things that must take place before you obtain this great blessing and I learned about those. One door after another opened. And as soon as that door was opened, the Lord sent information to Margie and me that we had never received before. It just seemed to flow to us. And one thing came right after another, after another, and after another. We started to experience things. We started to have **great** experiences, spiritual experiences—great pearls that came our way—and it all started because some guy that lives in Sandy, Utah, wrote a book and in it testified that he had seen Christ. And he said, "I don't want to say this. I'm a private person. It goes against everything I believe in to say this, but the Lord has commanded me to say these words." And regardless of who this guy is or what his book is when I read it the Holy Ghost testified to me and said, "Mike Stroud, you can obtain this, and you should seek for it, and not quit until you have obtained that witness." And that's been in one of the greatest blessings in my life, that some guy **testified** that he had this experience. And it was just an ordinary Latter-day Saint like me. Since that time, I've talked to and read many examples from Latter-day Saint men and women, most of them anonymous examples, of people who have had these experiences; men and women. And it's just been a marvelous experience for me. I have zero unbelief that this can happen to me, zero. I know it can. I know it will. But like the scriptures say, it will be in *Mine own way, and in Mine own time, and according to Mine own will.* And I'm willing to leave it at that. But, I boldly approach the throne of grace daily. **Boldly**! Joseph Smith said this in the *Words of Joseph Smith, "Weary the Lord until he blesses you."* How about that one? *"Weary the Lord until he blesses you."* Sometimes the Lord withholds blessings to see how just badly you want them. I found that to be a true thing. I can testify of that.

So, next week we'll talk a little more about the priesthood, but just some thoughts on what I said tonight; some musings based on what I feel. A lot of what I talked about on the priesthood was all me, Mike Stroud. I usually just give you doctrine and words of the prophets, but tonight I shared with you some of my thoughts, and I want to make you understand that they are my thoughts. Comments as we close? Weary the Lord until he blesses you. Go boldly. Paul says, *"Go boldly before the throne of grace."*

Student 1: Do you say your prayers out loud?

Mike: I don't.

Student 1: I've heard two things. If you speak out loud, the adversary can hear it. If you pray in your mind, he can't. So, sometimes I do, but most of the time I do silent.

Mike: Now, the only time I pray vocally is in public. All my prayers, except for certain times, where the prayer has to be vocal; other than that, very limited times. All my prayers are in silence. They are in my mind.

Student 6: Wouldn't it make sense, or doesn't it make sense that we could call down the powers of heaven to be around us. This is what I have done. I have called down the powers of heaven to be around me, that I may speak with Him freely and I have felt protected during that communication. That's my experience.

Mike: Amen, amen, and amen. That's a three amener! I think that's marvelous, that's wonderful. I'll share with you a little experience I had with the priesthood this week. It was interesting. I bought a couple of little turkey chicks; little polts, they are $7.50 each, and about three and a half inches tall. They are just little guys. On the second day, I noticed one of them had his eyes closed. By the third or fourth day, I was worried because he couldn't find the food or the water. He was chirping, was in distress, and was bumping against the walls. For two or three nights, I had pulled him out and held him in my arms. I'd take a little cotton swab with warm water on it and just rub it over his eyes to see if there was some stickiness in there, or something; if he had a cold, you know? And it would temporarily help a little bit. But, by the next morning, both eyes were just shut. And when I saw that, Margie and I both said, "If we don't do something this little guy is going to die because he can't eat. He's not finding his food, and he's not finding his water." I'd take him and push his little beak down into the water with my hands, and he would get a little bit of water, but it just wasn't enough. Bit by bit I could see this chick starving to death. So, I picked him up in my hands and held him in one hand, and I just talked to The Father. I just said, "This is Your creation. He is here to fulfill the measure of his creation and find joy. But if something doesn't happen, he is going to die tonight and won't make it to the next morning." I said, "In the name of Jesus and by authority of the Melchizedek priesthood, I bless you to be healthy and strong, your eyes to open up, to survive and be strong and fulfill the measure of your creation." The next morning both eyes were wide open and have had no problems since. I know that sounds like a small thing, but for this little bird, there was no question in my mind that he would have been dead by the next morning. No question about it.

Student 6: Fantastic! That's wonderful!

Mike: The Lord notices the sparrow's fall. I have found out that that can be taken literally. There's not one of His creations; I don't care how insignificant it is, that He is not intimately in touch with. And when a sparrow falls, He does notice the sparrow's fall, and so I think that's literal. So, I blessed that little chick and what do you think that does for Mike Stroud's confidence, a little thing like that, see? What does that do for my faith? Does that do anything for my confidence? It really does. Maybe sometime in the future, when I have a dying child, and there is no medicine, no hospitals, no EMTs, and no ambulances, because I once laid hands on a chick and his eyes were opened, maybe I can have the confidence to raise up the dead, and heal the sick when there's no other alternative. What do you think?

Student 6: Absolutely!

Mike: So, I leave those thoughts with you and thank you again.

References:

D&C 84:54-58
Autobiography of Parley P. Pratt, p.259-261 Joseph Smith speech in Pennsylvania
General Conference Oct 1988 Ezra Taft Benson "I Testify."
James 1:5-6
Ensign May 1989 Ezra Taft Benson, "Beware of Pride."
Mormon 9:20-27
Ether 4:15
D&C 121:36-45
JST, Genesis 14:30 – 31
3 Nephi 12:1
D&C 88
Words of Joseph Smith

Chapter Fifteen
Podcast 015 Priesthood

I'd like to start out with a quote from the Prophet Joseph Smith. This is in the *Discourses of the Prophet Joseph Smith*, page 364. Now, that's different from the *Teachings of the Prophet Joseph Smith*, so you have a couple of couple books there. This is a great quote, and we've used it already in some of our lessons, but we're going to use it in a little different application tonight.

> *The Savior has* ***the words of eternal life****. Nothing else can profit us. There is no salvation in believing an evil report against our neighbor. I advise all to go on to perfection and search deeper and deeper into the mysteries of Godliness. A man can do nothing for himself unless God directs in the right way,* ***and the Priesthood is revealed for that purpose****.*

There are a couple of things in that quote, and I'll have Margie put it up so you can have access to it. He talks about *the words of eternal life. The words of eternal life* are when Jesus Christ speaks to you personally and promises you from His own mouth to you, in your own name, that you shall inherit eternal life. That's what *the words of eternal life* mean. I know we can interpret that in several different ways. We can say, "Well, the *words of eternal life* are any of the words spoken of by God in the scriptures or through His prophets." But, at a higher level, *the words of eternal life* will sound something like, *"Sharon Whitmore, I now seal upon you your exaltation, that where I am you may be also, and that you have part and portion, you have a lot, an inheritance with Christ in the celestial world."* When He says those words, those are *the words of eternal life*. According to the Prophet Joseph Smith:

> *Nothing else* [short of that] *can profit us.*

Then he says,

> *Go on... and search deeper and deeper into the mysteries of Godliness.*

We don't hear it so much now, but what we've heard in the past is, "Leave the mysteries alone." That is counter to everything the scriptures and the prophets say. And then he says,

> *The priesthood is revealed for that purpose.*

You see? The priesthood was revealed for these purposes.

I have another quote that I want to give you on priesthood. These are remarkable things! This is found in the *History of the Church*, again Joseph Smith, Volume 4 page 207, and it says this:

> [The Melchizedek priesthood] *is the **channel...***

There's that word; it really helped me. When I read this, it helped me start to get a feel for what priesthood is:

> *the **channel** through which all knowledge, doctrine, the plan of salvation, and every important matter is revealed from heaven.*

Isn't that a great statement? I think that ***channel*** is just a marvelous word that helps us get a better feel for it:

> *It is the **channel** through which the Almighty commenced revealing his glory at the beginning of the creation of this earth, and through which he has continued to reveal himself to the children of men to the present time, and through which he will make known his purposes to the end of time.*

All of that is a definition of Melchizedek Priesthood. So, when God reveals Himself to man, He reveals Himself through this ***channel*** called the Melchizedek Priesthood. Let me give one more to you. It's in the *History of the Church*, Volume 5, pages 1 and 2 and was given in May 1842. This is where the very first endowments were given in the Red Brick Store by Joseph Smith. The history, content, and context behind this are that it is a Joseph Smith journal entry, written on May 4, 1842. He said this:

> *I spent the day in the upper part of the store...*

And then he listed the men that were there and said he was:

> *instructing them in the principles and order of the Priesthood, attending to washings, anointings, endowments and the communication of keys pertaining to the Aaronic Priesthood,* ***and so on to the highest order of the Melchizedek Priesthood,***

The *"highest order of the Melchizedek Priesthood"* was the part I wanted you to pay attention to. Then he says:

> *setting forth the order pertaining to the Ancient of Days, and all those plans and principles by which any one is enabled to secure the fullness of those blessing which have been prepared for the Church of the Firstborn.*

Now, in that quote, Joseph Smith was officiating in the endowment ceremony, as it was at that time, in the upper floor of the Joseph Smith Red Brick Store. In that place, in Brigham Young's home, and in the mansion house, are three places that we know of historically, that the endowment ceremony, as it was that at the time, was introduced and administered to certain brethren, and later to certain men and women. The Nauvoo Temple was not above the first level at this point. These ordinances are designed to be performed in the upper floors of the temple, and at this point, all that was completed at this late date was the basement and part of the first story. The Prophet Joseph Smith knew that he was never going to see the temple completed so that he could officiate in these ordinances himself, in the upper floors of the Nauvoo Temple. So, he just went into his Red Brick Store and hung some veils, brought in some potted plants, and assigned certain individuals to play certain roles. Heber C. Kimball played the role of Satan. Others played the roles of Elohim, Jehovah, and Michael, Adam and Eve, etc., and he administered the endowment there in that upper floor. Here he says that he instructed:

> *them in the principles and* ***order*** *of the Priesthood...and so on, to the* ***highest order of the Melchizedek Priesthood.***

That is the part I want to emphasize. When we talk about the priesthood, we have to use the word *order*. That brings us to the point that we find out that there are various *orders* or degrees of the priesthood. Over in *Doctrine and Covenants* section 107, we can see in the very first verse that the Lord introduces this concept of *orders of priesthood*. In verse 1, He says:

> *There are, in the church, two priesthoods, namely the Melchizedek and the Aaronic, including the Levitical Priesthood.*

Joseph Smith said, *"All priesthood is Melchizedek."* Now, that's a great clue there, too. So, all priesthood is Melchizedek; it's just that there are various orders of this priesthood.

Student 6: So, there are Deacons, and that's an office—

Mike: Yes, that's an office.

Student 6: But it's the Aaronic Priesthood; is it Melchizedek too?

Mike: Yes. Joseph said that all priesthood is Melchizedek; it's just that you have various orders within that priesthood. In section 107, verse 2, it says:

> *Why the first is called the Melchizedek Priesthood is because Melchizedek was such a great high priest.*

Now, the Prophet Joseph taught, that Melchizedek is Shem, the son of Noah, which has interesting implications. So, later you have Abraham who is paying his tithes to Melchizedek. And then, Abraham receives an order of the priesthood from under the hand of Melchizedek. So, we have all these great patriarchs who are contemporary. Now, in verse 3, it says:

> *Before his* [Melchizedek's] *day, it* [this priesthood] *was called The Holy Priesthood, after the Order of the Son of God.*

Then later on in Enoch's day, it's called *The Priesthood, after the Order of Enoch*. A lot of people don't know that. So, these *orders* have different names. The Aaronic Priesthood is an *order* called after Aaron and is a *preparatory order*. We have talked about this in the past and said that everything in the gospel of

Jesus Christ is designed to move us from where we are at any given time, upwards. One of the ways that we move upwards in the priesthood is through various *orders*. Brigham Young said in Kirtland, and later in Nauvoo, that the purpose of the School of the Prophets was to prepare the brethren to receive that order of the Melchizedek Priesthood that was called *The Order of Enoch.* So, we know from scriptures that this priesthood has three names. In the early days of the patriarchs, in Adam's day, it was called the *Holy Priesthood, after the Order of the Son of God.* Then later on in Enoch's day, it's called *The Priesthood, after the Order of Enoch.* You see, Enoch is before Melchizedek; Enoch is between Adam and Melchizedek. Then later when we get down to Shem, who has his name changed and his new name, his temple name, is Melchizedek. And so, because of who Melchizedek was, the priesthood then, and up to this day, is referred to as the *Holy Priesthood, after the Order of Melchizedek.* And that's what we have today; we have an *order* of the priesthood. In the *Teachings of the Prophet Joseph Smith*, page 322 – 323 that:

> *There are three grand orders of priesthood referred to here.*

He is referring to Hebrews chapter 7. Paul talks about these orders of priesthood. It's one of the great mysteries of the Christian world. They have no idea what he's talking about in the seventh chapter of Hebrews, but we do because we have the great prophet and seer Joseph, that opens up the mystery for us. He said:

> *There are 3 grand principles or orders of Priesthood portrayed in this chapter....[There] is what is called the* ***Levitical*** *priesthood, consisting of priests to administer in outward ordinance, made without an oath.*

Then number two:

> *The second priesthood is* ***patriarchal*** *authority. Go and finish the temple, and God will fill it with power, and you will then receive more knowledge concerning this priesthood.*

We'll come back to that one in a minute. He also said that there's another one:

> *Those holding the fullness of the* ***Melchizedek*** *Priesthood are kings and priests of the Most High God, holding the keys of power and blessings.*

Now, out of those three, the highest is the *Patriarchal Order.* The *Melchizedek Order* that we have in the Church today is an administrative order of the priesthood. All these orders have *priesthood keys.* For example, when John the Baptist laid his hands-on Joseph and Oliver and gave them the keys to the Aaronic Priesthood, he said:

> *I confer the Priesthood of Aaron, which holds the* ***keys of the ministering of angels****, and of the gospel of* ***repentance****, and* ***baptism by immersion for the remission of sins****.*

See, those are **keys**. Melchizedek Priesthood, the administrative priesthood that we have in the Church of Jesus Christ of Latter-day Saints, also has keys and we hear a lot about that. These are keys to administer ordinances, these are keys to direct missionary work, and these are keys to various things that make the Church function in an orderly way. And then we have this other priesthood called *Patriarchal Priesthood.* And the *Patriarchal Priesthood* in the *Book of Mormon* has a name. It's called *The Holy Order.*

Let's go to section 84 and let me show you one other thing here that is kind of interesting, as we talk about these various orders. We do not have all of the priesthood orders. There is much to come. There is so much on this in sections 84, 88, 107, and 121; and all are great priesthood sections that the Lord gives us. They are a little confusing sometimes, and we misinterpret a lot of this in the Church. I'm going to give you an example of one of those misinterpretations that we have on something we have called *the Oath and Covenant of the Priesthood.* Let's go to verse 18:

> *And the Lord confirmed* ***a*** *priesthood...*

Notice he said, *"**a** priesthood,"* not **the** priesthood, **a** priesthood. When you put the word "**a**" there, that now tells you that you have more than one.

> *And the Lord confirmed* ***a*** *priesthood also upon Aaron and his seed, throughout all their generations, which priesthood also continueth*

> *and abideth forever with the priesthood which is after the* ***holiest*** *order of God.*

You should notice the word *holiest*. You can't use that word *holiest* unless there are at least two other priesthoods that tie in with this. Here it is: you have to have *holy*, *holier*, and *holiest*. Right? Does that make sense? We don't have this *holiest order*. When we read verse 18, we think we are talking about the Melchizedek Priesthood that's confirmed upon a 19-year-old when he is ordained an elder. That is a priesthood, but that isn't the one that is talked about here, because look at verse 19:

> *And this greater priesthood* [the one that is called *the holiest* in verse 18]
> *administereth the gospel and holdeth the key* [not keys], *of the mysteries of the kingdom, even the key of the knowledge of God.*

Now, that's found in this *holiest order* that section 84 is talking about. Read a little bit further, verse 20:

> *Therefore, in the ordinances thereof,* [in this holiest order of the priesthood] *the power of godliness is manifest.*

See, we ought to stop and ask ourselves questions. What does that mean, *the power of godliness*? What is that? Verse 21:

> *And without the ordinances thereof* [of this holiest order of the priesthood], *and the authority of the priesthood, the power of godliness is not manifest unto men in the flesh;*
> *[22] For without* ***this****...*

Without what? The key, power, and authority of this holiest order of the priesthood:

> *For without this no man can see the face of God, even the Father, and live.*

This *holiest order of the priesthood* is designed to open up a conduit, a ***channel,*** which takes you right into the presence of the Holy Father, to commune with him face-to-face. Go over to section 107, and I'll show you a little bit further. You have to pull all of these together; you can't just take one. You have to look at them all and ask yourself, "What is all of this talking about?" So, in section 107, we see something in verse 18:

> *The power and authority of the higher, or Melchizedek Priesthood, is to hold the keys of all the spiritual blessings of the church—*

What are these? Look at this:

> *[19] To have the privilege of receiving the mysteries of the kingdom of heaven,*

Now, this is not reserved for just the president of the Church. These orders of the priesthood and these great privileges are not just reserved for fifteen men. This is open to every man and woman regardless of station, race, creed, color. Priesthood station and priesthood ordination have nothing to do with it. You come up, and you receive this, as you'll see in just a minute. These are the priesthood orders we're talking about in verse 19:

> [1] *have the privilege of receiving the mysteries of the kingdom of heaven,*
> [2] *to have the heavens opened up to them* [that's literal, not symbolic],
> [3] *to commune with the general assembly and the church of the Firstborn* [That's the heavenly church. It isn't the Church of Jesus Christ of Latter-day Saints],
> [4] *and to enjoy the communion and presence of God the Father, and Jesus the mediator of the new covenant.*

Those are all privileges that go with this *holiest order of the priesthood.* So, here's the question. In the days of the patriarchs, there was no administrative priesthood because there was no church. For all of the patriarchs from Adam down to Noah, there was no church anywhere. The first church that we see with the word *church* was with Mosiah and Alma in the *Book of Mormon.* We have the tendency to think that they had buildings that they met in and ward houses and that they had bishops, relief society presidents, stake presidents, and high councils, and so on. In reality, the definition of the church was: people who had repented of their sins, exercised faith in Christ, entered the waters of baptism, and met together. That was the church; they met together oft. So, we have a tendency, now, to think in terms of buildings, and organizations and so on, because we use the word church. Comment?

Student 4: Mosiah is 183 years before Christ, right? I was going to mention that they start talking about churches in the *New Testament*.

Mike: We are talking about people meeting in groups, whether it's in synagogues, or whether in catacombs. Prior to that time, they met together in groups of baptized people, to discuss the welfare of their own souls.

Student 4: So, what you are saying is that Jehovah was meeting with these people and started setting this up, and the *Book of Mormon* is really the pattern that we've got to live in our day.

Mike: Well, in the *Pearl of Great Price*, in Moses chapter 6, verse 7, it says:

> *And now this same Priesthood, which was in the beginning, shall be in the end of the world also.*

So, <u>this is Mike Stroud's opinion now</u>: what the Church of Jesus Christ of Latter-day Saints is trying to get us to do, is come to that ancient order that has been on the earth before, but is not now. In fact, I want to take it a step further. You might find this a little bit interesting. When the Prophet Joseph Smith had the heavens open to him, and he started receiving this communication, this information, I don't believe it was his intention to ever organize a New Testament Church. As I read some of his writings, I noticed that this whole idea of putting together the New Testament Church came from the new converts that were coming into the Church by the hundreds. The Lord had already prepared many, many people in the early days of the Church, by visions and dreams and having the scriptures open, and the Holy Ghost speaking to them; they were looking for a church patterned after which they read about in the *Bible*. And they were looking around themselves at the Baptist, the Methodist, and the Presbyterian, and what they saw in the *Bible,* they did not see in their institutions. They were looking for something. So, when Joseph Smith comes and talks about angelic ministrations, ancient prophets using the laying on of hands, the gift of the Holy Ghost, and different things like that, these people really got excited. And they said, "Here it is! This is what we've been looking for." But it's my feeling that what Joseph had in mind was something much more ancient. He had in mind something that he called *The Order after the Ancient of*

Days. Of course, we know the Ancient of Days was Adam. So, he was looking for something to come back onto the earth that the patriarchs enjoyed, and that was not an institution that had officers and callings. It was something the *Book of Mormon* had. The *Book of Mormon* enjoyed it. It's called *the Holy Order.*

Now, go with me and let me show you this *Holy Order* in the *Book of Mormon.* We'll just glance off this a little bit. Go to Alma chapter 13, which I believe, is one of the great chapters in the *Book of Mormon,* if not the greatest priesthood chapter in the *Book of Mormon.* Now, the thing you have to understand is that the first nine verses in Alma 13 are talking about the premortal life. That will help you. You'll see words like this: *being called and prepared from the foundation of the world.* That goes back before the Fall, before the Garden of Eden. The whole nine verses are talking about something called *the Holy Order*:

> *[1] And again, my brethren, I would cite your minds forward to the time when the Lord God gave these commandments unto his children; and I would that ye should remember that the Lord God ordained priests, after his holy order, which was after the order of his Son, to teach these things unto the people.*
>
> *[2] And those priests were ordained after the order of his Son, in a manner that thereby the people might know in what manner to look forward to his Son for redemption.*
>
> *[3] And this is the manner after which they were ordained—being called and prepared* ***from the foundation of the world*** [that's premortal life] *according to the foreknowledge of God, on account of their exceeding faith and good works;*

Where? In the premortal world:

> *in the first place* [meaning the premortal life] *being left to choose good or evil; therefore they* [these people that we see who are ordained in life to the *holy order*] *having chosen good, and exercising exceedingly great faith, are called with a holy calling, yea, with that holy calling which was*

> *prepared with, and according to, a preparatory redemption for such.*
> *[4] And thus they have been called to this holy calling on account of their faith* [in the premortal life], *while others would reject the Spirit of God* [in the premortal life] *on account of the hardness of their hearts and blindness of their minds, while, if it had not been for this* [this rejection] *they might have had as great privilege as their brethren.*

So, what Alma is telling us is that if we are able to come and obtain these orders of the priesthood in this life, it is because we were foreordained to them before we came. Joseph Smith taught that every man who was ordained to the Melchizedek Priesthood in this life was ordained to that same priesthood before he came here. So, you're receiving a second ordination to that priesthood. Let's leave that for just a second. Here's the question we want to ask: Where do we come into contact with this higher order of the priesthood as members of The Church of Jesus Christ of Latter-day Saints, or do we?

Student 6: In the temple.

Mike: In the temple is where you come into contact. So, this higher order of the priesthood is called Patriarchal because it's family order. There are no offices, and there are no callings, etc. In the Patriarchal Priesthood, you have men who are Kings, and you have women who are Queens. You have men who are Priests, and you have women Priestesses. That's *the Holy Order* because in heaven you don't have elders and apostles. In heaven, you have fathers and mothers. So, this priesthood that we have today, even the Melchizedek Priesthood that we have in the Church, is preparing us for something greater, something higher, something that's family centered. Does that make sense? Now, it's interesting that you can't get to the temple unless you've been ordained to this institutional Melchizedek Priesthood that's found in the Church of Jesus Christ of Latter-day Saints. You can't get to the temple and even be introduced and initiated into this higher order of things until you have had this Melchizedek Priesthood in the Church conferred upon you. And then you have a period of time to see what you do with it; to see if you're going to honor it and to see if are going to be true to your covenants, etc. When you go to the temple, the initiatory is an initiation. *The Holy Order of the Priesthood* belongs to a church, and that church is called *the Church of the Firstborn*. That's a heavenly church, a heavenly order. The Melchizedek order that we're involved with now belongs to The Church of Jesus Christ of Latter-day Saints, and it is a necessary, preparatory institution, and priesthood order. Don't you find it interesting that you're not going to be ordained to the Melchizedek Priesthood until you have some experience with the lesser order called the Aaronic Priesthood? For 12-year-old boys, it takes six years, and they're going to move up through three different callings of this preparatory priesthood. If a man comes into the Church and he is an adult convert, they're at least going to ordain him to a priest in the Aaronic Priesthood, and give him some experience with ordaining other people, in blessing the sacrament and baptizing, which are ordinances that belong to that priesthood. Everybody that I know of who comes into the Melchizedek Priesthood needs to have some time and some experience with the preparatory priesthood of that order called the Aaronic Priesthood. So, if you're going to enter into the higher order of the priesthood, which is temple-centered, you're going to have to have some experience with the Melchizedek Priesthood in the Church of Jesus Christ of Latter-day Saints, which is preparing you for something higher.

Student 6: How are the women prepared? Women are not prepared like men. In our modern day, women don't go through a preparation. My husband did, but I didn't.

Mike: Well, it's interesting that for you to go to the temple as a woman, and be introduced into this order, you also have to make covenants and be baptized into the Church. It's true that ordination to Melchizedek Priesthood and the Aaronic Priesthood are not required, but you still must have some preparation as a member of the Church before you can to go to the temple. Nobody comes to the temple without first being baptized into the Church. So, you have to do that. Now, the initiatory is very interesting because the words of the temple initiatory ordination are different for women than they are for men. Maybe you can discuss that in the temple the next time you go there. Both of you should have those wordings memorized.

But it's very, very different. A woman is not responsible for missionary work and for preaching the gospel to mankind on the earth. They do not have a priesthood responsibility. They are not responsible for the blood and sins of this generation. If you think about the initiatory, you will see that is true. A man in the initiatory has the ordinance performed, and it says that he **can** become clean from the blood and sins of this generation, but it depends upon his faithfulness. That is not at all mentioned for a woman. A woman has no responsibility for the blood and sins of the generation in which they live. Look at The Family Proclamation, and you can see the roles of men and woman played out there. Priesthood, in the future, will be a part of the woman's role because we are told women will become Priestesses. You can't be a Priestess unless you bear the priesthood.

Student 4: Remember you told us that women have wisdom?

Mike: Yes.

Student 4: So, they have enough wisdom that they can get themselves up to the temple.

Mike: Men need the *channel* of the priesthood. There is a different refinement for a man, and a different process to make a man holy than there is for a woman. It's a whole different ballgame and priesthood is part of that whole formula of making a man holy. Women don't need it. The priesthood is no more required for a woman than motherhood is required for a man.

Student 6: Why do you think that is the case?

Mike: I just don't know all of it. I've pondered that a lot. I just know that it's a lot harder for men to obtain holiness. There's nothing more majestic, nothing more glorified than a holy man. But it takes a **good woman** to get him there. And no man can obtain this level of holiness and sanctity without a good woman. Women, by nature, obtain this more readily than a man does. This is Mike Stroud now: I believe that a woman can obtain holiness without a man, but there's no way a man can do it without a woman. That's just my opinion. This is why the Lord says in the temple, among other things, *"It is not good for man to be alone."* There's more to that than just being lonely, you know; being a loose cannon, a danger to himself and everybody else. There is more to that. Once a man is perfected in Christ, sanctified in Christ, and made *"holy, without spot,"* there's nothing in all of eternity more glorious and more powerful than that. But, to get him there is a real tough deal.

Brigham Young taught that all of the ordinances of the temple are the ordinances of the *Church of the Firstborn.* So, what that means now, is that when you get your temple recommend and you are considered worthy to enter the house of the Lord when you pass that recommend desk you are now entering into a whole new order of the priesthood. And the initiatory, which is the first ordinance of the endowment, is an **initiation.** You are being initiated into the *Church of the Firstborn.* You don't have a membership, but you're being initiated in. You're being instructed, and you're having ordinances performed that will help open up doors of understanding. You're having keys turned that will give you the knowledge that you need and that you can get in no other way, to move upward and ultimately claim membership in the *Church of the Firstborn.* The endowment and everything in it is an allegory teaching you what you must do. It's a step-by-step formula; if you will, a **template**. You have the word temple in the template, showing you in an allegorical form, what you need to do to be reclaimed from your fallen nature, and redeemed from the Fall, to re-enter into the presence of the Lord, and receive from Him these orders of the priesthood, these ordinations, these promises. The temple is a template; the temple is not the real deal. It's just like there is no power of the priesthood, or power of the gospel that comes in and of itself through an ordination, or through an ordinance. There is no power in an ordinance, in and of itself. It's what the ordinance is teaching us. The ordinance is opening up doors. The ordinance is taking a key and putting it into a lock that prior to that is secure. That ordinance is now giving you the knowledge that you need to go forward and obtain the real deal.

Student 6: When I was very, very sick and felt like I was dying every day, the only thing that gave me the power to go on was the initiatory ordinances. I went to the temple every day at that point in my life. It was like I was going there just to save my life. And I now know why it was able to do that. I knew that it gave me hope, but there was more to it than I knew then. I understand that now.

Mike: Well you know, the Prophet Joseph said, and we quote this a lot, he said, *"A man or woman is saved no faster than they can get knowledge."* Notice that salvation comes through knowledge. The ordinances, the temple allegory, the priesthood, and everything are trying to teach us, to give us knowledge, so that we can actually do something that opens up the powers of heaven.

Student 6: And that's what happened to me going to the temple every day.

Mike: Without these ordinances, which are teaching us something, you just don't have the key to open those doors, to turn those locks.

Student 6: Yeah, I can see that!

Mike: Let's look at this order of the priesthood in action in the life of Melchizedek. Go over to the *Joseph Smith Translation* in your *Bible*; it's just before the maps. Go to JST, Genesis 14:25-40. This order of the priesthood, this Holiest Order, this Patriarchal Order; the Holy Order that we're talking about, comes from God. You're being initiated through allegory with mortal men and women in the temple. You're being shown the way on how to come to this point. When it actually happens, it's not going to happen under the hands of a mortal. For example, when you go through the temple you receive the initiatory, followed by the endowment. Then you are promised that if you proved faithful, the day would come when you will be chosen, called up and anointed kings and queens, priests and priestesses, whereas, you have now only been anointed to become such. So, there is another anointing. When you go into the initiatory, you receive a washing and an anointing. You receive a garment, and you receive a name, etc. You go through the allegory, and you're taught how fallen man is redeemed from his fallen state, step-by-step, and brought back into the presence of the Lord. What happens when you're brought back into the presence of the Lord? He is going to lay His hands on your head, and He is going to ordain you to a higher order of the priesthood. You're going to obtain membership in the *Church of the Firstborn.* Prior to that, you're going to hear His voice before you see Him. He is going to call you by name, and you're going to obtain promises from Him. You're going to obtain from Him the *words of eternal* *life* because He is going to seal you up with His own voice. Keep that in mind. You're going to see that now in Genesis. He is going to seal you up with His own voice, calling you by name, to eternal life and exaltation, and you're going to obtain promises from Him. Now, that's your first time to the veil. Notice that you go to the veil twice. The obtaining of this promise has some names. It is called *the more sure word of prophecy*; it's also called *making your calling and election sure*. It's obtaining the promise of eternal life and an inheritance with Christ in the presence of His Father, and that comes from Him. Now, the second time you go to the veil, you are brought into His presence. This is called the *Second Comforter*. So, before you enter into the presence of God, you're going to obtain from Him, without seeing Him, information and obtain promises. So, let's see if we can see that here in these verses. That is what the temple is teaching us. JST Genesis 14, verses 25 through 40:

> *And Melchizedek lifted up his voice and blessed Abram.*

Now, notice this is Abram. This is before Abram received his name change, his new name. Abram's new name is Abraham. His wife's new name is what? Sarah. What was her name before? Sarai. So, with his new temple name, he goes from Abram to Abraham. With her new temple name, she goes from Sarai to Sarah. Now, look at what it says, keeping in mind that Melchizedek is Shem, the son of Noah:

> *[26] Now Melchizedek was a man of faith, who wrought righteousness; and when a child he feared God, and stopped the mouths of lions, and quenched the violence of fire.*

This is as a child!

> *[27] And thus, having been approved of God, he was ordained an high priest after the order of the covenant which God made with Enoch,*

So, what was *the Priesthood after the order of the Son of God* called at the time that Melchizedek receives his ordination? It's called *The Priesthood after the Order of Enoch*. The priesthood that Adam had was called *the Priesthood after the order of the Son of God*. It is the same priesthood that is going to honor Melchizedek's name, because of these things that we're reading about here. And today, we have access to that same order of the priesthood with his name on it, because he *wrought righteousness, obtained favor with God,* and *was ordained a high priest*. Now, in verse 28:

> *It* [this order of the priesthood] *being after the order of the Son of God; which order came,* ***not by man****, nor the will of man; neither by father nor mother; neither by beginning of days nor end of years;* ***but of God****;*

There's your key. When you're knocking on the door of these higher orders of the priesthood, you're going to receive this from God Himself, under His hands. I suspect it's Christ that ordains you to this. In verse 29:

> *And it* [this order of the priesthood] *was delivered unto men* ***by the calling of his own voice****, according to His own will, unto as many as believed on His name.*

Do you see how this comes first? Whose own voice? God.

This is not the Melchizedek Priesthood that we are receiving in the Church of Jesus Christ of Latter-day Saints. I guess that if there's one thing I want you to get out of this lesson tonight, it is that this order that we're talking about here is not the Melchizedek Priesthood that we are getting in the Church. The Melchizedek Priesthood we're getting in the Church is preparatory to this and is necessary to this. Verse 30:

> *For God having sworn unto Enoch and unto his seed with an oath by himself; that every one being ordained after this order and calling should have power, by faith,*

Now watch. Here are the fruits of **this** priesthood:

> *to break mountains, to divide the seas, to dry up waters, to turn them out of their course;*

Moses had this order, so did Enoch, so did Melchizedek:

> *[31] To put at defiance the armies of nations, to divide the earth, to break every band, to stand in the presence of God; to do all things according to his will* [God's will], *according to his command, subdue principalities and powers; and this by the*

> *will of the Son of God which was from before the foundation of the world.*

Now, here we go:

> *[32] And* ***men having this faith****, coming up unto* ***this order of God****, were translated and taken up into heaven.*

You see, that's a little different than what we're talking about when we're in stake conference and we raise our hands when it is proposed "that the following man be ordained to the Melchizedek Priesthood." Right? "As we read your name please stand." See, we are not talking about the same thing. Look at verse 33:

> *And now, Melchizedek was a priest of this order; therefore, he obtained peace in Salem, and was called the* ***P****rince of* ***P****eace.*

Now, when you capitalize those words, you are now talking about a person. You're not talking about a state of being, but about a person. And he was called ***the*** *Prince of Peace*. Who else do you know that had that title? That's one of the names of Christ, Isn't it?

> *[34] And his people* [Melchizedek's], *wrought righteousness and obtained heaven,*

Do you know how they obtained heaven? They were taken up off the earth and were translated:

> *and sought for the city of Enoch, which God before had taken, separating it from the earth, having reserved it for the latter days, or the end of the world.*

So, brothers and sisters, here we have such a marvelous thing, and there is more there that you can read about.

Now, *the oath and covenant of the priesthood*: we don't have time for it tonight, but I'll do it next week. The way we teach *the oath and covenant of the priesthood* is okay but incorrect. Who am I to say that it is incorrect? Well, I'll show you from the scriptures. We take section 84 and teach that it is referring to when a person comes up and is ordained an elder in the Church of Jesus Christ of Latter-day Saints. In verse 33 through 39, only the first two verses of those scriptures are referring to what we do in the Church with the Melchizedek Priesthood ordination, under the hands of man. The rest of the verses are talking about *the Holy Order* that can only be introduced in the temple, through the ordinances and the allegory of the temple. We have taken and lumped that all together and we say that verses 33 through 39 are all talking about the same thing. And next week, what I'll do is go through that step-by-step and show you that we're not teaching that correctly. It's not that we're doing it on purpose. It's not that we are trying to deceive or anything, but, if anyone is like me, having read those verses all of my life, carefully, I always had a big question about the way that we teach it in the Church that could never be resolved. We could never resolve that, and we will talk about that next week. So, next week what we want to do is take this a step further, now that we've introduced and shown that there are various orders of the priesthood. Outside of the Church, you can't enter any of those, so none of these orders come into play until you are baptized a member of the Church. Then these priesthood orders become what Joseph Smith calls *channels,* through which God reveals Himself to man. Each priesthood order has with it greater responsibilities, but also huge privileges. Each order opens up different levels of privileges, rights, keys, and knowledge. Something I just find interesting is in the Nauvoo period; they went through the temple endowment like we do in the temple, and we have the Aaronic portion of the endowment, and we have the Melchizedek portion of the endowment. Right? So, there's an Aaronic Order in the temple, and there's a Melchizedek Order. We get confused thinking that it's the Aaronic Priesthood in the Church and the Melchizedek Priesthood in the Church. It is not. They have the same names, but the Aaronic Priesthood in the Church, which is deacon, teacher, and priest, is different than from the Aaronic Order that's being talked about in the temple that has signs, tokens, keywords, and names. It's a whole different ballgame. You have to think in terms of Aaronic as being preparatory to Melchizedek. We get mixed up because we see those same words used in the temple and say, "Oh, that's talking about a deacon, teacher, priest, or an elder, seventy, high priest, apostles, bishops, etc." But it's not because the Aaronic Order and the Melchizedek Order in the temple have nothing to do with institutional orders that govern the Church of Jesus

Christ of Latter-day Saints. They just carry the same name, but it's a whole different ballgame.
Student 6: Mike, so there's *holy, holier,* and *holiest.* Will you tell us, again, the three Orders of the Holiest Priesthood?
Mike: In the Holy Priesthood, the lower level would be Aaronic Levitical; it's holy because it's a priesthood.
Student 6: Ok, in the temple?
Mike: Well, in the temple and the Church. We can lump those together. They are two different things, trying to achieve two different things, but the bottom line is that all Aaronic Priesthood, the temple order or the Church order, is designed to prepare you for something higher. It's a **preparatory** priesthood. But keep in mind that Joseph also referred to the Aaronic Priesthood as being an order of the Melchizedek Priesthood. "All priesthood is Melchizedek," he said. It's just divided up into different orders. So, the first order would be Aaronic Levitical, which would be *Holy*. The second order would be Melchizedek, which would be *Holier*. And the third order would be Patriarchal or Family, which would be *Holiest*. There's some controversy on that. Some scholars want to put Melchizedek as the Holiest and Patriarchal as Holier. I disagree with that because in the Elohim, in the realms of eternity, it's a Family order with Father and Mother presiding; that's Patriarchal. And you're not introduced into Patriarchal Priesthood in the Church of Jesus Christ of Latter-day Saints until you get a temple recommend and go to the house of the Lord. That and other reasons is why I put patriarchal as the Holiest. Then Joseph also said, "Let's get the temple built and as soon as the temple is built I'll give you more information in this higher order of the priesthood." See, they already had the Melchizedek Priesthood. They got that from Peter, James, and John passed on through ordination. But Joseph said, "I want to tell you more about this one, but I can't tell you about it until the temple is finished." That tells me it is higher.
Student 6: So, the position of stake patriarch is an office in the Melchizedek Priesthood?
Mike: Yes, and that's an institutional order. That belongs to the Church of Jesus Christ of Latter-day Saints. You have to ask yourself the question: which order, what offices, and what

responsibilities belong to the Church of Jesus Christ of Latter-day Saints?
Student 6: I see.
Mike: There is no stake patriarch mentioned in any temple allegory, but there is in the Church.
Student 1: Oh, that's true.
Mike: Ultimately, Brigham Young taught that if we were worthy, we wouldn't need stake patriarchs, because every father could lay hands on his children's heads, and declare their lineage through revelation. But, as a Church and as fathers, we're short of that. So, we have a substitute father as a stake assignment that comes in and declares that lineage.
Student 6: Wow!
Student 4: That's kind of sad, isn't it?
Mike: Kind of sad. That goes along with what the Lord would say to us, "You live way below your privileges, and below My expectations." But that's all right. We can turn it around because Brother Packer said (like in section 1) that the day will come when every man would speak in the name of the Lord, every man. So, every father becomes a prophet, a priest and a king, a patriarch, for his own kingdom, his own posterity, and his own family. And we're working on that! The whole temple program is designed to help us come up to that level. I believe that Joseph wanted to just go right over to a New Testament church. I believe he wanted to take us right into this order and give us something Adamic. But the people said, "No." The people wanted a New Testament church, and they got it. And that is what we have today. I believe that. That is Mike Stroud's opinion. I believe that if Joseph had his way, we would not have a New Testament church, but we would have a priesthood order that focuses on the family with husband and wife, mom and dad, being the center of that thing. Now, the Church is trying to get us to go that way, and the temple is trying to get us to go that way, and they use the Church organization to try to move everything to that end. I think Joseph wanted to go right there from the beginning, but the members of the Church rejected it. The Lord gives us what we want. If you want something bad enough, the scriptures tell you, He will give it to you. So, I hope that is some information that will help. Next week, we'll talk briefly about

the Oath and Covenant of the Priesthood, and I'll also talk to you about the *second anointing* and what that is, and *making your calling and election sure* through the *second anointing* **or** *making your calling and election sure* through *the more sure word of prophecy*. We will talk a little bit about that next week.

Resources:
Discourses of the Prophet Joseph Smith, page 364.
History of the Church, Vol. 6, p. 363 Prophet Calling, Defense of
Discourses of the Prophet Joseph HC, Vol. 4, p 207
History of the Church, Vol 5, p 1-2
Teachings of the Prophet Joseph Smith, page 247
D&C 107:18
Teachings of Joseph Smith, page 109, "*all priesthood is Melchizedek*"
Teachings of the Prophet Joseph Smith, page 322 – 323
Alma 13
Genesis 14:25-40

Chapter Sixteen
Podcast 016 Priesthood Part II

Let's go over to *Doctrine and Covenants* section 84 for just a minute. I want to talk to you about something called *the oath and covenant of the priesthood.* Now, that's something we talk about in the Church, but I'd like to share with you that the way we're teaching it (and I've done this for thirty years) is incorrect. We are not teaching it correctly. I'd like to point out a couple of things to you and show you how just a few subtle little words will change things. *The oath and covenant of the priesthood* starts in verse 33 and we quote it as ending in verse 39. You see, in verse 39 it says this:

> *And this is according to the oath and covenant which belongeth to the priesthood.*

But actually, it goes all the way down to verse 43 in order to get a feel for it. Anytime a young man is going to receive the Melchizedek Priesthood, and he is interviewed by his bishop and the stake president, they go over with him what is called *the doctrine of the oath and covenant of the priesthood.* They quote verses 33 through 39, but I would like to share with you that what we're quoting isn't what this scripture is teaching. And I know we don't do it maliciously. We're just not looking carefully. <u>I believe</u> this is one of those examples where we have not done well in preserving what God restores, and we allow the precepts of man and the traditions of the fathers, to come in and alter what God reveals. I'm not finding fault because this is something that is so explainable. Whenever God reveals Himself to man, immediately all the powers of the earth do everything they can to alter and change that revelation. So, it becomes a great challenge to successfully preserve God's revealed work. We have to ask ourselves the question: how well did we preserve that which Joseph received from God in the doctrinal purity that it was given? And again, I'm not finding fault. I don't want to do that. I just want to point out to you that we need to be careful. Again, it's evidence, brothers and sisters, of why we need to not put our trust in man. We all need to come to a point where we put our trust in the Lord, seek personal revelation, and the companionship of the Holy Ghost. Otherwise, in any other way, anything short of that, we're in jeopardy to one degree to another. Remember in section 45 it says that the only ones that will survive in the coming days, up to and into the coming of Christ, are those that have done two things. Number one: *"have received the truth."* That your first criteria. And number two: *"have taken the Holy Spirit for their guide."* Anything else is not from God. This is His word in the scripture. Do you want to make it from 2016 through the Second Coming and have an inheritance in the millennial world? Those are the two things you've got to do; *receive the truth* and *take the Holy Spirit for your guide.* So, here is an example of something that we teach as doctrine, and we have to ask ourselves these questions: are we receiving the truth, or have we missed it a little bit? Are we a little bit off the mark? And if we're off the mark, does it alter the end result? What we want is to have a relationship with the Father and the Son. In verse 33, I'm just going to point out a couple of things to you, and it says:

> *For whoso is faithful unto the obtaining these **two** priesthoods*

Now, this verse is telling us that we're talking about two priesthoods. In the previous verses, those priesthoods are the Aaronic, which is the lesser preparatory priesthood; and the Melchizedek, which is the everlasting priesthood and a higher priesthood. It says, *"Whoso is faithful unto the obtaining these two..."* I want you to pay attention to **two priesthoods**:

> *of which I have spoken, and the magnifying their callings, are sanctified by the Spirit unto the renewing of their bodies.*
> *[34] They* [those who receive these **two** priesthoods] *become the sons of Moses* [Melchizedek] *and of Aaron* [Aaronic] *and the seed of Abraham, and the church and kingdom, and the elect of God.*

Stop right there. We're not going to go into what it means to be sanctified and have your bodies renewed. I just want to point out that verses 33 and 34 are talking about **two** priesthoods, agreed? It's pretty obvious, isn't it? Now, look at verse 35, and it's a whole different ballgame. Here is where we mess up:

> *[35] And also all they who received* ***this*** *priesthood*

We're talking about something different here. We have gone from **two** priesthoods, now, to **one**. And everyone, including myself having taught this for thirty years, missed that. I have read these verses hundreds of times and taught them hundreds of times, and missed that distinction. Now, in verse 35 we're talking about something that is different from the two priesthoods mentioned in verse 33 and 34:

> *And also all they who receive* ***this*** *priesthood receive me, saith the Lord;*
> *[36] For he that receiveth my servants receiveth me;*
> *[37] And he that receiveth me receiveth my Father;*
> *[38] And he that receiveth my Father receiveth my Father's kingdom; therefore all that my Father hath shall be given unto him.*
> *[39] And this is according to the oath and covenant which belongeth to the priesthood.*

In these verses, we are talking about **three**, not two priesthoods. We're talking about two in verses 33 and 34, and in 35 we're talking about another order of priesthood. Remember, last week we talked about it? When you talk about priesthood, you have to talk in terms of orders. *The Aaronic order*, *the Melchizedek order*, *the order after the Son of God*, *the priesthood order after Enoch*, *the order of the Son of God after Melchizedek*, etc. Now watch, ***this*** priesthood that we're talking about goes on in verse 40:

> *Therefore, those who receive* ***the*** *priesthood, receive this oath and covenant of my Father, which he cannot break, neither can it be moved.*

What we teach in the Church is that all of this pertains to that young 19-year-old who is being interviewed to receive the Melchizedek Priesthood and the ordination he is about to receive under the hands of his stake president, his bishop, his father, or some other Melchizedek priesthood bearer that can track his lineage back to Peter, James, and John, through the three witnesses of the *Book of Mormon*; which every Melchizedek Priesthood bearer in the Church today can do. **This** order of the priesthood does not come down through mortal hands. **This** order of the priesthood that we're talking about from verse 35 through 40 is an order of the priesthood that comes under God's hand. This is the highest, holiest order of the Melchizedek Priesthood; it's called *Patriarchal*. Here's the part that throws everybody off. If you stop right there, you could probably get by with this, but verse 41 throws a monkey wrench into the whole works. And we never go to verse 41, so therefore, nobody ever asks or challenges the idea of the way we teach *the oath and covenant*. Verse 41:

> *But whoso breaketh* ***this covenant****...*

Now, the way we teach it is that *this covenant* is from verse 33 through 40. The way I'm teaching it is from verse **35** to verse 40:

> *But whoso breaketh this covenant after he hath received it, and altogether turneth therefrom,* ***shall not have forgiveness of sins in this world nor in the world to come.***

Are we talking about a young man who receives the Melchizedek Priesthood from his stake president, or bishop, or his father and then he goes inactive? Does he become *a son of perdition*? That's what verse 41 is talking about. You just described *a son of perdition*. There is no way that verse 41 can refer to *the oath and covenant of the priesthood* the way we teach it in the Church.

Student 6: A 16-year-old cannot take that kind of responsibility. The Lord wouldn't put that kind of responsibility on them, first of all.
Mike: Well a 16-year-old is still in the Aaronic priesthood, but let's take it up to a 19-year-old.
Student 6: Yes, I mean 19-year-old.
Mike: A 19-year-old who has been tutored in the Aaronic Priesthood and is now ready to be ordained an elder, receive the Melchizedek Priesthood, have it conferred, and then be ordained an elder. You see, under that circumstance, every returned missionary that leaves the Church and goes inactive turns against the Church, and breaks his covenant becomes *a son of perdition* according to verse 41. It can't be!
Student 6: Even if they were 40, 50 or 60.
Mike: Even if, it can't be. So, there has to be something else we're teaching here that we are missing. Now, let's look at verse 42:

> *And wo unto those who come not unto* ***this*** *priesthood...*

Notice it's not the two mentioned in verse 33, it's one. So, from verse 35 through to verse 42, is talking about the highest order of the Melchizedek Priesthood that doesn't come by man, but comes under the hand of God, and is administered by an oath under His hand. It is referred to as priesthood that is without mother and father, without beginning of days or end of years and is everlasting. The reason it is called *the everlasting priesthood* is because it is administered by Him who is everlasting. So, why do I show you this? Let's go back to verse 42:

> *And wo unto those who come not unto this priesthood which ye have received, which I now confirm upon you who are present this day,* ***by mine own voice****...*

Here is another thing you want to triple underline. This isn't something that is happening in an institution or something that is happening by mortal man laying fleshy hands upon another person's head. This is coming by revelation under the direction of God's own voice, and there is an ordination here where God puts His hands on these men and ordains them to ***this*** priesthood:

> *...out of the heavens; and even I have given the heavenly hosts and mine angels charge concerning you.*
> *[43] And I now give unto you a commandment to beware concerning yourselves, to give diligent heed to the words of eternal life.*

If you notice in the temple, we break the *Old Testament* time into two sections: From Adam up to Moses and from Moses to Christ. Do you remember that? *They offered up the first fruits of the field and the firstlings of the flock, which continued until the death of Christ and which ended sacrifice by the shedding of blood.* Do you remember that statement? Why is the *Old Testament* broken up into two parts? Why do we go from Adam to Moses? It's because from Adam to Moses there was only Patriarchal Priesthood on the earth. Now, you can see that referred to in section 84. This priesthood was designed to be handed down from father to righteous son: Patriarchal. Section 107 shows us this through giving us the priesthood lineage from Adam to Noah. And that priesthood that was there, from Adam up to Moses, is something that God was about to restore through the Prophet Joseph Smith. ***This*** is the priesthood that we talk about, and the order you enter into, in the temple. ***This*** order of the priesthood is not administered in the Church of Jesus Christ of Latter-day Saints. You have to go through the Church to qualify, but it is temple-centered. Now, go over to section 50, and let me show you what the blessings of ***this*** priesthood are. So, I'm showing you this as an example that this is something that is taught thousands of times every Sunday, throughout the world in priesthood meetings, and in interviewing and preparing men to receive the Melchizedek Priesthood. We're teaching this, and obviously, we stop at verse 39 because if you go to 40 and 41, it raises questions that you can't answer. Go to section 50 and let me show you this Patriarchal Priesthood that comes under the hand of God Himself. Section 50 verse 17, we've talked about this little bit so we will go over it quickly:

> *Verily I say you, he that is* ***ordained of me****,*

Take that literally. It doesn't mean ordained by My servants or ordained by My authorized ministers. It's "*ordained [by] me.*" And then go to verse 26:

> *He that is **ordained of God** and sent forth,*

Take that literally. God is laying His hands upon your head and ordaining you. That's the priesthood we're talking about in section 84, that if you turn against this, you become *a son of perdition*. So, this is obviously not what we usually teach. Now, here are the blessings; look at the power involved in this order of the priesthood. Verse 26:

> *the same is appointed to be **the greatest**, notwithstanding he is the least and the servant of all.*

Whoever receives his ordination from God has the title of *the greatest*:

> *[27] Wherefore, he is possessor of all things;*

Think about that for just a minute. He obviously isn't talking about a 19-year-old being ordained to the Melchizedek Priesthood in the Church. *"Possessor of all things,"* is number one. Number two is:

> *For all things are subject unto him, both in heaven and on the earth, the life and the light, the Spirit and the power, sent forth by the will of the Father through Jesus Christ, his Son.*

That's the power associated with ***this*** order of the priesthood that comes under the hand of God; that if you turn against this, you commit the unforgivable sin against the Holy Ghost and your destination is outer darkness, *a son of perdition*.

> *[28] But no man is possessor of all things except he be purified and cleansed from all sin.*
>
> *[29] And if ye are purified and cleansed from all sin, ye shall ask whatsoever you will in the name of Jesus and it shall be done.*
>
> *[30] But know this, it shall be given you what you shall ask; and as ye are appointed to the head, the spirits shall be subject unto you.*

In other words, you have the power of God. Would you like to see an example of where a man received this priesthood and what he was able to do with it, in the *Book of Mormon*?

Let's go to Helaman chapter 10; this is Nephi. Now, look at the chapter heading, and you get an idea of a man who has a priesthood that is not like what we talk about in the Church. Just look at the chapter heading:

> *The Lord gives Nephi the sealing power—*

This sealing power that Nephi has here is not the same sealing power we see used in the temples. There are different kinds of sealing powers, not just one, but there are different orders and different levels of that. Notice, it says:

> *He is empowered to bind and loose* ***on earth and in heaven****—He commands the people to repent or perish—*

And look at this:

> *The Spirit carries him from congregation to congregation.*

This is all because this man has received ***this*** order of the priesthood and ordination, under the hand of God. So, now let's look at it and see what it says in verse 2:

> *And it came to pass that Nephi went his way towards his own house, pondering upon the things which the Lord had shown unto him.*
>
> *[3] And it came to pass as he was thus pondering—being much cast down because of the wickedness of the people of the Nephites, their secret works of darkness, and their murderings, and their plunderings, and all manner of iniquities—and it came to pass as he was thus pondering in his heart, behold, a voice came unto him saying:*

Who do you think is speaking to him here? A stake president? A bishop? It's God saying, "*Blessed art thou, Nephi.*" Now, notice he doesn't see God at this point. This is something that we've talked about. He hears a voice come unto him. This is called *the more sure word of prophecy*, and it's also *making your calling and election sure*. That is the key that opens the door for you to have a personal encounter with the Lord Jesus Christ and receive the *Second Comforter*. This precedes all of that and goes right along with ***this*** priesthood that we're talking about:

> *[4] Blessed art thou, Nephi, for those things which thou hast done; for I have beheld how thou hast with unwearyingness declared the word,*

> *which I have given unto thee, unto this people. And thou hast not feared them, and hast not sought thine own life, but hast sought my will, and to keep my commandments.*
> *[5] And now, because thou hast done this with such unwearyingness, behold, I will bless thee for ever;*

That is Nephi's *calling and election made sure*. He has now obtained from the voice of the Lord, direct to him, a promise of eternal life, and with that promise comes a promise of an inheritance in the celestial world with the Father and the Son. Now, you are asking, "Where are you getting that from, Brother Stroud?" I'm taking from many sources, and many scriptures, and many words of the prophets, and putting that all into one place and telling you that what's happening here embodies all of that:

> *I will bless thee forever; and I will make thee mighty in word and in deed, in faith and in works; yea, even that* ***all things*** *shall be done unto thee according to thy word,*

Remember section 50 where it says *possessor of* ***all things*** in heaven and earth? Here is your key to why. Why is Nephi able to have obtained such tremendous power?

> *for thou shalt not ask that which is contrary to my will.*

There's your key. Now, when we get up to a point in our progression where the Lord can say that or similar things like this about and to us, we will find the same opportunities, privileges, and blessings bestowed and endowed upon us because He is no respecter of persons. How does a person get to a point where God says, "I will give you all of My power because I know you won't ask anything contrary to My will." How do you get to a point like that? You have to be tried and proven in the furnace of affliction and the crucible of fire. There is no other way. God has to know that He can trust you because, remember, brothers and sisters, if Nephi receives this and altogether turns from this covenant, these promises, and these privileges, what is his fate? He becomes *a son of perdition.* Here's the whole picture and we are pulling section 84 together. This is what constitutes committing the unpardonable/unforgivable sin. Now, look at verse 6:

> *Behold, thou art Nephi, and I am God. Behold, I declare it unto thee in the presence of mine angels, that ye shall have power over this people, and shall smite the earth with famine, and with pestilence, and destruction, according to the wickedness of this people.*
>
> *[7] Behold, I give unto you power, that whatsoever ye shall seal on earth shall be sealed in heaven; and whatsoever ye shall loose on earth shall be loosed in heaven; and thus shall ye have power among this people.*

Read the rest of the story, and you can see that he was faithful and true to everything that had been given to him. This man was translated. Nephi obtained translation and was translated up into the city of Enoch.

Student 1: What I find interesting is when the people become so wicked that he asked the Lord to send a famine. He didn't want the people destroyed by the sword because *Thou shalt not kill,* right? He had to seek righteousness for all.

Mike: Interesting. He had the power to do that without asking the Lord to intervene. He could do it. It also shows the great humility, and lowliness of heart, and the meekness of this man. This is a great example for of all of us priesthood brethren. This is what we're doing.

So, you get a feel for what we're saying here, brothers and sisters? We now kind of conclude our discussion on the priesthood. Understand that when you go to the temple, you're entering into a whole new realm of things; a whole new paradigm of gospel living; a whole new level of spiritual excellence that the Church of Jesus Christ of Latter-day Saints **prepares** you to receive. And everything in the temple is designed to move men and women towards this higher, Family order of the priesthood, where men become kings and women become queens; men become priests and women become priestesses, fathers, and mothers. This is the launch pad to become like the Elohim. The Elohim are men and women who live in the highest degrees of exaltation and are Heavenly Fathers and Heavenly Mothers. That's the Elohim. We are Their children. Telestial worlds like this one, are the school houses/schoolrooms of the children of the Gods. We're in school. A test is being administered, and we're in the midst of it. Any questions or comments on that order of the priesthood?

It's my feeling that in his Restoration, Joseph had in mind the desire to move us into what he calls *the Ancient Order of Adam* or *the Order after the Ancient of Days*. When he first administered the endowment in Nauvoo in May of 1843, he called that whole experience the *Order after the Ancient of Days*, and it was Adamic. It had nothing to do with the *New Testament* church. It was something much more ancient, something much more significant of a higher order, something designed to move you quicker into the presence of God, and redeem you from *the Fall*. When the Lord brought the children of Israel out of Egypt, and out of bondage with an outstretched arm, His desire was to take that whole nation of former slaves, bring them to the temple and introduce them into the initiatory/endowment, and to administer Himself to them on Mount Sinai. Okay? You can read this in Exodus 19 through 23. (And then He's also talking about it in the *Doctrine and Covenants*, and section 84 alludes to it.) Moses was commanded by God to prepare this whole nation, to sanctify them, take three days to sanctify them, wash their bodies, and wash their clothes. There were to be no sexual relations between the husbands and wives. They were to put up a barrier around the mountain. They were not to go past the barrier unless commanded to do so. And on the third day, he was to bring them up there, and the God of heaven would come down in their midst, and He would see them face-to-face. This was designed to be a mass, national *Second Comforter* experience. The only thing similar to that is what we read in 3 Nephi, where 2,500 people at the Bountiful Temple had this experience. But it's estimated that the children of Israel, here, were anywhere from 1,500,000 to 3,000,000 people. Now, take the children out, and you still have a huge number, and he wanted to bring them into the presence of God. And God told him to prepare them to do it. It was His desire. So, the day comes, they go up the bounds (the little wall that was around the base of the mountain), and the Lord comes down in smoke and fire. There are earthquakes, the whole mountain is trembling, and it scared the heck out of the people, so they ran and stood afar off. And they said to Moses, "We don't want to see Him. You go talk to Him and then tell us what He said." As a result, the Lord took Moses and the Patriarchal Higher Order of Melchizedek Priesthood out of their midst and gave them a lesser preparatory priesthood and the law of performances and ordinances. They failed the test. Now, here's a question. Are we much better than that, because, guess what? We don't want to do anything either. We tell our leaders, "You go talk to Him and tell us what He said," instead of us going to the Lord and claiming our right to have these experiences. We cut ourselves off by telling our leaders that. That's what we do as a church. I believe that's one of the reasons why in 1832, the Lord said the whole Church was under condemnation. This is in section 84:

> *[54] because [they] have treated lightly the things [they had] received—*
> *[55] Which vanity and unbelief [has] brought the whole church under condemnation*
> *[56] And this condemnation resteth upon the children of Zion, even all.*

Something to think about. We look at our ancient ancestors, the children of Israel and ask, "How can they be so stupid? How can they make such mistakes? Why did they do what they did?" We need to stop and ask, "How are we doing? Are we falling into the same traps that they did?"

Student 6: When this priesthood is bestowed upon you, is it in the temple? Is it an actual ordination in the temple?

Mike: The people that I know that have received this ordination, have not received it in the temple. It can be done in a temple. Certainly, God can do it wherever He wants, but it's not limited to a temple. I know of one person who has received this priesthood ordination under the hands of the Savior, and it was done in a wilderness area, in a solitary place away from man and his polluted feet. So, it's just another example of how we want something like this to be done at a certain point, but the Lord can do it whenever and wherever He sees fit. And it certainly can be done in the temple. There's no reason that it could not be done there.

Now, all of this priesthood and this higher priesthood is tied in with the doctrine of *making your calling and election sure.* The Prophet Joseph Smith said:

> *I advise all to go on to perfection, and search deeper and deeper into the mysteries of Godliness. A man can do nothing for himself unless God direct him in the right way; and the priesthood is for that purpose.*

Having your *calling and election made sure* falls into the category of *the mysteries of Godliness.* It was taught openly by Joseph Smith. He also said:

> *I would exhort you to go on and continue to call upon God until you make your calling and election sure for yourselves, by obtaining this more sure word of prophecy, and wait patiently for the promise until you obtain it.*

That was his admonition to all the brothers and sisters of the Church. Now, *calling and election made sure* is not limited to the priesthood. It's my feeling, and this is Mike Stroud, that women don't need to hold the priesthood. Men need priesthood because it is a schoolmaster. It is a tutor. It's an instrument to help us become what women already are by nature. That's not to say that there are not women who make mistakes, but by nature women are holy. I was teaching this the other day; that anciently all covenants were made by the shedding of blood. This ancient priesthood order that we're talking about, covenants were entered into, and there was blood shed. I want you to think about a woman shedding her blood monthly, and that blood is shed in behalf of another person. It has to do with life. A woman sheds blood monthly, and there's a great lesson in this! A woman gives up everything, even her own identity, and name when she enters into a marriage relationship. Men don't do this. A woman's whole life is a life of sacrifice. There is never a time if she is doing what her nature persuades her to do, that she isn't sacrificing her life throughout her lifetime. And the token of that sacrifice is the monthly shedding of blood. It's a token. Priesthood, brethren, is designed to help us come to a point of holiness by sacrificing, which is difficult for a man. By nature, men do not sacrifice easily. We have to learn this process, and priesthood is the instrument and channel through which God reveals himself, gives us keys, helps, and gifts to help us become holy and without spot. Now, why do I say this about women and men? When you go to the temple, the initiatory for women is significantly different than the initiatory for men. Significantly different. If you haven't ever made a comparison, the next time you go to the temple and you're in the celestial room, or you're in a holy place there, you talk to your husband or your wife about the wording in the initiatory. Ask him about it. It is significantly different. So, women can also have their *calling and election made sure*. The priesthood is not required in order to obtain this. Women are not required to be married to a man in order to have their *calling and election made sure*. It's an individual, private, intimate, experience between the man or woman and his or her Savior. And it comes as a result of being tested, and tried, and proven, to see if God can trust you. The first step is for you to get to a point where you trust Him, which is a major hurdle for us in this world. It's like in the *Old Testament,* Proverbs 3:5-6 says:

> *Trust in the Lord with all thine heart; and lean not unto thine own understanding.*
> *[6] In all thy ways acknowledge him, and he shall direct thy paths.*

It is difficult for us to trust what we don't see. But you have to be able to trust God before He can put you in a position where He can find out if He can trust you. So, this trust is on both sides. Go ahead.

Student 6: Mike, doesn't He already know if He can trust us or not trust us? I mean, He knows all things.

Mike: He knows all those things, so basically, it's you finding out for you, isn't it?

Student 6: It's what?

Mike: It's you finding out. This is about you. You're right; He knows everything about you. But, you are finding out, so you have to put yourself in a position where He can extend promises and blessings to you and then you can have those come into your life to be sanctified and redeemed. A good point.

Now, let me just say this: you can make your *calling and election sure* in at least two different ways. One is through a priesthood ordinance that is performed in the temple. Go to section 132 though, and then let me show you something that we sometimes don't teach quite right. You would be surprised how many members of the Church there are that think that once they have had a marriage sealing in the temple, that it's binding. That once the ordinance is performed, that ordinance is now binding in life and death, and that they will be husband and wife in and after the resurrection of the dead. All of these ordinances are conditional; **all** of them are conditional. So, when you are married in the temple, the sealer pronounced blessings—*the blessings of Abraham, Isaac, and Jacob, the blessings of kingdoms, thrones, principalities, and powers and dominions, and exaltations,* etc.—but we don't hear the last little step. *All of these blessings I pronounce upon you according to your faithfulness*. That's the condition, which means that if you walk out of the temple and within a week you're not faithful to the ordinances and covenants, you have no temple marriage. It is conditional up and until the Holy Ghost places the seal on that marriage ordinance. There are so many members of the Church that feel once the ordinance has been performed, that's all there is to it. I know a lady that I tried to get to go back to the temple. She went once, and received her endowment blessings and figured that was all that was necessary. And she immediately came back home and shortly went inactive and didn't go back to church. So, she became active long enough to get a temple recommend, go and get her endowment blessing, and then went back and resumed her former lifestyle of inactivity. She felt that all the promises and all the blessings that she'd heard in the initiatory in the temple and the endowment allegory, were hers because she had been there. She just couldn't fathom that it's conditioned upon your faithfulness and that it didn't even happen. I've had people look at me and argue until they're blue in the face and say, "That's wrong." Here's the law in section 132, verse 7. Here it is right out of the Lord's own mouth:

> *And verily I say unto you, that the conditions of this law are these: All covenants, contracts, bonds, obligations, oaths, vows, performances, connections, associations, or expectations, that*

> *are not made and entered into* ***and sealed by the Holy Spirit of promise****...;*

Now, skip to the end of verse 7:

> *for all contracts that are not made unto this end* ***have an end when men are dead****.*

There it is! So, all ordinances, vows, contracts, conditions, obligations, connections, performances, and associations, unless they are sealed/ratified by *the Holy Spirit of Promise*, have no power and are not in effect, and are void when that man or woman dies. What we're trying to do here is take our ordinances that we've entered into and live our lives, **all** of our lives, so that when we leave this life, we have the Holy Ghost, which is *the Holy Spirit of Promise. The Holy Spirit of Promise* is a function of the Holy Ghost. You can lie to men, to apostles, to prophets, to bishops, and stake presidents, and you can get away with that; but you cannot lie to the Holy Ghost. That's why the Holy Ghost **has to seal these ordinances** because any other way there can be deception, but you cannot deceive the Holy Ghost. We want to live our lives so that when we breathe our last breath, we're what Elder Ballard used to call, "safely dead," which means our covenants are in effect. If you die within your covenants and you have been faithful and true, then the Holy Ghost places that seal and seals that ordinance, and it is now in effect after you're dead and in eternity.

There is an ordinance that is performed in the Church called the *second anointing*. When you go through the temple for the first time, you go into the initiatory and receive a first a washing and a first anointing. Then, you go into the endowment and you are instructed in allegory form. In the endowment, it says this, "Brothers and sisters, if you are true and faithful the day will come when you will be chosen called up **and anointed**." That is said after you have been anointed. You have already been anointed in the initiatory. You are now hearing this after that anointing has taken place. So, you are now talking about a *second anointing*. "...Chosen, called up and anointed as kings and queens, priests and priestesses, whereas you are **now** anointed only to become such." That is your first one. The *second anointing* is an ordinance that **declares** you a king and a priest, a queen and priestess, and gives you, what the Church calls and what the Lord calls, the *fullness of the priesthood*. That also is a *calling and election made sure ordinance*. That's performed in the Church, in the temple, under the direction of the President of the Church and can be performed by the First Presidency, members of the Quorum of Twelve Apostles, and I believe, members of the First Quorum of the Seventy, but I'm not sure about that. I know the First Presidency and the Twelve can. Temple presidents do not perform that; mission presidents do not perform that. It was done in a Salt Lake Temple for years and years in the Holy of Holies, in the celestial room, and the president of the Church performed that ordinance. There used to be only two temples that had a Holy of Holies, where these ordinances that we're talking about, the *second anointing ordinances*, were performed. The stake presidents had two recommend books. They had a recommend book that recommended you for your first time to the temple, and then the stake presidents had a second recommend book that would recommend you go back to the temple and receive your *second anointing* blessings. And for years and years, the stake president held those interviews. Then later on the Church got larger, and the recommend process for the *second anointing* was refined, came under the direction of the First Presidency and the president of the Church, and you received an invitation. And by the way, the *second anointing* blessings are only given to husbands and wives. These blessings are not administered to individual men and women. They are husband and wife ordinances. So, every endowment you go into and you hear, "If you are true and faithful the day will come," it's referring to some future day. So, from the day that you're in the temple, at some future day, you will be invited to come back to the temple and receive **the rest** of the endowment blessings.

Student 6: But the stake here also does that *second anointing.*

Mike: Yes, I'm going to come to that. You're exactly right. Now, here's the thing that we want to remember. Go back to section 132, verse 7 it says, *"All covenants, contracts, bonds, obligations."* Notice the word, *"All **covenants**."* That includes the *second anointing covenant*. You can go into the temple and have this ordinance performed, but unless it is sealed by the Holy Spirit of Promise, just like your temple marriage, it is of no efficacy in and after the resurrection of the dead. It's an ordinance, like all other ordinances, that was conditional. And what's the condition? The condition is: **it has to be sealed by the *Holy Spirit of Promise***. That's the condition. If it's not done, you've just had an ordinance performed in a holy place, but it has no power in eternity until ratified by the Holy Ghost. As I understand, these ordinances are still being performed, but on a limited basis, throughout the Church. It's not something that is generally being done. The Holy of Holies was found in only two temples for the first hundred plus years of the Church restoration, and that was in the Salt Lake Temple and the Manti Temple. If you wanted to receive your *second anointing,* you had to make a trip to Salt Lake City, and then later on people could go to Manti, because that's where the Holies of Holies were and where these ordinances were performed. Every temple in the Church today, has within it a place that is under lock and key. It's a small room, and only the temple president and general authorities hold the key to that little room. It's a little closet. That little closet is not the Holy of Holies. That little closet contains furnishings that are necessary in order to perform these ordinances, which are similar to your first initiatory but are the concluding ordinance. The sealing room that contains that closet that is locked is the Holy of Holies for that temple when so dedicated. For those of us that go to the Snowflake Temple, it is the North sealing room, the large one. And if you look down in the corner of that room, you will see a door. And it is a locked door. I went to the Manhattan temple, and I've been to temples all over the world. I walk around and look at the various sealing rooms until I can find the room that has that little closet that has a locked door. And that room is, can, and does function, when so dedicated, as the Holy of Holies for the performance of these *second anointing* blessings. And every temple that's built has that facility set up to do that. It's my feeling that we're not doing that generally, but the Church is certainly prepared for that to become a more general application among the membership than it is now.

Now, in closing, [student] brought this up: these same blessings, these same promises, these same ordinations, these same bestowals, and endowments that are incorporated with the ordinance of the second anointing can be performed by God

Himself with you personally. When you receive *the more sure word of prophecy*, and you converse with the Lord through the veil, and then you enter into His presence with the *Second Comforter*, you've received all that there is to receive. The interesting side of this is that when God administers this to you, there is no condition. There is no need for the sealing of the Holy Ghost. The Holy Ghost is already there and has prepared you and taken you into the presence of God, who performs this ordinance, so it is in effect. And if you sin against that, you become *a son perdition* if you're male. So, there are at least two ways that these higher ordinances and blessings of the Melchizedek Priesthood can be received. All that we've talked about tonight, including *the oath and covenant of the priesthood*, are talking about priesthood orders and steps that take us step-by-step until we enter into the presence of the Lord and receive all that He has for us.

Student 2: Elder Stroud, all of this that we have spoken of leads to that highest blessing.

Mike: They do.

Student 2: They are not all one and the same.

Mike: All of them are parts and portions, and they come in sequence. It's hard for us to say that this comes first, or that comes first. It's just all part of the package. And for me to say that God won't do *three* until *two*, and *one* are done, that's just my thinking, but I'm not about to limit Him and tell Him in what sequence He can or cannot do things. He can do things according to His own good will and pleasure. But, the answer to your question is that all of these things are a part of the total package that the Lord has kept reserved from before the foundation of the world, to be reserved and revealed to babes in *the dispensation of the fullness of times*. We're receiving things, brothers and sisters! We're talking about things here tonight that have not been known in previous dispensations. These are the *mysteries of godliness* that the Lord has promised to give us in this day.

Student 2: So, they were not performed in those dispensations, or what? I mean obviously, we know of transfigurations, and we know of—

Mike: Go to section 121, and let me anticipate your question there. Go to the end of verse 31, just the last sentence:

...shall be revealed in the days of the dispensation of the fullness of times—

So, that tells you that whatever verse 26 through verse 31 is talking about has been reserved to be revealed *in the days of the dispensation of the fullness of times*. Now, go to verse 26. Let's look at some of these things:

God shall give unto you ***knowledge*** *by his Holy Spirit, yea, by the unspeakable gift of the Holy Ghost,* ***that has not been revealed since the world was until now;***

Skip down to verse 28:

A time to come in the which ***nothing shall be withheld****, whether there be one God or many gods, they shall be manifest.*

And then it talks about the universe, and it talks about powers of the priesthood. Verse 29:

All thrones and dominions, principalities, and powers, shall be revealed...

All to be revealed in our day. Things that have never been revealed before are now being revealed to us in our day. We've gone an hour and seven minutes. This kind of wraps up our three-week discussion on priesthood, *the oath and covenant of the priesthood*, *second anointing*, and *the fullness of the Melchizedek Priesthood*, which we are initiated into at the time we go to the temple for our first blessings. And it's concluded, either by a priesthood ordinance sealed by *the Holy Spirit of Promise*, or an ordinance performed by God Himself, in which the conditions are all removed, and you are sealed up unto eternal life as a king and a queen, or a priest and a priestess, with an inheritance with God and Christ in the celestial world.

Student 2: May I ask one more question?

Mike: Sure.

Student 2: You have alluded before to *the new name* that is received in the temple. Would you elaborate on that for just a minute?

Mike: Just for a second on names: names are identities. Whenever you receive a name, it's referring to an identity. And that identity carries with it privileges, rights, blessings, responsibilities, and obligations. The *new name* represents a new position in the eyes of God, a new identity, a new position, a new authority, a new privilege, a new responsibility, and obligation. So, all the names that we talk about are things that identify men and women at various places in their progression, on the journey back to the Father. An example of that is: Christ is known as a Man of many names; His Father is a Man of many more names. Mike Stroud has a few names. A name is the same as a title or the same as a position. Some of Mike Stroud's names are: a son, Mike Stroud is a son, and as a son, he had a name. Mike Stroud is now a father. Now Mike Stroud, who is still a son and father, is now a grandfather and great-grandfather. And there are names that go along with that. What's the name? They are son, father, grandfather, and great-grandfather. They are all the same person, but they just indicate where I am in my progression back to the Father.

Student 2: How many names do you receive in the temple?

Mike: There are four names that are mentioned in the temple. There is the *new name*, your own name, a name that is associated with the Melchizedek Priesthood, and then there's a fourth name that you receive at the veil. The fourth name is the Father's name. And it's the same for women; just change it to Mother in Heaven, wife, princess, queen, and mother. They're the same things. They are names that represent and indicate where you are in your progression, and if you've been successful in completing various estates of progression. Does that help, without going into it? We can't, on an open forum like this, because they are things that belong to the temple. But, let's just say that each one of us has, have had, do have, and will have, many names, slashes, titles, positions, etc. There is significance in taking upon you the **name** of Christ. There is deep significance on that. That is something that you need to ponder and think about. What does it mean to take upon you the name of Christ? What is the name that King Benjamin speaks of in Mosiah chapter 1 and 2, by which his people will be known? Why did he give them **a new name** by which they will be known? Abram's new name is Abraham. Sarai's temple name is Sarah. Enoch's new name is Raphael. Noah's new name is Gabriel. Every name that ends with the word EL, that's the name of God. Names that end in EL are Elohim names: Michael, Ezekiel, Gabriel, Raphael, Uriel, Israel.

Those are all names of God. EL is the Hebrew word for God. Elohim is the plural word, which means gods. Well, it's been fun. I hope that's helpful. Next week, what I want to talk to you about is something that has been on my mind. I want to chat with you about devils and unclean spirits. And we may take a couple of weeks on that. For sure it will take all of next week.

References:
D&C 84:33-43
D&C 107:40-52 Father to Son
D&C 50:17 and 26-30
Helaman 10:2-7
Exodus Chapters 19-23 Israelites and Moses
3 Nephi Chapters 9-26 Christ to Nephites
Joseph Smith, Discourses of the Prophet Joseph Smith, pg. 364, "I advise all to go on to perfection…"
History of the Church Vol. 5, page 387, "I would exhort you to go on to continue…"
D&C 84: 54-56
Proverbs 3:5, 6
D&C 132:7
D&C 121:26-31

Chapter Seventeen

Podcast 017 Devils and Unclean Spirits

Tonight, we're going to talk about something special that Margie and I were discussing recently. She said I need to talk about it at this particular time: devils and unclean spirits. This subject isn't talked about much in our day, and it's a very important subject. In the early days of the history of the Church, Joseph Smith and the brethren talked about it extensively. It started to diminish in our Church conversations and doctrinal discussions in the 1890's, and by 1930, it became a topic that is almost never talked about in our church doctrinal discussions.

Let's go to 1 Nephi 11:31 for a take-off scripture. Nephi 11 is Nephi's commentary on his father's vision of the tree of life. He sees the ministry of the Savior in vision. Verse 31:

> *And he spake unto me again, saying: Look! And I looked, and I beheld the Lamb of God going forth among the children of men. And I beheld multitudes of people who were* ***sick, and who were afflicted.***

Underline *"sick, and who were afflicted."* Those are two groups of people: those who were sick, and those who were afflicted. You can be afflicted and not be sick, or you can be sick and not be afflicted, or you can be both. Now, look at the next line:

> *And I beheld multitudes of people who were sick, and who were afflicted* ***with all manner of***

> ***diseases,*** [that ties into the sick part] ***and with devils and unclean spirits;*** [and this ties in with the afflicted part]

You have two groups of people now: those who were sick with diseases and those who were afflicted with devils and unclean spirits. If you're like me, over the years, you've heard in prayers, "Bless the sick and the afflicted." It's quite a common usage of words in our prayers. In this scripture, it seems to specify groups of people who are challenged with certain things. So, He goes forth, and he heals:

> *and the angel spake and showed all these things unto me. And they were healed by the power of the Lamb of God; and the devils and the unclean spirits were cast out.*

So, those sick with diseases were healed, and those who were afflicted had the spirits cast out. Isn't that interesting? We read those things quickly and don't pay a lot of attention, but if we start to look at words and see how they're formed and separated by semicolons, commas, etc. and it gives a whole new meaning.

Now, what I want to chat with you about tonight is something that Margie and I discovered when we were on a mission in the Philippines. This might challenge some of the ideas that you've held. It did for me, and it took a little bit of time for me to wrap my mind around what I want to discuss with you tonight. **The power of devils and unclean spirits lies in their anonymity**. It's like a secret combination. A secret combination is at its most deadly and most effective when the people think there is no secret combination. At that point, when people think that it is nonsense and hysteria, then know that the secret combination is working very well, and it's at its most dangerous when people think it doesn't exist. It's the same thing when we're dealing with spirits from the dark side. They want to remain as anonymous as possible. When we start to talk about them and to expose their signs and tokens and their plans and strategies, then at that point they begin to lose power over us. So, as long as they can remain in the background, and do what they do, with us thinking that there are no such thing as organized, dark intelligences that can make war against us; as long as we remain oblivious, then they exercise huge power over us. And, what we experience from them we blame on all kinds of other things instead of recognizing the source from which these afflictions come. We may blame it on chemical imbalances, or we may blame it on emotional disorders, or we may blame it on mental illness, schizophrenia, bipolarism, and a host of other things that we use to describe disorders in human beings.

So, let me read a quote to you from the Prophet Joseph Smith. This was given in April of 1842, and Joseph was shot to death in June of 1844. So, this quote represents now, the Prophet's experience and thinking throughout most of his ministry, as he's now coming to the end. It is called the *Discerning of Spirits by the Power of the Priesthood.* Now, they were having big problems with evil spirits in the early history of the Church. Section 50 and other sections in the *Doctrine and Covenants* were given to address the situation that was going on. There was a lot of dark spiritualism taking place among the members of the Church. They were without the keys to understand what was going on, and so many people were assuming that these supernatural phenomena that were taking place on a regular basis among the members of the Church, were coming from God. Not only among the membership, but they were seeing a lot of this at camp meetings, revival meetings, and in that great spiritual awakening that was taking place on the frontier in those early days. So, let me just read this to you, and I will emphasize a couple of points that we want to talk about tonight.

> *Every one of these professes to be competent to **try** his neighbor's spirit, but no one can **try** his own, and what is the reason?*

It says, "**Try** the spirits." Have you ever thought about that? That's a phrase that Joseph used, *"We need to **try** the spirits."* Now, if you'll think of the temple for a moment, there's an example of where spirits are *tried.* In essence, a human being would ask the question, "How do I know you are who you say you are?" See, what you're doing now is you're "**trying** the spirit," rather than taking it at face value. Just because a person is standing three feet above the floor and doesn't seem to be bound by the physical laws of this world, we assume automatically that it is from God. Now, that's the problem that was there. They were having these manifestations, and they were assuming that it was coming from Heavenly Father just because it appeared to be supernatural or otherworldly. So, Joseph says: You need to **try** the spirits." Now, the first covenant that you enter into in the temple with its accompanying name, sign, and token is a detection sign. It was given to Adam and Eve in the Garden of Eden before they were cast out. It was given to them so when they come into a telestial world in a fallen condition, and start to interact with fallen dark spirits; they would have a key whereby they could **try** the spirits and detect false from true messengers. The Prophet Joseph Smith goes on to say:

> *Because they have not a key to unlock, no rule wherewith to measure, and no criterion whereby they can test it.*

This means they had no way to test this appearance or experience. Notice the three words he uses: key, rule, criterion to use to test these spirits:

> *Could any one tell the length, breadth or height of a building without a rule? Test the quality of metals without a criterion, or point out the movements of the planetary systems, without a knowledge of astronomy? Certainly not; and if such ignorance as this is manifested about a spirit of this kind, who can describe an angel of light?*

These dark spirits from the dark side that we'll be talking about tonight have the ability to muster even a portion of light, so that when they appear, because of the light that they possess, mortals will think that they come from God. Korihor, in Alma 30 was deceived and said that the devil appeared to him as an *angel of light*. Joseph says that without a criterion, who could tell whether you are describing an angel of light? He goes on to say:

> *If Satan should appear as one in glory, who can tell his color, his signs, his appearance, his glory? —or what is the manner of his manifestation?*

Notice the key words again: glory, color, signs, appearance, manifestations. This is really tricky. Joseph goes on and says this:

> *Or who can drag into daylight and develop the hidden mysteries of the false spirits that so*

> *frequently are made manifest among the Latter-day Saints?*

See, this was a big problem. And I would ask you this, brothers and sisters; if it was a big problem in 1842, do you think that problem has diminished in 2016? Do you think that Satan has backed off, or conceded ground, or has become less dangerous and less deceptive in 2016 than he was in 1842 when the Prophet wrote these words? Are we in as much need today of the key, measure, rule, and criterion to test what is going on around us as they ever have been in the history of the world? That's my question. My feeling is that there has never been a time where this knowledge and these laws are needed more than now. Joseph goes on to say:

> *We answer that no man can do this without the Priesthood, and having a knowledge of the* ***laws by which spirits are governed****;*

If you go to the temple, you get a little clue when the Lord is speaking about using Lucifer as opposition to providing experience for his children. "We will **allow** Lucifer to tempt them." I want you to notice that word; do you remember that at the temple? "We will **allow**." That indicates that all of these dark spirits, no matter what they do, could not do anything that they do if it were not **allowed** by the Father and the Son and by the Gods that sit enthroned in the Heavens. They can only do what they are **allowed** to do, and there are laws that govern them, according to Joseph's statement. Joseph goes on and says:

> *for as "no man knows the things of God, but by the Spirit of God," so no man knows the spirit of the devil, and his power and influence, but by possessing intelligence which is more than human, and having unfolded through the medium of the Priesthood the mysterious operations of his devices;*

This is our take-off verse for tonight's lesson. Now, it's interesting that the Prophet Joseph Smith lists eight things or characteristics that define organized evil. Here they are:

> *without knowing the* ***angelic form****, the* ***sanctified look*** *and* ***gesture****, and the* ***zeal*** *that is frequently manifested by him for the glory of God, together*

> *with the **prophetic spirit**, the **gracious influence**, the **godly appearance**, and the **holy garb**, which are so characteristic of his proceedings and his mysterious windings.*

Now, I would submit that every one of those eight things could easily refer to Godly things. This whole statement is available at the end of this chapter. You'll want to look at this again and again. These are all talking about dark satanic things, but listen, they each could easily be describing something Godly. So, with those eight things, you and I don't stand a chance at detecting this evil that surrounds us day in and day out, unless we have a **key, a rule, and a criterion,** that we can test the spirits and **try** them. Ending up this comment:

> ***A man must have the discerning of spirits*** *before he can drag into daylight this hellish influence and unfold it unto the world in all its soul-destroying, diabolical, and horrid colors;* ***for nothing is a greater injury to the children of men than to be under the influence of a false spirit when they think they have the Spirit of God.***

I want you to remember this because the worst thing that can happen to men is, *"to be under the influence of a false spirit when they think they have the Spirit of God."* Let me show you how subtle Satan is on this. I want to go back to where he says, *"A man* (man/woman, because it's not limited to men, as I'll point out to you tonight) *must have the* ***discerning of spirits**."* In the Church, we use the term *the spirit of discernment* and the *gift of discernment*, but those are not scriptural terms. Did you know that? We use them all the time in the Church, but they are not scriptural. The correct scriptural term is ***discerning of spirits***. Now, I want you to note the subtle sophistry of the devil to divert attention away from him by simply changing word structure. Notice that the *spirit of discernment* doesn't point towards anything that is negative, whereas the *discerning of spirits* tells you that you have to have a gift to discern spirits, good and bad. He has successfully buried that term the *discerning of spirits* in Latter-day jargon among the members of the Church—it's not there. In place of that, we use *the gift of discernmen*t or *the spirit of discernment,* which takes us away from the direction of looking at intelligent beings and effectively keeps them in a state of anonymity. This is a very, very subtle and a very powerful, suggestive thing. The *discerning of spirits* is one of the *gifts of the Spirit* listed in 1 Corinthians, *Doctrine and Covenants*, section 46, and in Moroni 10. That is one of the *gifts of the Spirit*, but we don't ever use that. So, here is something, as we seek for the *gifts of the Spirit*, we should pay attention to that wording and in our prayers, ask the Lord to bless us with *"the gift of discerning of spirits."* Be specific. Don't ask for the *gift of discernment*, but call the gift by its scriptural term, and at that point, we begin to shed light on this darkness that needs to be dragged into the light. What did Joseph Smith say? *"A man must have the discerning of spirits before he can drag into daylight this hellish influence and unfold it unto the world in all its soul-destroying, diabolical, and horrid colors."*

So, now we're dealing with laws. Something that we have in the Church that has developed over time is what the *Book of Mormon* calls the *"precepts of men,"* and the *Doctrine and Covenants* calls *"the traditions of the fathers."* We've talked about this in the past, that when God reveals Himself from heaven, what a challenge it is to preserve that truth and keep it as unsullied and unadulterated as possible. It's the nature of God's truth being revealed in a telestial world, that the minute His word comes into a telestial world and is found among the children of men, all the forces of Hell will do everything they can to alter it, adulterate it, and change it, so that it loses its original purity. That's not finding fault with anybody, that's just a fact. So, with that in mind, we go back to that scripture in 1 Nephi 11:31. When we were in the Philippines, I came across an article as I was just perusing the internet. It was an anonymous article written by a man who was a bishop, and I'll put that up so you can see what it was that put Margie and me on this little adventure, which turned out to be quite a great adventure! In that article, he talked about devils and unclean spirits and said this, "That these are two different, distinct groups of people." All my life as a teacher in the gospel, I had taught that these two words were basically referring to the same group of people. I had never thought about them as being different and distinct groups of people: a group that the Lord refers to as **devils**, and another totally separate group that the Lord refers to as **unclean,** and in some other places in the scriptures, **foul** spirits—unclean and foul. By the way, I will have a 164-page document available for you to look at, that is probably the most extensive compilation of quotes by the early Brethren on this topic that I've ever seen before. I just came across it this last week (See reference section at the end of this chapter). What we are trying to do is identify that there is a warfare going on and we're afflicted with it every day. We need to learn some things and gather some information and intelligence on this, so that we can effectively and successfully combat this evil and complete our journey back to the Father, with the necessary experience and advantage for the world to come.

So, this is what we have on devils. The scriptures talk about a war in heaven and a third **part** of the host of heaven. A third part, it's not one-third. That's another thing we don't quote correctly. We say, "a third of the hosts of heaven," and that's not scriptural. Nowhere in the scriptures does it say one-third. It says, *"A third part,"* which indicates there are three groups, and that third part could be 5%, 10%, or 27%, but if it were one-third, it would be 33%, so that's not correct. It's a third **part** of the hosts of heaven that were cast out, and they became devils. They are called ***sons*** *of perdition*, and this is my opinion: there are no women in this group. They are all men. It doesn't matter what the percentages are, it's a third part, and these men are never to have a birth, or have a body, or ever experience marriage, nor will they ever be the father of children. They are **unembodied**. Now there's a difference between **un**embodied and **dis**embodied. They are unembodied. They are cast down, and they are on the earth, and they represent the organized, supreme, evil, leadership that presides over all other evil, that afflicts men and women in this world. The second group—unclean spirits—are subject to the first group. The devils run the show. As I have studied the gospel, one of the things that have helped me understand things and has opened up personal revelation to me, is the study and pondering on patterns. Patterns have ended up being a powerful way for me to receive revelation from my Father in Heaven. One of the things we know about these devils, the *unembodied*, the third part, is that they are in a constant state of rebellion against the Father and the Son. It's my opinion, and this is Mike Stroud now, that the gift of repentance—and it is a gift, brothers and sisters—is not extended to them. This is another interesting thought that we ponder and if you read the scriptures closely, we just think that repentance is available to anybody at any time and all they have to do is go out, like a book on a shelf that says *The Book of Repentance*, reach up, grab it, open it up and access all the blessings. Repentance is a gift that is extended because of the Atonement of Christ and is extended to mankind. This group does not have that gift extended to them. They cannot repent because it's not available. Here's another thought: since they've never had a physical body, they don't relate to the feelings, passions, emotions, and sensations associated with a physical, mortal body. Now, it's important to remember that, because the second group does.

Student 5: I have a question about the repentance gift. Now, repentance is a gift given to us **because** of Christ, or **by** Christ?

Mike: *The Book of Mormon*, Alma chapters 40-42, talks about the Atonement bringing about the *conditions of repentance and* that because of the Atonement, there is a condition now available to men and women that without the Atonement, doesn't exist. That condition is called the *conditions of repentance.* It brings about the bowels of mercy and answers the demands of justice, but it's a *condition* that exists because of Christ's perfect atoning sacrifice. Okay? And, if you will start looking at these terms, "Is repentance a gift that is extended to God's children?" you'll read scriptures that all of a sudden will open up your mind. You'll be illuminated, and you'll say, "Oh, my gosh! There it is right there!"

Now, let's go to this second group of people. So, the first group that has never had bodies can't relate to certain things. It's my feeling that the first group is more or less centered on power, control, and captivity. The second group of people that the scriptures refer to as *"unclean spirits,"* are simply men and women who have lived in mortality, had a birth, and died in their sins, unredeemed and unchanged because they didn't take part in the gospel laws, the power of the Holy Ghost, and the other things that can change them from their natural element into a sanctified element. They die in their sins. There are many degrees of that. These people who had a body understand very well, and in their disembodied state, can still remember the feelings, passions, desires, appetites, compulsions, and addictions. These things that they had in the flesh follow them into the spirit world. So, Lucifer and the third part enlist and captivate these people and use them to torment men and women in the flesh; they truly afflict us. Now, here's something else, and you can do your own homework on this as I have. Alma 34:34 says that when a person dies, they are the same person in the next world that they were here. You know that scripture:

> *Ye cannot say, when ye are brought to that awful crisis, that I will repent, that I will return to my God. Nay, ye cannot say this; for that same spirit which doth possess your bodies at the time that ye go out of this life, that same spirit will have power to possess your body in that eternal world.*

There is no such thing as personality changing, or a huge changing in a person just because they experience death. They remain the same person. Now, here's an interesting thing. The early Brethren taught that when you die, everything that describes who you are, whether good or evil is intensified when you lay the body down. Everything is enhanced and intensified. So, if you are a man or woman of integrity and honesty, and that was an important trait for you while you were in the flesh, when you die and go into the spirit world, that trait, characteristic, or attribute is intensified and becomes even more so than it was while you were in the flesh. Now, the opposite is also true. If you were a liar and loved and made a lie, a compulsive liar, that lying spirit is intensified and you are more of a liar, more captivated, and more compelled and prone to lie in the spirit than you did while here in the flesh. Everything is intensified, the good and the bad. It has something to do with laying the body down and finding yourself in the spirit realm. Brigham Young said that it would be ten times harder for a person to repent of a sin in the spirit world after death than it would have been while in the flesh. There is something about the body that acts as a tool to help us in our journey, and when we lay that aside, it can either be to our betterment or our disadvantage. So, here's the thing I want you to remember. These unclean spirits, men and women who have lived on the earth, who now find themselves in various positions of captivity based on their compulsions, addictions, and habits they had in life, seek to find some kind satisfaction or a relief from these things, by tormenting men and women still in the body in the telestial world. It appears, from the things I've read, that they can never completely get a full satisfaction in what they try to do, but it's enough to keep them coming back for more. I don't know how else to explain it. You have a man who has a serious pornography addiction in this life and dies with that addiction; he's going to have that same addictive behavior, desires, and compulsions in an intensified state in the spirit. The only way he's going to find any relief from that is by tempting mortals still in the flesh, to participate in the sin that he died in. There seems to be some kind of perverted satisfaction, almost a relief of some kind when they're successful in that endeavor.

One word that the Lord uses to describe his children in a telestial world is *"warfare."* It's used over and over again. Hence, we have all kinds of allusions to us needing to take upon ourselves protective armor. Go with me to section 10 in the *Doctrine and Covenants*. Let me show you just one example of this to give you a feel for what is involved here. If you want to have fun, go to the hymnbook and just peruse and see how many hymns there are about warfare and battle. Verse 5 talks about these two groups. Now, you'll never see these two groups—devils and unclean spirits—until you have made that leap that we're talking about two separate groups; one group that is larger than the other, but subject to the first group. The second group of unclean spirits is a continually growing multitude of people. The first group is fixed. It is a third part, and they are devils. The second group grows with the death of every man and woman who dies in their sins, that is unredeemed, without a knowledge of the gospel. So, look at what the Lord says in verse 5:

Pray always, that you may come off ***conqueror****;*

Think about the times we use the word conqueror. It's always used in a warfare situation.

> *yea, that you may conquer* ***Satan****, and that you may escape the hands of the* ***servants of Satan that do uphold his work.***

There are your two groups: *Satan and the third part* and then the servants of Satan who uphold his work and are the *unclean spirits.*

I thought about whether to tell you this tonight, and I think I will. While I was serving in the Philippines, I had an experience, and I don't know if it was before I found the anonymous article explaining the difference between devils and unclean spirits, or if it was after. But, it was early in the morning, and the Lord allowed me to have a vision of these devils. I saw them. They were all men. I watched them and heard their voices. I saw what they were doing to human beings, or what they wanted to do to them. The worst Hollywood horror movie that you could think of didn't hold a candle to what I saw in that vision. It made me so upset; it traumatized me badly. I was a witness of what these brutal men either were doing or would like to be doing, to Father's children who are in the telestial world in a mortal probation. Then I woke up and went back to sleep, or went into a vision, and saw it a second time. That happened three times, and it was so traumatic that I didn't get over it for weeks. I was able to see who these people are and what they want to do to us. This was either before or after we found the internet article. The point was, it set our feet on something. I've never forgotten what I saw, and I have no illusions about what the warfare is and what the enemy is that's out there. I think this vision was seen by many people in the early history of the Church and it just points out the warfare that we're involved in. And they do not want to be exposed.

What we'll do is continue this a little bit further because I have all kinds of different things to share with you. These beings are subject to certain law. For example, if you are to come into contact with any of these and command them, they may want to know *"by what authority"* you make that command. And that authority is simply embodied **in the name of Jesus Christ**. That is the authority necessary. It's interesting, in the scriptures (Mark 16:17) when the Savior called The Twelve, both in America and in the New Testament era, and sent them out, He said, *"And* *these signs shall follow them that believe;"* And the first thing he mentioned was, *"In My name shall they cast out devils."* That was the very first thing mentioned. Then he goes on to talk about healing the sick, taking up serpents, etc. But it's interesting that the **first thing mentioned** is that those who have bodies, in the name of Christ, and through their belief, would have the power to cast out devils.

Student 1: Do you know how difficult it is to say those words? I have experienced that. You have it in your mind, and it doesn't want to come out of your mouth.

Mike: There's also a sign you can use by raising your right arm to the square. It's a power sign, and you can do your homework on that sign. There's plenty of information on it and why it's a square, and not straight up, etc. There's great symbolism that connects you with heaven when the right arm is raised to the square. Men and women can use that sign, and **in the name of Jesus Christ** can command these devils and unclean spirits **and they have to obey**. That is one of the priesthood laws that the Prophet Joseph Smith was talking about when he said that if we have a knowledge of these things, then we can not only bless our lives but also be an instrument in blessing the lives of many, many people.

Student 5: Why do they have to obey, seeing that they are so disobedient and rebellious?

Mike: Good question. There are certain laws and signs and tokens set up in heaven that were foreordained before the foundation of the world so that there would be a certain order in chaos. Now, the telestial world is a world of entropy and chaos. The only order in this world comes because of ordinances. The root word of ordinance is *order*. Elder Packer taught this. So, for there to be any kind of order in a world that thrives on disarray and disorder, laws have to be in place. Once you discover these laws, you can help God's children bring order to an otherwise disorganized, chaotic life. That's the purpose of what we're talking about. Go to section 123:7 in the *Doctrine and Covenants* and let me show you a little scripture that relates to this in a way. Through the prophet Joseph Smith, the Lord said that the "***mainspring of all corruption***," is the *false traditions of the fathers,* who passed those traditions on to their children. Think about the term the *"mainspring of all corruption."* Think about all the corruption in a telestial world. In verse 7, it talks about the children who:

> *have inherited lies...* [from their fathers] *and filled the world with confusion... is now the very* ***mainspring of all corruption****, and the whole earth groans under the weight of its iniquity.*
>
> *[8] It* [false traditions of the fathers, inherited by the children] *is an iron yoke, it is a strong band; they are the very handcuffs, and chains, and shackles, and fetters of hell.*

Skip to verse 11:

> *And also it is an* ***imperative duty*** *that we owe to all the rising generation, and to all the pure in heart—*

I would submit that what we are doing here tonight is exercising the beginnings of something the Lord calls our *imperative duty*:

> *[12] For there are many yet on the earth among all sects, parties, and denominations, who are blinded by the subtle craftiness of men, whereby they lie in wait to deceive, and who are only kept from the truth because they know not where to find it—*
>
> *[13] Therefore, that* ***we should waste and wear out our lives in bringing to light all the hidden things of darkness****, wherein we know them; and they are truly manifest from heaven—*

Now, if you go down to your footnote *13b,* where it talks about *"hidden things of darkness"* you can see it says, *"Secret Combinations."* I want to tell you that what we are talking about here tonight is the ultimate *secret combination.* It's a group of people who have **combined** to destroy the souls of men and to keep it as secret and anonymous as they possibly can, so that in the midst of the destruction when souls are perishing, they point in a completely different direction at the cause of their very destruction. What a huge success this is! So, in verse 13, the Lord says that *"We should waste and wear out our lives in bringing to light all the hidden things of darkness"*:

[14] These should then be attended to with great earnestness.

And that's what we are trying to do here, brothers and sisters; to begin a dialog where we will begin to drag into the daylight all of this hellish combination that surrounds us, that is afflicting people continually, and they do not know what's going on. They are completely in the dark.

Margie and I have had the opportunity many, many times now since the Philippines, to have this discussion with people on a one on one basis. We've started to talk about these things. As we've talked about these groups of organized, intelligent beings and people start to feel the spirit of that, it starts to resonate with them, and to distil upon them; they know that it's true. We teach the concepts and principles, and then the Holy Ghost starts to distil upon people. We have people who will start to say things like, "You mean, I'm not crazy?" I can't tell you how many times this has happened, brothers and sisters. They don't want to talk about it because they literally think there's an imbalance. Some of the common things that are going on with afflicted people are that they think there is something wrong with them: they're bipolar, or schizophrenic, or something like that. They think that people will think badly of them, and they don't want people to think badly of them. So, we start to say, "This isn't you, there is nothing you are doing here that's wrong. You're being afflicted by organized, dark intelligence." It's almost like you can see a huge burden that's being lifted off their shoulders when they start to have exposed to the daylight, this combination that's been afflicting them. It's been such an interesting thing to watch that in people. "I thought that I was crazy!" they say. And some of the things they have in common are that they hear noise, they hear voices. The word that they use to describe this is "chatter." This is the word that we hear over and over. Most of the time it's unintelligible chatter. It's just background, human voices, male and female, but they can't really decipher what is being said. In some cases, they'll see shadow beings. They'll see dark shadows and different things like that.

So, when we start to talk about this, it's a great liberating doctrine for so many people. Tonight, this is an introduction to this subject, to introduce you to a concept that hopefully, the

Spirit will persuade you to want to continue to look into. There's an old falsehood in the Church, and I can tell you where its origin comes from, and the paper I'm going to put forward for you to look at, has that origin. The origin says we shouldn't talk about these things, because if we talk about them, then we'll invite them into our presence. Now, don't believe this. You don't have to invite them; they're already here. You're surrounded day in and day out. This isn't a question of something being away from you and that if you start to talk about it, it's going to bring it into your proximity. You are surrounded day in and day out by these personages. They're here. They're not on another planet. They are here in a different dimension. There are people listening to this talk tonight. There are people who are listening to and observing this. Question or comment?

Student 6: Mike, I think what happens a lot of times is that they create fear in your mind. In fact, that very thing you talked about, "not to talk about it" and that is, in my experience, the very thing that keeps us from this truth. And they torment you by making you fear to talk about it or looking into it in your own life and seeing how you have been tormented by these types of things. So, I think the big thing is fear. I know when I feel fear I know exactly what's going on in my life.

Mike: Well said. Can I end tonight's class with three quotes from the Prophet Joseph Smith that point to the concept of gaining knowledge? The Prophet said:

> *Knowledge is necessary to life and godliness. Woe unto you priests and divines who preach that knowledge is not necessary unto life and salvation. Take away the apostles, etc., take away knowledge, and you will find yourselves worthy of the damnation of hell. Knowledge is revelation. Hear all ye brethren, this grand key: knowledge is the power of God unto salvation.*

One other quote:

> *As far as we degenerate from God, we descend to the devil and lose knowledge, and without knowledge we cannot be saved, and while our hearts are filled with evil, and we are studying evil, there is no room in our hearts for good, or*

> *studying good. Is not God good? Then you be good; if He is faithful, then you be faithful. Add to your faith virtue, to virtue knowledge, and seek for every good thing.*

And then this last quote pertains exactly to what we have been talking about tonight. The devil knows this truth that I am going to read to you right now, and he wants to keep this from you. The Prophet said:

> *A man* [/woman] *is saved no faster than he gets knowledge, for* ***if he does not get knowledge, he will be brought into captivity by some evil power in the other world****,* [why?] *as evil spirits will have more knowledge, and consequently more power than many men who are on the earth.*

How are you going to overcome evil in the world to come, if you haven't learned the laws, the keys, the tests, the measurements, and the laws of the holy priesthood that govern all spirits, good and evil? How are you going to have an ascendency over these people and not be brought into captivity, if you don't learn everything you can in this life so that we can have an advantage in the world to come? Let me testify to you from what I've seen and what I know. The last thing these evil spirits want you to do is to learn about them and the laws that govern them. That's the last thing they want.

Well, that's the beginning. I've got lots more to share with you, so I'll put some papers up and some things for you to look at. Some of the things we believe and teach are not quite the way it is. We teach that the devil can have no power over children, and that's not true. He cannot tempt them, but he can afflict them. One of the classic stories is the father, who brought the little boy that was tormented by an evil spirit, and the apostles tried to cast that spirit out, but they couldn't do it. So, the father brings the little boy to the Savior. The Savior asks, *"How long is it ago since this came unto him?"* And the father said, *"Of a child."* For the word *child,* the Greek, Hebrew, and Aramaic takes it back and puts it as a *baby/infant*. So, interesting things, even though children are not tempted and not accountable before age eight, they certainly can be afflicted. We've got some things to learn, and I would say do your study and homework on this.

The more you learn about this, then the Lord will slowly begin to open up a ministry for you so that He can use you and the knowledge you have to bless the lives of men and women, who are afflicted with devils and unclean spirits. You will be a blessing in their lives.

In closing, I'll just say that when we were in the Philippines and came across that article, I was just astounded because I had taught for so many years in the Church classrooms, and had not seen the difference between devils and unclean spirits. I just thought it was one group, two words describing the same group. As soon as that door was opened, the Lord began to provide Margie and me with a flow of information that I was just driven to understand. I was so driven that it even got to the point that Margie looked at me becoming obsessed with this knowledge, and she said, "You know, you're overboard." I agreed that I really was, so I tried to put it away and tried to get away from it. But, I was driven to go back to it! Toward the end of our mission, I told Margie that there must be some reason why the Lord wants me to have this information. We weren't home a week before the purpose for having this information started to unfold. It was a great blessing on our mission in New Jersey, and here in Eagar, and everywhere we've gone, and specifically among our own family members. It has been a great power and a great blessing to use this knowledge to bless and free and deliver people from this power. I hope that's helpful to you and I hope this begins some pondering for you.

References:

1 Nephi 11:31
Joseph Smith in *Discerning of Spirits by the Power of the Priesthood.*
Alma 40-42 Conditions of Repentance
D&C 138:19 Conditions of Repentance
Alma 34:34
D&C 10:5
D&C 123:7-14
Teachings of Joseph Smith
History of the Church

Anonymous article:
http://lastdaysigns.blogspot.com/2011/11/dealing-with-demons-devils-and-unclean.html

For a free PDF of the 164-page document, "Pornography, Sickness, Evil Spirits and the Priesthood" by Brother Scott J. Gillespie, see:
https://www.dropbox.com/s/uyosftjnar58hkj/Porn%2C%20sickness%2C%20evil%20spirits%20and%20the%20priesthood.pdf?dl=0

Discerning of Spirits by the Power of the Priesthood

By Brother Scott J. Gillespie

Every one of these professes to be competent to try his neighbor's spirit, but no one can try his own, and what is the reason? Because they have not a key to unlock, no rule wherewith to measure, and no criterion whereby they can test it. Could any one tell the length, breadth or height of a building without a rule? test the quality of metals without a criterion, or point out the movements of the planetary systems, without a knowledge of astronomy? Certainly not; and if such ignorance as this is manifested about a spirit of this kind, who can describe an angel of light? If Satan should appear as one in glory, who can tell his color, his signs, his appearance, his glory?—or what is the manner of his manifestation? Who can detect the spirit of the French prophets with their revelations and their visions, and power of manifestations? Or who can point out the spirit of the Irvingites, with their apostles and prophets, and visions and tongues, and interpretations, &c., &c. Or who can drag into daylight and develop the hidden mysteries of the false spirits that so frequently are made manifest among the Latter-day Saints? We answer that no man can do this without the Priesthood, and having a knowledge of the laws by which spirits are governed; for as "no man knows the things of God, but by the Spirit of God," so no man knows the spirit of the devil, and his power and influence, but by possessing intelligence which is more than human, and having unfolded through the medium of the Priesthood the mysterious operations of his devices; without knowing ***the angelic form, the sanctified look and gesture, and the zeal that is frequently manifested by him for the glory of God, together with the prophetic spirit, the gracious influence, the godly appearance, and the holy garb***, which are so characteristic of his proceedings and his mysterious windings.

A man must have the discerning of spirits before he can drag into daylight this hellish influence and unfold it unto the world in all its soul-destroying, diabolical, and horrid colors; for nothing is a greater injury to the children of men than to be under the influence of a false spirit when they think they have the Spirit of God. Thousands have felt the influence of its terrible power and baneful effects. Long pilgrimages have been undertaken, penances endured, and pain, misery, and ruin have followed in their train; nations have been convulsed, kingdoms overthrown, provinces laid waste, and blood, carnage, and desolation are habiliments in which it has been clothed.

Joseph Smith Jr.
Doctrinal History of the Church 4:587
April 9, 1842

Chapter Eighteen

Podcast 018 Devils and Unclean Spirits Part II

Tonight, we are going to continue our discussion of *Devils and Unclean Spirits*. That's distasteful for some people. Every week when we post the podcast, we choose a little picture for the thumbnail. The one we used last week was an image of a dark, cloaked figure, and when we found it I said, "Oh, I like that one! That's a good one!"

Margie said, "Oh, that is spooky! We don't want to put that up there," but I think it fits with what we are trying to do here. I've had several comments on our discussion from last week, and one of the main questions that comes up is, "Why don't we talk about this more? Why isn't this subject discussed?" Although I don't have an answer for that, I did mention last week that in the early days of the Church, it was a topic of general discussion in conferences, priesthood quorums, and different places. From 1890 onward, it started to wane, and by 1930, it was almost non-existent. I'm not finding fault with anybody, I don't want to do that, but I do wonder why we don't discuss something which Joseph Smith and the founding brethren of the Church talked about so expressly. I think one of the reasons for that is that some false traditions have taken the place of what was once considered very important doctrine and we have allowed this to kind of slip away.

Over in *Doctrine and Covenants* 123:7, the Lord talks about the *"mainspring of all corruption."* Now, think about that for just a minute. The *"mainspring of all corruption"* (meaning the fountain, or the origin of all corruption) in the world is what He calls *"the creeds* [traditions] *of the fathers"* and how the children *"inherit lies"* from the fathers. So, these traditions that are passed on to the children go from generation to generation, until they take on the appearance of truth. What was originally truth is supplanted by these false traditions. The *Book of Mormon* calls these *"the precepts of men."* The temple refers to them as *"the philosophies of men mingled with scripture."* Satan has been very subtle in this process of hiding his tactics and strategies and the way he promotes this warfare. So, last week a comment was made that one of the things that stuck out most from that lesson was that the desire and ability of these unclean spirits to remain anonymous is their great power source. Their anonymity gives them power. The *Book of Mormon* talks about it in 2 Nephi 28:22. Nephi is talking about the tactics of the devil in the last days and that the day would come when people would say that there is no devil and would actually deny his existence, because:

> *...he sayeth unto them: I am no devil, for there is none.*

In that 164 page, long article I gave you last week on devils and unclean spirits, the statistic that came out was that somewhere around 59% of the membership of the Church do not believe there is an active conspiracy involved in captivating the souls of men by organized evil. 59% of the members of the Church! They believe in a devil, but don't believe that there is active warfare where he is conspiring to captivate and control them.

Student 1: That's odd. Why would he be here if he doesn't do anything, right?

Mike: Right. And he's been very successful. You can tell when a secret combination is most effective because it's when people believe that there is no secret combination. While that very combination is destroying them, spiritually and physically, the people say it doesn't exist. That's an example of when it is most deadly and working well.

It's the same thing with this doctrine of devils and unclean spirits. One of the false traditions that we talk about is, "We should not discuss these things because in discussing them it provides an invitation for them to come into your life and cause you problems." That's a false doctrine because you're in hell right now! All telestial worlds are hell places. Now, I don't mean that in the term of the Christian world "Hell," meaning places that are forever burning and never consumed and all of that garbage. Hell is a place where evil spirits dwell and evil spirits are here. They are in the telestial world, and these groups of evil spirits and unclean spirits provide a very critical, crucial opposition for the sons and daughters of God, necessary for them to progress and become like Father in Heaven and Jesus Christ, to become *saved* men and women. You can't do it without devils. Did you know that? There is no way you can become a god without active opposition from a devil. It just can't happen. So, here we are in this place, and we're surrounded by them, and they are trying their best to remain in the darkness, remain hidden, and remain anonymous. As we talk about these kinds of things and we bring them to light, that's one thing that they really would rather not happen. They would rather remain in this anonymous condition to do their work behind the scenes, and even as it were, to blame it on something else. They blame their work on man's physical body. They may say, "Well, your body is inherently evil. Man is inherently evil." That's a very subtle doctrine since man's body was created by God, and if you believe that principle, then it's God's fault that you're evil. It removes all personal responsibility from you and puts it on God for you doing what you do because your body was made by Him. You see that subtle doctrine that slips in there? In reality, President Boyd K. Packer said, *"Our physical body is the instrument of our spirit."* Now, it is true that our physical body in the telestial world has weaknesses in it. These weaknesses have to do with mortality. But, by and large, the body responds to the spirit. For years and years, I taught it differently. I taught that the spirit was imprinted with what the body did, and I have since changed my feelings on that. The body is pretty much obedient to whatever the spirit wants it to do. That ties with President Packer's comment when he said that the body is the instrument of the spirit. Now, it's true that the body can have an effect on the spirit, both for good and for evil. But, by and large, we know that the body without the spirit in it does nothing. Take that spirit out, and it's inanimate. So, as the spirit overcomes and becomes godlike, through the power of the Holy Ghost and is sanctified, the body will reflect that sanctification. Likewise, the opposite is also true: that if the spirit makes choices which lead it away toward captivity and toward misery, then the body will reflect that captivity and that misery. So, what we're striving to do here in this world, is to have the spirit become supreme and rule in righteousness and subject the body to the spirit.

I want to look at some scriptures tonight. Let's go over to 2 Nephi 2:27:

> *Wherefore, men are free according to the flesh; and all things are given them which are expedient unto man. And they are free to choose liberty and eternal life, through the great Mediator of all men, or to choose captivity and death, **according to the captivity and power of the devil*** [remember that phrase right there]; for *he seeketh that all men might be miserable like unto himself.*
>
> *[28] And now, my sons, I would that ye should look to the great Mediator, and hearken unto his great commandments; and be faithful unto his words, and choose eternal life, according to the will of his Holy Spirit;*
>
> *[29] **And not choose eternal death**,*

Now, it's not the body making a choice here. These choices are not physical. These choices are being made by the spirit. Remember that the body, in and of itself, is an instrument of the spirit. The body either acts according to what the spirit does or is acted upon, according to what the spirit does. The spirit is the controlling center of activity and agency in all of God's children. Let's continue with verse 29:

> *according to the will of the flesh and the evil which is therein* [there are some weaknesses there that the devil uses], *which giveth the spirit of the devil **power to captivate**, to bring you down to hell, that he may reign over you in his own kingdom.*

Every choice we make is either going to be a choice toward light or a choice toward darkness, and your spirit and body will descend to and reflect those choices. So, let's talk about when a person has become addicted, and we'll use pornography for the example.

Pornography is the major sin of our day that is captivating the Melchizedek Priesthood in the Church. It's a huge major problem! When you make a choice to view that, it is the spirit that chooses. The weaknesses in the flesh are inherent in our body because it's made up of the same elements of the telestial world. So, that choice to go against light, and the weaknesses in the body, lead toward captivity and death, and that's what Lehi is talking about.

On the other side, when you make a choice toward light, then your body also responds to that, and the physical weaknesses, inherent in the telestial world, are changed and burned out. The result of that is called *sanctification*. The process of going through that is called *"the baptism of fire and the Holy Ghost."* So, either you can descend to a devil, or you can ascend to a state of righteousness that qualifies you for all the gifts and blessings of the gospel in this life, and it's your spirit that makes that choice. Now, when you die, and you lay your body down, the body in and of itself, does nothing but deteriorate back into earthly element. Again, the body is the instrument of the spirit. It can either help sanctify the spirit, or it can help lead the spirit into a captive, destructive state; either/or. Brother Packer taught that the body is the instrument of the spirit. He was told that in his patriarchal blessing and taught that doctrine all of his life. That's where it comes from. Now, here's another thing that he taught in at least the last ten years of his life:

> *All beings who have bodies have power over those who have not. The devil has no power over us only as we permit him. The moment we revolt at anything which comes from God, the devil takes power.*

Even *sons of perdition* who resurrect with physical bodies will have power over devils who have never received a body, nor a resurrection. So, physical bodies in all statuses, from devils to gods, have power over beings who do not have physical bodies. That's important to remember too, as we discuss this tonight.

As we talked about last week, an interesting thing that happens when you lay the body down is that the good characteristics and attributes that you've developed through your mortal life follow you into the next world, and—this is the important part—they are **intensified and enhanced.** That's an important thing to remember. You will be the same person there that you were here, but in an enhanced and intensified state, both good and bad. This is why Brigham Young taught that it's ten times harder for a person, who dies in their sins, to repent in the spirit world than it would be to repent having a mortal body in the telestial world. When you lay that body down, having died in your sins, your sins are intensified and enhanced: your addictions, your compulsions, everything is intensified. Hence, it is harder for that person to obtain a state of grace in the spirit, than it would have been if they had repented while in the physical body. Those are good things to remember. Everything is intensified, everything is enhanced, both the good and the evil. So, if you're an honorable, charitable person, who's filled with love and good will; if you had the gifts of the Spirit with you when you died, those go with you into the next world, and are intensified and enhanced, and give you an advantage in the next world. Remember that we're always progressing from one estate, one existence, into another. And, what you want to do when you leave one place and go to another is, you want to go there with an advantage. You don't want to go into the next world disadvantaged. This is why the Lord says in this great scripture in *Doctrine and Covenants* 130:

> *[18] Whatever principle of intelligence we attain unto in this life, it will rise with us in the resurrection.*
> *[19] And if a person gains more knowledge and intelligence in this life through his diligence and obedience than another, he* [/she] *will have so much the advantage in the world to come.*

So, as we talked about last week, we have two groups. We have a static group that's not increasing in number, and that's the *"third part"* that were cast out, not to have bodies. They have no relative experience with what it's like to have a physical body in the telestial world. Everything that they can relate to, as far as a physical body, has to be in the abstract. It has to be something they view in others that they cannot relate to in themselves because they've never had a body and they never will—they're denied a birth; that's the *"third part."* However, there's also a growing group of people called unclean or foul spirits. Those are men and women who died in their sins and are taken captive as they pass into the spirit world, by that same spirit that had an influence on them while they were alive. To one degree or another, and it's not all the same, but they are in a state of captivity, needing some deliverance.

Let's look at a couple of scriptures. Let's go on over to Ephesians 2:1-2 in the *New Testament* for just a minute. It gives us an interesting little statement about Lucifer. This verse refers to the devil as *"the prince of the power of the air."* Paul says this:

> *[1] And you hath he quickened, who were dead in trespasses and sins;*

Now, *quickened* is an interesting word. Quickening is one of the ways that persons who are dead are brought back to life. Quickening is not the same as resurrecting, but that's another lesson so just kind of tuck that aside:

> *[2] Wherein in time past ye walked according to the course of this world, according to* ***the prince of the power of the air,*** *the spirit that now worketh in the children of disobedience.*

Ephesians 2:2 refers to one of the titles of Satan as the *prince of the power of the air.* Now, without going into any details, we could expect to see miraculous things take place in what we call *the air*, the atmosphere, the area above the earth.

Remember that when Christ prepares to come at His second coming, some of His signs that will appear prior to the Second Coming, take place in the heavens and the atmosphere above the earth. One of them is called *"the sign of the coming of the Son of Man."* Joseph said it would be a universal sign that everybody on Earth sees at once. Many people will think that it's a comet or some planet moving into our planetary space. You'll be able to see it. Now, remember that for everything that God does, Satan has his counterfeits and there's an opposition in everything that God does. So, if God is going to show signs in the air and in the heavens, that point toward the Second Coming of His Son, you will also see signs in the heavens and in the air that are counterfeit signs. They will come from the dark side that will try and deceive you into thinking that they are coming from Christ. You will see that.

Interestingly enough, starting on May 27, 2016, and lasting three days, a sign was in the heavens that the Hopi Indians call the Kachina Blue Star. Now, whether you believe this is true or not, is not the point here. The point is that there is a sign that the Hopi Indian Tribe has seen. You can google this and look up the Kachina Blue Star, and it was seen in various places around the earth. It was seen in the United States, Asia, the South Seas, and in Europe. They photographed it, and it is a blue planet. According to Hopi tradition, this is the ninth sign in a series of signs, which indicates the cleansing of the earth by cataclysmic events. Now, I'm not saying it's true, and I'm not saying it's false, but I am saying is that there are signs in the air. You and I need to develop this *gift of discerning of spirits* so that when these things happen, we can discern between the true signs that come from The Father and His Son, and the false signs that come from *the prince over the power of the air.* Those false signs will be so closely aligned with the true signs that you will need knowledge, priesthood power, and revelation to discern the difference. That's how close it's going to be.

Let's go to Luke 4 in the *Bible* and look at another one. God has given Satan power over the riches of the earth. I remember when I was a missionary in Germany that the most famous play was about a man named Faust. He was a man who sold his soul to the devil for the wealth and riches of the earth. I'd never heard of that before, and I thought, "Wow! Is it possible to do that? Is it possible for you to enter into a covenant with the devil, and does he have the power to bestow the wealth and riches of the earth?" So, are there actual people out there who have become fantastically wealthy by selling their souls, as it were, to the devil? The answer is, yes. Now, let's go to Luke 4:5-7. This is Luke's account of the temptation of the devil, where Jesus fasted forty days. (But also look at verse 5 in the *Joseph Smith Translation* because the word *devil* is changed to *spirit*):

> *And the* ***spirit*** *taketh Him up into a high mountain, and he beheld all the kingdoms of the world, in a moment of time.*
> *[6] And the devil said unto him, All this power will I give thee* [all the kingdoms of the world], *and the glory of them: for that* [the ability to give it] *is delivered unto me; and to whomsoever I will I give it.*

[7] If thou therefore wilt worship me, all shall be thine.

So, there seems to be an indicator in there that he has power to bestow the wealth, treasures, prestige, and honors of men. He seems to be doing a pretty good job of that because in the *Doctrine and Covenants* section 121, the Lord says this:

[34] Behold, there are many called, but few are chosen. And why are they not chosen?

[35] Because their hearts are set so much upon the things of this world, and aspire to the honors of men, that they do not learn this one lesson—

[36] That the rights of the Priesthood are inseparably connected with the powers of heaven.

I'm going to give you another thing, later on, to show you that Satan, in our day, has been given certain powers quite unlike what he's had in the past. He's always had his witches, soothsayers, sorcerers, and magicians, etc. The greatest example was in Egypt, where the Pharaoh had his magicians, Jannes and Jambres, and how they duplicated fantastic miracles. They were able to turn water into blood. They had power over elements. They were able to turn staves into snakes. And it was only because a prophet of God was there with the power of *discerning of spirits* and God backing him up, that the miracles of these dark magicians were exposed for what they were; coming from the dark side of things. You're going to see more of that. I am going to prophesy now, and this is Stroud 23:3. The deceptions, miracles, sorceries, and witchcrafts in the past, will be nothing compared to what's coming. If we have not prepared ourselves by seeking for and obtaining these marvelous gifts of the Spirit, I don't know how we'll be able to come through the deception that's facing us.

Let's go to Luke 13:16. If you read in that document I sent you, the Brethren taught a lot that Satan has the power to cause people to be sick. One of the things that I have learned through my studies and personal experiences is that one of the signs of having sickness induced by dark spirits is vomiting. The Prophet Joseph Smith was attacked by an evil spirit, and he vomited so violently that he dislocated his jaw. He had to put his jaw back in place with his own hands before he could administer to another priesthood leader who was ill and afflicted. Once you start learning these doctrines, then you'll start to see this. Look at this little pearl in Luke 13:16. This was a woman who was brought to Him to be healed:

> *And ought not this woman, being a daughter of Abraham, whom Satan hath bound, lo, these eighteen years, be loosed from this bond on the Sabbath day?*

What was her infirmity? Look back at verse 11:

> *And, behold, there was a woman which had a spirit of infirmity eighteen years, and* ***was bowed together, and could in no wise lift up herself.***
> *[12] And when Jesus saw her, he called her to him, and said unto her, Woman, thou art loosed from thine infirmity.*

He laid his hands on her and immediately she was made straight and glorified God. And then that little ditty down in verse 16:

> *Satan hath bound [her], lo, these eighteen years.*

If you read the handout, you will notice that the early brethren like Brigham Young, Heber C. Kimball, George Q. Cannon, and Jedediah M. Grant, specifically pointed toward certain infirmities. They said that rheumatoid arthritis, pains, being bound in the back, in the spine, across the shoulders, and up the neck—these kinds of bindings are caused by unclean spirits and devils; not all of the time, but many times, just like the woman in the scripture that was bent in half and couldn't straighten up. If we have the *discerning of spirits,* we can see this, when the Lord wants us to discern what it is, and take appropriate action.

Let's go to Mark 9. This is probably my favorite story of all. This is referred to in all of the Gospels, but this is the one giving the most detail. Starting in verse 17:

> *And one of the multitude answered and said, Master, I have brought unto thee my son, which hath a dumb spirit;*

How are we to interpret that? In our day, dumb means you can't speak.

> *[18] And wheresoever he* [the spirit] *taketh him* [my son], *he teareth him:*

Look at the footnote for *teareth.* In Greek, it translates to dashes on the ground, convulses, and lacerates.

> *and he foameth, and gnasheth with his teeth, and pineth away: and I spake to thy disciples that they should cast him out; and they could not.*

This is a pretty sorry looking situation, isn't it?

> *[19] He answereth him, and saith, O faithless generation, how long shall I be with you? how long shall I suffer you? bring him unto me.*
> *[20] And they brought him unto him: and when he* [the spirit inside the child] *saw him* [Christ], *straightway the spirit tare him; and he fell on the ground, and wallowed foaming.*

What's the lesson we can learn here? These spirits knew Christ. I had an experience this week in casting out some unclean spirits. The person who came to me had to be brought here by a friend because the spirits that were in her were trying to do everything they could to keep her from coming here. They know when a person is blessed by the Lord with a gift to help deliver them:

> *[21] And he asked his father, How long is it ago since this came unto him? And he said, Of a child.*

The Greek, Aramaic, and Hebrew on that, translates *child* as *an infant/baby*. Now, if this is true then this also changes us and the way we think about things because in the Church we say that Satan has no power over children. The scriptures say that he cannot tempt children and they are not accountable until age eight, as revealed in *Doctrine and Covenants* 68. But, it doesn't say that they can't be afflicted, and here's an example of a child being afflicted for many, many years:

> *[22] And ofttimes it hath cast him into the fire, and into the waters, to destroy him: but if thou canst do anything, have compassion on us, and help us.*
> *[23] Jesus said unto him, if thou canst believe, all things are possible to him that believeth.*
> *[24] And straightway the father of the child cried out, and said with tears, Lord, I believe; help thou mine unbelief.*

Interesting. I wish we had the rest of the story there. What took place between *"Lord, I believe;"* and *"help thou mine unbelief?"* Was there a conversation there? A look? Did the Savior look at him a certain way? But something happened, and the father said, "I don't know if I have what it takes here to be part of this."

> *[25] When Jesus saw that the people came running together, he rebuked the **foul spirit**,*

Now, that's an identifier that the spirit has had a birth, has lived on the earth and died in their unsaved, unclean condition. It is not a devil:

> *saying unto him, Thou dumb and deaf spirit, I charge thee, come out of him, and **enter no more into him**.*

This is the only place in all the scriptures where an unclean spirit or devil has been cast out, and the Lord said, "Don't come back."

> *[26] And the spirit cried, and rent him sore, and came out of him: and he was as one dead; insomuch that many said, He is dead.*
>
> *[27] But Jesus took him by the hand, and lifted him up; and he arose.*
>
> *[28] And when he was come into the house, his disciples asked him privately, Why could not we cast him out?*
>
> *[29] And he said unto them, **This kind***

You should triple underline those words: ***this kind***. What does that tell us? There are all kinds of degrees of these spirits. And this particular kind:

> *can come forth by nothing, but by prayer and fasting.*

I want to share with you an experience that Margie had shortly after coming back from the Philippines. We had been learning these things that I'm teaching here, but as of yet, had no practical application. It was just a period of an intense gathering of knowledge. When we came home, we were here a few weeks, and two or three times my wife said, "We need to go see Sister [name omitted]." I'd been her home teacher in years past, and since we had been home from the Philippines, we hadn't been over there. So, we went to see her. The first thing she did after embracing us was that she got very emotional and teary-eyed and said, "I have been praying for months and months that the Lord would send you here to help me. You're the only one I know of that can help me." We found out that she had been troubled for months and months by some spirits. She could hear them talk. They would carry on conversations, and she could hear them. It wasn't all intelligible, but she could hear them enough to know that they were talking about her in her presence. There was a conversation going on that she could hear. She is a feisty lady, and she'd get angry and tell them, "Quit talking about me in my presence, as though I wasn't here. I can hear you!"

I asked, "If you can understand them, will you do me a favor? Will you start to keep a log and write down everything they're saying?" Now, I've since found out that people who are afflicted by spirits hear something, but most of the time it's not intelligible. Most of the time it's what they describe as *chatter*. Sometimes they see things, almost all the time they hear noises, sometimes they see shadows, and sometimes they catch things moving from one place to another. The point is, there's nothing *Hollywood spooky* about all of this. You're dealing with people, very real people, alive people, who just live in another dimension, and sometimes that dimension, that veil, can become very thin if the Lord allows it for His purposes, which are always wise.

So, back to this lady. We performed an ordinance, using the priesthood, in the name of Christ, and cleansed her house. We told any unclean, dark, foul spirits, or devils to leave those premises, that they weren't welcome there, that they were intruders and trespassers, and they needed to leave. Then I laid hands on her head and gave her a blessing, and said the same thing, rebuking these spirits, and in the name of Christ, commanded them to leave. This had some short-term success. When I'd go back, she'd say, "Yes, I noticed some difference, but it seemed like they would come back."

Some of these spirits were threatening her to have me stay away, saying things like, "If you call him over to help you again, you think you've been miserable before, well, you haven't seen anything yet. Unless you tell him to stay away, we will double and triple our efforts on you, and you will be more miserable than you have ever been before." And, they would threaten her, but like I said, she's feisty, and it didn't matter.

We went back maybe three or four times doing the same thing, with only limited success. Finally, at one point, I said to my wife as we left, "Gosh, maybe these aren't spirits after all. Maybe she's mentally suffering a breakdown." People had told her she was in the beginning stages of Alzheimer's. They wanted to commit her, and nobody believed what she said. At this point, after a few episodes, I started to doubt it myself. That same afternoon, or the next day, I was tilling in my garden, and this story in Mark came to my mind. The Lord brought to mind that story in Mark that we were just discussing. *"This kind can come forth by nothing, but by prayer and fasting."* I went in and talked to Margie and said, "We need to go on a fast." I know this was on a Saturday because we started a fast that day, and made an appointment to see this lady the next day to break our fast. We told her we were going too fast with her. The next day, we went over there in the spirit of fasting and prayer and did the same thing we'd done four or five times before. I laid my hands on her head in the spirit of fasting and prayer, commanded these spirits to leave in the name of Jesus Christ, and they left and never came back. She died a couple of years later, delivered from this awful thing that had been tormenting her so much.

They have to obey certain laws, and in the temple, you will see where a devil asks the question, "By what authority?" And the authority is in the name of Jesus Christ. A right arm to the square and invoking the name of Jesus Christ is a powerful sign and a name that causes spirits to obey by law unless there are other circumstances involved that require priesthood power, fasting, and prayer. Fasting, prayer, and priesthood power and authority are additional sources to break loose particularly stubborn people who, for whatever reason, have the power to resist an ordinary command and it takes additional signs and authority to break them loose.

Over in Matthew 12:43, in the middle of the Savior giving parables, he talks about an unclean spirit being cast out of a person. This is just in the middle of nowhere. It has nothing to do with the verses that precede it or that follow it. Then, He says that the spirit, after it is cast out of its house, which is the body it illegally had stolen and possessed, returns:

> *[44] Then he saith, I will return into my house from when I came out: and when he is come, he findeth it empty, swept, and garnished.*
> *[45] Then goeth he, and taketh with himself seven other spirits more wicked than himself, and they enter in and dwell there: and the last state of that man is worse than the first.*

It makes you wonder why the Lord, in the middle of these parables, sticks this interesting little item in there. This is what I've learned, and I've since found out it's true because I've done this now, multiple times; if you excuse, cast out, expel, or invite to leave (and those are all words you use, depending on the spirits you are dealing with), remember that devils cannot repent. We talked about that last week. The *third part* does not have the gift of repentance offered to them. They need to just be expelled, and the word in the scriptures is "*cast out*." The other group of unclean spirits may also be expelled and cast out, but remember this: they've had a physical body in a telestial world and are still offered the ability to repent, access the power of the atonement, and find deliverance and peace. They can escape the employ of the *third part*. If you have the discerning of spirits, and the Lord tells you in the midst of blessing a person who is afflicted (if the Spirit whispers to do so), you can invite those spirits that you're addressing to repent and turn to the Savior. You can talk to them through the blessing that you're giving this person, and remind them, "You have been deceived. Satan has deceived you again in the spirit world like he did when you were in life. You do not need to remain here." Usually, when the Spirit directs you to speak in this way and carry on this dialogue, there will be a messenger from the Lord, standing by in the spirit world, who is prepared to receive that spirit if they will turn to Him and repent. So, it's an interesting way of doing missionary work. What do we try to do in this life? We try to find people who will turn from their deceived course, listen to the missionaries, pray about the *Book of Mormon* and the message of the restoration, enter into a covenant, and begin newness of life. Sometimes you can do that same thing with those who are on the other side of the veil. I testify from personal experience that it's possible for you to turn a key in their behalf through the blessing. Keep in mind that you're blessing a mortal here, who's afflicted. You can speak to that spirit who is intruding, who is causing the affliction, and if the spirit is right, you can get them to go to the Lord, repent, and be delivered from Satan's captivity. Isn't that fascinating? It's a possibility, you see? I had that opportunity where the Lord prompted me, not every time, to talk to the person. Do I see them? No. Do I hear their conversations? No, even though some do. I've not developed that gift to that extent. So, I'm simply following the promptings that come, ever so subtlety in the form of thoughts in my mind and feelings in my heart, and I try to be obedient to those things. They come as you have your hands on the head of the person who is seeking for a blessing.

This last week I had an opportunity to give a blessing to a lady who was sorely possessed, and her friend brought her to our house. It was probably one of the most dramatic times I've had doing this. I anointed her head with oil, and then she became very physically active, to the point that as I laid my hands upon her head, I didn't think she was going to remain in the chair. I had the feeling that the spirit in her was an unclean spirit, not a devil, and a very active one. It was one who did not want her to be there participating in this. All through this blessing, she was highly physically agitated to the point that I didn't know if she was going to be able to remain in that chair or not. As we closed the blessing, the activity didn't seem to settle down. I was a little bit concerned. I was through with the blessing, the ordinance, and yet, she remained still agitated to the point that I started to doubt that we were going to be able to have the results we wanted. Then the Spirit spoke and said, "Do this...," and I did that, and then the Spirit said, "Do this...," and I did that. Then the Spirit said, "Say this word...," and I did that. You could see that the Spirit of the Lord replaced this unclean spirit, and this peace washed through her. You could feel her whole body relax. All the tension left. All the agitation left until there was just total peace and serenity. I was so grateful that the Lord had blessed her. In that blessing, we also invited angels to come in, and the spirits of *just men made perfect*. You see, that little story back there in Matthew, when one spirit is cast out, and he comes back and the place where he was **empty,** and he brings seven others with him, and the fate of the latter was worse than the former. **You cannot leave an open place here**. That's why the Savior said in this one instance, "And come not again unto him." One of the things I've learned through this is that you need to invite light and power from God to fill the place where darkness and confusion was.

Here's something else to remember. These devils and unclean spirits have no respect, no reverence at all, for the agency of man. They are truly intruders, interlopers, and trespassers. They are loud and fast. They are always in a hurry, and there is nothing slow or peaceful about them. Everything is in a hurry. Everything is now. Everything is loud. The opposite spirit comes from the Lord. So, the spirits of good people, angels, spirits of *just men made perfect*, deceased departed ancestors, especially those who are endowed, family members, need to be invited and given permission to come in and help you. They have absolute respect and absolute reverence for the agency of man. To access their light, power, peace, serenity, and strength, they need to be invited and given permission to do that, whereas the others come uninvited and intrude. These are things that I have learned. The spirits of the just, the spirits of the righteous, there's a serenity and peace that accompanies them, where the others are confusion, chaos, everything's in a hurry, everything is loud. You can discern the difference. What a marvelous blessing it was to see this sister's faith answered for asking for a blessing, and to see deliverance given to her because of her faith in the Lord, Jesus Christ. What a privilege it was to participate in that.

Student 1: Did you have another priesthood holder with you when you administered the oil?

Mike: I gave her two blessings, one earlier in the week, and that helped. And then, three days later she came back. I had a person to help me in the first blessing. Where possible, when we do this, it's good to have a quorum. This is another thing I've learned. The smallest priesthood quorum is three men, and then quorums go in odd numbers from three, five, seven, nine, and twelve. If I can, and have the time, I like to be able to fast and invite two other men who've been instructed in this, and have some knowledge in it so that they can add their faith. That becomes a very powerful thing. She called that morning and needed that blessing. Her friend called for her and said, "She needs a blessing, can you come?" and I said that I would, so I didn't have anybody on the second time around. I've also learned that you need to anoint with oil. In this blessing that I gave this lady, the Lord revealed to me through the Spirit the following term: "the oil of gladness." And there was one other term that talked about that oil, and I have since found out that they are scriptural terms that I had not known. This oil is a powerful symbol of deliverance. Oil always represents the Holy Ghost. In reality, if we do anything, it's not us as men, it's simply that as we try to be clean, we access the power of the Lord. He can work through us. In answer to your question, it was just me the second time, but I did have two women in the room who have tremendous faith, and both of them understand these principles, so that was a great boon.

This is an article that was written in the Church newspaper April 30, 1853, in *The Millennial Star*. Keep in mind, the Church was in Utah, and I believe this is the newspaper that was printed in England. This article was attributed to John Taylor, who was the editor-in-chief of the Church newspaper. I just want to read certain parts of it. Now, this article is called "The Coming Crisis and How to Meet It." It will be with this week's lesson so that you can read it. It is well worth reading. I just want to read a few short little parts:

> *A great and awful crisis is at hand—such a crisis as was never known before since the foundation of the world.*

Now, that should get our attention! This was written in 1853:

> *Perhaps you will be disappointed if I tell you that the time is coming, and now is, when, not only God, the Highest of all, shall be revealed in spirit and in mighty power, but the Devil or Satan also, will be revealed in signs and wonders and in mighty deeds! This, reader, is the great key to all the marvelous events that are to transpire shortly upon the earth.*

So, what Brother Taylor is giving us now is a great key to understanding what's happening in our day:

> *Now just stop right here, and pause, and mark emphatically this key. Then you and I will proceed to unlock the mysteries and to prepare ourselves to the battle. For there will be no neutrals in the approaching controversy. I say again, that God the Highest of all will make bare His arm in the eyes of all nations. And the heavens even will be rent, and the lighting down of His power will be felt by all nations.*
>
> *But this is not all. Satan also will be revealed.*

I want to testify to you that I'm seeing that Satan is being more revealed, being more obvious, and less anonymous than ever before, and it's just the beginning:

> *He has made some manifestations of his power in different periods of the world, but never before has there been such an array of numbers on his side, never before such a consolidation of armies and rulers, never before has there been such an imposing and overwhelming exhibition of miracles as Satan will shortly make manifest. Don't suppose for a moment, that I am uttering dark sayings or speaking unadvisedly upon speculation or the strength of mere human opinion. Don't tell me about Popes and Prelates sitting in the Temple of God as God.* [That's in 1 Thessalonians.] *One far greater than any Pope or Prelate is soon to be revealed and he will claim to be worshipped as God. Now, remember, that it is no modern wicked man that is going to claim divine honors. No, it is that old Serpent, the Devil. He it is that will head the opposition against God and His Christ. And he, the son of perdition it is, that* ***will be allowed a much longer chain than heretofore****. And such will be the greatness of his power, that it will seem to many that he is entirely loose. He will be so far unshackled and unchained that his power will deceive all nations, even the world. And the elect will barely escape the power of his sorceries, enchantments, and miracles!*
>
> *And even God, Himself, the true God, will contribute to put means and instruments in his way and at hand, for his use, so that he can have a full trial of his strength and cunning, with all deceivableness of unrighteousness in them that perish.*

That is the prelude to this article that is about ten pages long, that I think you should read and look at. So, I'll put it up as a handout on the link to this class.

Let me just close by saying that we should not fear this. We have available at our means the where-with-all to obtain knowledge concerning this arch enemy and his tactics. It is possible for God's children to come to a point where Satan has no power over them. That's a part of the temple endowment ceremony. There's a point where Satan is cast out of their midst. They are still in the mortal world, but he can't tempt them anymore. He's lost power. I submit to you that the loss of the power of Satan over God's children primarily comes in the accumulation of *knowledge*. The Prophet Joseph Smith said:

> *A man is saved no faster than he gets knowledge, for if he does not get knowledge, he will be brought into captivity by some evil power in the other world, as evil spirits will have more knowledge, and consequently more power than many men who are on the earth. Hence it needs revelation to assist us, and give us knowledge of the things of God.*

So, we should be learning all that we can, from all these sources. We have a 164-page document, and the appendix is the most comprehensive compilation of statements by latter-day restoration prophets and apostles that I've ever seen assembled anywhere. May the Lord bless us to obtain this knowledge, so that we can have power over those who are unembodied and disembodied, to have their works of darkness brought to light, and we can be instruments in the hands of our Father and His Christ in delivering his children while in this telestial world, I pray, in the name of Jesus Christ, amen.

Just a little addendum quickly: to the brethren that are listening to this (and sisters if you don't have a Melchizedek Priesthood brother in your home), sit down with your spouse and write out a dedicatory prayer. Take the knowledge you have, pray for the spirit of revelation, take the information that you're in possession of and that the Spirit has testified to you that is true. You should take none of this information from me. I'm just teaching you some things. You should pray to know if anything you hear in any of these classes is true. If it's distilled upon you by the Spirit then, that's wonderful. Sit down and write out a dedicatory prayer as dictated to you by the Spirit of revelation. If you're a husband and wife, participate together in that process. Then, choose a day when you want to dedicate your home. You want to clean out your home. You want to put a shield over your home. You want to have angels block the doors and protect your property. You want to be able to walk into your home and have the same spirit as you come into your home as you have when you enter into the temples, the Houses of the Lord. You want to have that spirit, that atmosphere. Your home should be second only to the Temple of the Lord. I think your home is a temple place, but it needs to have a dedication process. It needs to be an ordinance. And, write that down, and then dedicate your home. I think that now more than ever before, you're going to need to have a holy place that you can reside in, that you can go into, that you can study in, that you can receive revelation in; A Holy Place, and that's your home. So, I would invite you to do that, and you'll have a marvelous experience, if you'll just sit down, pray, and ask the Lord to reveal to you what words you should put down in this dedicatory ordinance. Especially use the information we've talked about on angels, *spirits of just men made perfect*, devils and unclean spirits, which are the opposite of light. They are the counterfeit of angels and *spirits of just men*. Then, you'll notice a difference, especially if you struggle with anything that causes you to be concerned, or you just don't seem to shake, such as addictions and compulsions. I have a daughter that calls on the phone every once in awhile and says, "I am having such an anxiety attack, I need some help." So, we'll go and place some hands on her head, and we'll give her a blessing, and specifically address unclean spirits. If there was ever an anxious group of people, it is those who are unredeemed in the spirit world. If you want to use a word that would describe them, it would be *anxiety*. So, you know, these are not us, but people who are *afflicted*, these devils and unclean spirits, want you to think that there is something wrong with you. In reality, what you are is being *afflicted*. They are intruders. They are not welcome. So, if you have those kinds of things, seek for a priesthood blessing, and in that blessing, specifically, address these things. Remember, and here's a rule, *general blessings* bring about general responses. *Specific blessings* bring about specific results. So, the more specific you can be, with anything that troubles you, or afflicts you, or causes you to keep from moving forward, the more specific you can be, the better. Anyway, I would admonish you to dedicate your homes and provide a safe, holy place where the Spirit of the Lord will come, and angels will not feel a need to hide their faces or cover their eyes. Something to think about. God bless you! Love you all!

References:
D&C 123:7
2 Nephi 28:22
2 Nephi 2:27-29
Boyd K. Packer *fireside address was given at Brigham Young University on 2 February 2003*
Teachings of the Prophet Joseph Smith, sel. Joseph Fielding Smith (1976), "All being who have bodies..."
D&C 130:18-19
Ephesians 2:1-2
Luke 4:5-7
JST Luke 4:5
D&C 121:34-36
Luke 13:16
Luke 13:11-12
Mark 9:17-29
Matthew 12:43-45 unclean spirit
Teachings of the Prophet Joseph Smith, page 217 Knowledge
Visions of Glory by John Pontius

The Millennial Star April 30, 1853:

The Coming Crisis & How to Meet It

by John Taylor
Samuel W Richards (Editor)

A great and awful crisis is at hand — such a crisis was never known before since the foundation of the world. All nations are looking through the misty future in order to descry, if possible, what is about to happen. Many sermons have been preached, many speeches have been made, and some pamphlets have been published, with the hope of lifting up the veil of the future. Yet none but the servants of God who have the testimony of Jesus, which is the spirit of prophecy, can unfold the mysteries of the future. They can give the trump a certain sound, and their counsel will not be guess work. God will do nothing except He reveal His secrets to His servants and Prophets. God, the Lord God of Israel, will take the control of these great events which are shortly to come to pass. Not a sparrow will fall to the ground without His notice. But His servants will be fully advised to every important event that is to transpire. They will be the heralds of blessings and also of vengeance. For the Lord hath a controversy with all nations, and the hour of recompense is at hand.

But, says the reader, I would like to know of what this crisis is to consist! Who are the contesting parties? Well, reader, if you will be patient and honest-hearted, praying withal, with unceasing diligence and thanksgiving to God, you shall have the keys of such knowledge as all the sectarian priests of Christendom are by no means able to reveal, because they are only revealed to God's servants, the Prophets.

Perhaps you will be disappointed, if I tell you that the time is coming, and now is, when, not only God, the Highest of all, shall be revealed in spirit and in mighty power, but the Devil or Satan also, will be revealed in signs and wonders and in mighty deeds! This, reader, is the great key to all the marvelous events that are to transpire shortly upon the earth.

Now just stop right here, and pause, and mark emphatically this key. Then you and I will proceed to unlock the mysteries and to prepare ourselves to the battle. For there will be no neutrals in the approaching controversy. I say again, that God the Highest of all will make bare His arm in the eyes of all nations. And the heavens even will be rent, and the lighting down of His power will be felt by all nations.

But this is not all. Satan also will be revealed. He has made some manifestations of his power in different periods of the world, but never before has there been such an array of numbers on his side, never before such a consolidation of armies and rulers, never before has there been such an imposing and overwhelming exhibition of miracles as Satan will shortly make manifest. Don't suppose for a moment, that I am uttering dark sayings or speaking unadvisedly upon speculation or the strength of mere human opinion. Don't tell me about Popes and Prelates sitting in the Temple of God as God. One far greater than any Pope or Prelate is soon to be revealed and he will claim to be worshipped as God . Now, remember, that it is no modern wicked man that is going to claim divine honors. No, it is that old Serpent, the Devil. He it is that will head the opposition against God and His Christ. And he, the son of perdition it is, that will be allowed a much longer chain than heretofore. And such will be the greatness of his power, that it will seem to many that he is entirely loose. He will be so far unshackled and unchained that his power will deceive all nations, even the world. And the elect will barely escape the power of his sorceries, enchantments, and miracles!

And even God, Himself, the true God, will contribute to put means and instruments in his way and at hand, for his use, so that he can have a full trial of his strength and cunning, with all deceivableness of unrighteousness in them that perish.

It is not to be expected that Satan will carry on his great warfare against Christ and his Saints by means of any one religion exclusively. It is not the Papal or Protestant religion alone that you have need to fear. But the great and abominable Church which you should expect to encounter is Anti-Christ. Whatever exalts and opposes itself to God, that is Anti-Christ, whether it is a civil or religious power. But the most formidable power that will be arrayed against Christ and his Saints in the last days, will consist of the revelations of Satan.

These revelations of Satan will come through every medium and channel by which the cunning and power of Satan can be brought to bear against the Saints and their Lord. It is a great mistake to suppose that Satan is altogether a religious personage. No, far from this. He is a politician, a philosopher, an erudite scholar, a linguist, a metaphysician, a military commander, a prince, a god, a necromancer, an enchanter, a diviner, a magician, a sorcerer, a prophet, and (if it were not railing) a clergyman and a liar from the beginning. With these universal endowments, he has never hitherto made a full and grand exhibition of himself, as it remains for him to do. But the Lord, who gave him an opportunity to try is battery upon good old Job, is fully designing to give him sufficient apparatus to deceive all the nations that love not the truth, and have pleasure in unrighteousness. His signs and tokens are as ancient as the apostasy of Cain, and as varied as will suit the secret designs of all ages. Through him men learn how to become "observers of time and seasons," with great skill and astonishing accuracy. He presides over the arts of astrology, clairvoyance, mesmerism, electro-biology, and all auguries and divinations. Being Prince of the power of the air he understands aeronautic and steam navigation, and he can compose and combine the various elements, through the co-operation of them that believe in him, with far more that human skill.

Now don't doubt what I say concerning this matter, but rather read the history of his skillful exploits and his mighty power, as they are recorded in the Old and New Testaments. Take a Bible and Concordance, (if you have any Faith in the Bible left, in an age when the Bible is perverted beyond all other books), and read attentively for yourselves, and you will there learn that I am telling you the truth.

Now there is a greater destruction coming upon the wicked nations of the earth, than was even experienced by Pharaoh at the Red Sea. But before that destruction can be made manifest, men's hearts will be hardened, and wickedness will rise to a more over-towering height than many bygone generations have been allowed to witness. God, through his Prophet, will roar out of Zion. His voice will be heard in spite of all the confusion and indignant opposition from many nations. After the testimony of His servants has been proclaimed to all nations, as a witness, then shall the scene of the end come. And great shall be that scene.

The Devil in the last stage of desperation, will take such a pre-eminent lead in literature, politics, philosophy, and religion; in wars, famines, pestilences, earthquakes, thunderings and lightnings, setting cities in conflagration, etc., that mighty kings and powerful nations will be constrained to fall down and worship him . And they will marvel at his great power, and wonder after him with great astonishment. For his signs and wonders will be among all nations. Men will be raised for the express purpose of furthering the designs and marvelous works of the devil. Every description of curious and mysterious arts that penetrate beyond the common pale of human sagacity and wisdom, will be studied and practiced beyond what has been known by mere mortals. The great capabilities of the elements of fire, air, earth, and water, will be brought into requisition by cunning men under the superior cunning of the prince and the God of this world. And, inflated with the knowledge of these wonderful arts and powers, men will become boasters, heady, high-minded, proud, and despisers of that which is good. But the God who is above all, and over all, and who ruleth in the armies of heaven, and amongst the inhabitants of the earth, will not be a silent observer of such spiritual wickedness in high places, and among the rulers of the darkness of this world. For the master spirits of wickedness of all ages, and of worlds visible and invisible, will be arrayed in the rebellious ranks before the closing scene shall transpire. Now just at this time, God will come out of His hiding place and vex the nations in his hot displeasure. By the mouth of His Prophet He will rebuke strong nations afar off, notwithstanding their strong armies and great miracles, and cunning arts.

His servant, the Prophet, in Zion will have a marvelous boldness to rebuke them, and to lay down before them in plainness and inflexible firmness the law of the Lord . As Moses laid down the law to Pharaoh, and then continued to multiply evils and judgments until he made an utter end of Pharaoh and the Egyptians, even so will the living God prescribe the line of conduct to be pursued, and the penalties of violation, to great and mighty nations, until they rally around the ensign established upon the mountains, and go up to the house of the God of Jacob to learn His ways, or are utterly overwhelmed in keen anguish and ruin.

The ways of the God of Jacob are easily recognized in these days of general wickedness. It is true, that they are clearly revealed in the Scriptures of truth, and by a living Priesthood of inspired men, yet they have been so long and so grossly perverted by the precepts and opinions of a hireling ministry, that doubts and contentions have sprung up in every land, and the plainest and simplest truths are denied, abrogated, or accounted obsolete. God is not allowed to speak from the heavens by the mouths of Prophets as in former days. Notwithstanding there is much preaching and praying, still there is a virtual acknowledgement among all nations that God, as He was known unto the Patriarchs and Prophets of old, has forsaken the earth. And men are therefore left to discover the way to heaven by the light of nature, or the misty nebulae of a hireling Priesthood. And it is a fact, undeniable, that infidels in the school of nature have more true piety towards the living God than the hireling ministry of Christendom have.

Hence priests are doing so much, often unwittingly, to blind the eyes of the people, so that they shall not see the approaching crisis in its true character until the catastrophe is completed, and Great Babylon and all her lofty cities, great wealth, princely merchants, chief captains, and mighty sovereigns, are laid low in one general ruin. Oh ye great and strong nations! ye philosophers and religionists! ye spiritual mediums and ye revelators, sitting upon thrones over great nations! how can you fulfill the prophecies that are so clearly revealed, concerning the destructions of the last days! Ye perhaps marvel that the great men and governors over one hundred and twenty-seven provinces in ancient Babylon, with a brave monarch at their head, should have been such firm believers in the astrologers, magicians, and interpreters of dreams, in their days! But marvel not, for when the greater power of the like class of persons, under the direction of Satan, shall be brought to bear in your own day, the delusion will be so much stronger that Princes, Presidents, Governors, and chief Captains, will be constrained to bow to it. Their credulity will be taxed beyond the power of resistance. The workers of these mysterious and supernatural arts will bring to their aid both natural and supernatural causes that will challenge and defy disputation.

The senses and judgment of men cannot withstand such imperative facts as will arrest their observations. For it cannot be denied that facts and truths will constitute such a measure of the ingredients of these mysterious and wonderful arts as to give them an irresistible strength of conviction to those who are unenlightened by the Spirit of God. And so far as facts and truth are mingled, it must also be acknowledged that God, the true and living Sovereign of Heaven and Earth, will contribute to produce the delusion. He has said that "He will send them strong delusions that they might believe a lie." He gives his reason and apology for acting after this stranger manner because, knowing the truth, they do not love it unadulterated. And knowing God, they do not choose to glorify Him as God. Therefore their foolish hearts become darkened, and God suffers Satan to compound and mix up truth and error in such proportions as to be captivating and strongly delusive. As a snare, this composition will be ingeniously mixed and administered to all nations, by skillful and practiced hands.

And who shall be able to withstand? Do you think that your great sagacity and the compass of your profound, philosophical turn of mind will enable you to detect the error and delusion of these arts? Oh, man, this is a vain hope. You will not be competent to detect the delusion. God Himself will allow Satan to ply your scrutinizing eye with powers and sophistications far beyond your capacity to detect. Do you say then, I will stand aloof from investigation, I will shun all acquaintance with these mysterious workings, in order that I may not be carried away with their delusive influence. Vain hope. Oh, man, you cannot be neutral. You must choose your side and put on your armor. Those that come not up to the help of the Lord in the day of battle, will be sorely cursed. The captive Hebrew Daniel stood up boldly against all the governors and whole realm of Babylon with their monarch at their head. Daniel readily acknowledged that it was not from any wisdom in him, above other men, that he could surpass the astrologers and magicians.

But holding intercourse with the God of heaven, he became endowed with supernatural comprehension that effectually shielded him against supernatural delusion. Thereby he escaped the snare that entwined around the great statesmen and governors of that immense empire of Babylon. Thereby, those who take refuge in the name of the Lord and in immediate revelation from heaven, will be safe, and no others. He that is not for God and the principle of immediate revelation, will inevitably be ensnared, overcome, and destroyed. Because he that is not for Him must be against Him. No man in any age was ever for God, that did not hold intercourse with Him personally, and receive for himself the revelations of his will. The rock of revelation, by which Peter knew Jesus Christ, is the only basis upon which any man can escape the strong delusion which God will send among the nations through Satan and his mediums and coadjutors. Reader, if you live long, you will be compelled to take a side for God or for Satan. Satan was allowed to try a compulsory process upon as good a man as Job. The whirlwind and tempestuous elements, with disease and death, were put into Satan's hand that he might compel Job to abandon his integrity. Had not Job possessed the key to revelation from God, he would have been compelled to have made peace with Satan, and forsaken the Lord. His wife urged him to do so says she, "Curse God and die"; or in other words, take the side of Satan against God.

Now, reader, if you have ships of precious merchandise, floating at sea, the time is fast coming when Satan will destroy those ships, unless you bow down to his power and become a co-operator with him. And if you do bow down to him, to work wickedness and say, no eye seeth me then God will destroy those ships and you too, and peradventure He will destroy your family also, and make a clean end of you, and blot out your name under heaven. Your beautiful mansion and flourishing family still have to be consecrated to God or to Satan, whichever you may choose. The controversy is begun and the war will never end till the victory is complete and universal, and there shall not be found so much as a dog to move his tongue against the Lord, and the immediate revelations of His will. Your being a minister of some Church, will not serve as the last screen for you against the hot indignation of God, unless you have the law and the testimony of the true and living God made known to you personally.

For the time has come that God will write His law upon every man's heart, that will receive it, not with ink, but with the Spirit of the living God. And against him that hath this law, the gates of hell never have prevailed and never will prevail. Heaven and Earth shall pass away before a jot of this law shall be made to succumb to wicked men or devils. The heavens have been shaken once when angels rebelled, and they are destined to another shaking even with the earth. Do you say you don't need any more revelation from God. Then the Devil will be allowed to give you some which you don't need. And by the time that he has revealed himself to you, and buffeted you, and trained you under his rigorous discipline to fight in this awful crisis against the heavens, peradventure you will not then feel so rich and increased in goods, but that you can take a little counsel from the Lord, and feel a little of your extreme poverty and destitution.

You cannot know God without present revelation. Did you ever think of this most solemn and essential truth, before? You may have been accustomed to pray, all your lifetime, and as yet you, even you, do not know God. You may have heard many thousand sermons, with a sincere desire both to remember and practice them, and yet you do not know God. But it has been decided in the court of heaven, that no man can know the Father but the Son, and he to whom the Son REVEALETH him.

Now, has Jesus Christ ever revealed God the Father to you, dear reader? Be honest with yourself, and do not err in your answer to this most important question. However much the Son may have revealed the Father to Prophets, Patriarchs, and Apostles of old, the question still remains in full force has he revealed Him to you? A revelation to another man is by no means a revelation to you. For instance, God revealed himself to Samuel, and called him by name to be a Prophet. But the call to Samuel is by no means a call to you to be a Prophet. God called Abraham to kill Isaac, but that is no revelation to you to kill your son. God revealed the baptism of repentance to John the Baptist, before Christ's death, but that is not a revelation to you.

He revealed authority to Paul to preach to the Gentiles, but what was told to Paul is not told to you, nor is it required of you. Again, you need the righteousness of God to go where God is, and be happy and how will you get it except it is revealed to you personally? You cannot get it any other way. Hence the Lord says, "The righteousness of God is revealed from faith to faith." Don't say now, as some do, that revelation was anciently given in order to establish the truth, and being once established is it no longer necessary to be revealed to subsequent generations of people. Don't say this for your life, for revelation is just as necessary to establish truth now as it was then. You need the ministry of angels now, just as much as people did then. They in past ages could not know God, nor say for a certainty, from personal knowledge, that Jesus Christ was the Christ, only by the Holy Ghost and you are just as weak and dependent as they were. You most assuredly cannot call Jesus, Lord, only by the Holy Ghost. If the Holy Ghost is confirmed upon you, by the imposition of the hands of the true Priesthood, then you can know God for yourself.

Why? Because the Holy Ghost teaches all things, even the deep things of God. This generation needs present revelations from heaven, as much as any other generation ever did, because they are quite as wicked as Sodom ever was. They practice as gross sensuality and beastliness, as glaring robbery and murder, as much treachery and lying, and are as ardent for war and blood — guiltiness, as ever the ancient Canaanites were. And among the many religions that have sprung up, calculated to confuse people's minds, there is, now, as must jargon and schism, contention and strife, and persecuting zeal, as there ever was before. Now, reader, you need present revelation from God to your own dear self, in order to help you out of this nasty, confused labyrinth, and to set your feet firmly upon the solid rock of revelation. Mere flesh and blood cannot help you now. It requires an Almighty arm to effect your deliverance. Therefore, put no more trust in man, for a curse rests upon him that will be guided by the precepts of man. I do not ask you to be guided by what I say to you, unless the Lord from heaven shall reveal to you that I speak the truth, even as it is in Christ. Although I know that I am declaring heaven's truth to you, in all sobriety, yet, my knowing it, does not suffice for you. You also must know it for yourself, and not for another.

This is your right and your privilege. For God has made this promise to you, and not to you, reader, only, but to all others whom He calls to repentance. Now, go and get revelation for yourself. If you are penitently desirous with all your heart to get revelation from God to your own self, go to some one whom God has called and ordained to confer the Gift of Reader, be resolute! This is a critical and trying moment with you. And this is God's call unto you. Don't refuse when He calls you! And if you are honestly, without prejudice, meditating upon what you now read, then God's Spirit is sweetly persuading you to believe what I say. The faint dawn of the Spirit is even now upon your mind. Now, reader, cherish this little dawn of light until the daylight of more truth shines more clearly upon your mind.

Pray mightily for the Spirit of Revelation to rest upon you, that you may know the things that are freely given to you of God . And follow the Spirit of revelation, as fast as you receive its whisperings, down into the water where Jesus went, for the remission of your sins, and you will very soon become a witness to the one truth, and put your own seal upon it even as I have done. And you will not barely believe, and hope, and fear, but you will know, from present and personal revelation, that the Lord is a God at hand, revealing Himself as freely as He ever did in Patriarchal days. Will you not, then be a happy man, O reader! and you a happy woman, O reader, to come into possession of the same gift of present revelation from heaven, that holy men and holy women enjoyed in ancient times? Yes, I know you will. You will then feel deep pity and sorrow for any one that says he doesn't need present revelation! You will then discover the pride of such an one's heart, and mourn over him as one that is blinded by the God of this world. But your peace will be great and your joy unspeakable. Although you can hardly believe me now, yet through your faithfulness, the Spirit of prophecy will in due time rest even upon you, O man! and also upon you, O woman! The spirit of prophecy has rested upon many sons and daughters in as humble walks of life as you are, and they, according to "promise", have prophesied and dreamed dreams. Now when this promise is fulfilled in your experience, you will feel very glad and very happy. And you will feel thankful that you ever read this article with a humble, prayerful heart. And when you see the promised signs following your faith, as thousands have done in this day, then you will exclaim, Surely this is not merely the form, but also the power of godliness this kind of gospel is in very deed the power of God unto salvation to every one that believeth! And then if you have money, which so many worship, you will not be afraid to give a tenth to rear up a Temple like Solomon's, in which God will place the ark of His covenant, and reveal His will, through His servants the Prophets, for the benefit of all the ends of the earth. When you yourself have the promised gift of discerning of spirits, then you will not have to ask your neighbor who is an imposter and who is not — you will know from the Fountain Head all about it just as well as the next person.

He that is spiritual judgeth all things. Many things are hard to be understood and reconciled, which the unstable and unlearned stumble at, even as formerly he that is spiritual can easily judge all things, but he that is not spiritual can judge nothing correctly, for he is blind, and he cannot see afar off .

And further, when you see also the gross and beastly sexual abominations that are practiced and are increasing among all nations, without shame or fear, you will not marvel that God is determined to raise up a righteous seed and glorious branch, by re-establishing the Patriarchal Order, as in the days of Abraham, Jacob, David, Solomon, and Elkanah . Neither will you marvel, while the Spirit of God is upon you, that man and even women should sneer at the sacred institution of marriage being an institution wholly under the control of God, as it was in the days of Abraham. Why should you not marvel at their sneers? Because, we have been distinctly and emphatically forewarned that in the last days there shall arise scoffers, walking after their own hearts' lusts, who shall speak evil of dignities and things that they know not, have men's persons in admiration because of gain. You would have more cause to marvel and disbelieve the scriptures of truth, if sensual men and women did not speak evil of the Patriarchal Order of marriage, and of men that conform to the pure sanction and penal restrictions of that most holy Order.

Now there are several ways in which the pure and obedient get revelations. It will be your privilege in due time to become acquainted with these various ways. One way is, through the inspiration of the Spirit. The Spirit is given to every man to profit withal. All men have such a measure of the Holy Spirit as to enable them to make a profitable use of the light and opportunities that they have and to obey the law under which they are placed. All the different methods of revelation are not probably given to all men now. God dispenseth His gifts severally as He will. The inspiration of the Almighty giveth understanding. Every various method of immediate revelation, however, always accords with the inspiration of the Spirit. If an holy angel talks with a man, what the angel speaks accords with the inspiration of the Holy Spirit. If the Urim and Thummim is consulted, it accords with the teachings of the Holy Spirit. An open vision or dream, each accords with the inspiration of the Holy Ghost. Now one mark of a dream from God is, that it is distinguished for the clearness and simplicity of the impress that it makes upon the mind of him that dreams. A dream from the Lord being always true in all its legitimate bearings, will be so disembarrassed from error and uncertainty to him that has the Spirit of truth in lively exercise, that he will know it perfectly in distinction from all false hallucinations or deceptions of the mind.

Reader, take your Bible and read the Bible account of dreams. There you will see that dreams from the Lord, for any important end, are plainly distinguishable from all deceptive influences. When Jacob went toward Haran and lay upon his stone pillow, and dreamed of seeing a ladder reaching up to heaven, etc., after he awoke he knew, beyond a doubt, that the dream was from God. Hence he says, "How terrible is this place," etc. When Laban wanted to cheat Jacob out of his just wages, the Lord appeared to Jacob in a night dream, and told him how to increase the number of his cattle, so that he could get the advantage of the cheating employer. Jacob understood the dream perfectly, and so managed as to have the best of the increase fall to his share. When Joseph told the simple dream of the sheaves, his brothers all understood it well. And when he told the dream of the sun, moon, and eleven stars bowing down to him, his father Jacob felt the force of the meaning, although he rebuked Joseph.

When God gives a dream to a wicked man, He makes him fully to understand it, unless He wishes to hide the meaning from him. Abimelech understood his two dreams from the Lord, concerning Sarah, Abraham's wife. The Lord gave Solomon wisdom, and riches, and dominion, in a dream, and yet Solomon knew the import of the dream, and that the Lord had appeared to him, in that dream. The Lord does not suffer wicked spirits to foul and blot and mar a dream, when he wants to communicate His mind and will in a dream. Foul spirits are rebuked and commanded to depart when God wants to indict the truth upon any one's mind. The Angel of God guards the dreamer till a clear and distinct impression is made. And that impression is of an unmistakable character, it cannot be misunderstood, any more than the light of the sun can be mistaken for the darkness of midnight. An open vision is another method of revelation. David saw an Angel of the Lord with a drawn sword, even the pestilence, standing between the heavens and the earth. The Prophet having prayed that the eyes of his servant might be opened, showed him that the armies of heaven were more numerous than the host of his enemies.

Another method of revelation is through the ministry of angels. An angel forewarned Lot to leave Sodom. Angels gave the Law to Moses, upon Mount Sinai. An angel opened a great iron gate that liberated the Apostle Peter. Again, God reveals things by Urim and Thummim, and by burnt offerings, and by diverse tongues, etc.

Now, reader, I entreat you to seek the aid of present revelations from God. You need them just as much as any poor creature ever did, that has been born into the world. Without them you never can know God, worlds without end. Don't flatter yourself that because others know God or have formerly known Him, you are any better off on that account, unless you know Him for yourself.

Are you poor and oppressed? Then you have the greatest need to receive revelations from God. There are very many poor people in these days, and in these lands. Even in England, rich men oppress you, and many cheat you and defraud you, and keep back your merited wages and you, who do the greatest part of the work that is done in the land, can hardly get an honest living, while your masters roll in pomp, and fare sumptuously every day. I have seen you and your little sons and tender daughters, hurrying off early in the morning to work for them, and returning late at night, poorly fed and poorly clothed often. And all the time that you are making others rich, they are keeping you in poverty and ignorance. And your daughters are often insulted and sometimes seduced by masters, and you are threatened with workhouse if you don't grind for the oppressor, and you have but little time to see your own families, and bless them with comforts, and educate and train them up for usefulness and salvation. Now, if you knew how to take counsel from the God of heaven, as Jacob did, you would not have to submit always to such fraud and oppression.

But God would help you out of your many difficulties, and your enemies could not help themselves. God has seen your afflictions, and has sent forth his servants to all nations to preach deliverance, for the acceptable year of the Lord has now come.

And ye rich men, the voice is to you. Gather up the poor and bless them, and your riches shall not waste, but increase fourfold and great shall be your reward in heaven. But blessed are the poor who shall obtain the gifts of revelation for themselves, for they shall rejoice greatly in the Holy One of Israel. For not many rich, not many noble, will be humble enough to seek revelations from God. But beware of the counsel of any priests or ministers who are hired and paid for preaching. God never hired any man to preach, nor did He ever authorize any man to hire himself out to preach for wages. Therefore beware of all such lest they deceive you. Go not after them, neither listen to them for a moment, for they are confederate with rich men and oppressors, and they are despisers of present revelation, and consequently they neither know God themselves, nor are they willing that others should know Him. And vengeance will shortly overtake all that know not God, and obey not the Gospel.

(Millennial Star, 30 April 1853, Volume 15, Pages 273-276, 289-292 - The article is attributed to Pres. John Taylor, and believed it was put together by Parley P. Pratt)

Star, 30 April 1853, Volume 15, Pages 273-276, 289-292 - The article is attributed to Pres. John Taylor, and believed it was put together by Parley P. Pratt)

Chapter Nineteen
The Spirit of Prophecy and the Spirit of Revelation

Tonight, I want to talk to you about something that is pure *Book of Mormon* doctrine. You don't find it anywhere in the *Old Testament*. It's only mentioned once in *the New Testament*, twice in the *Doctrine and Covenants*, and twenty-four times in the *Book of Mormon*. If we didn't have the *Book of Mormon*, we wouldn't have this doctrine at all because you would not be able to understand the *New Testament* reference without the *Book of Mormon*. The topic is *the spirit of prophecy* and *the spirit of revelation*.

Let's go to a take-off scripture. Let's go to Alma 17:2-3. That's where we'll start and see where it takes us tonight. Now, these are two famous verses that missionaries and mission presidents use throughout the world. What I want to share with you tonight is a little different and deeper insight into what we're talking about here. All gospel topics have layers of truth. You've read these verses over and over, but tonight I want to take you into them and show you some interesting things. This is where the sons of Mosiah are returning from a fourteen-year mission among the Lamanites, and they meet Alma the Younger. They have a reunion. That's in verse one. Now, verse 2:

> *Now these sons of Mosiah were with Alma at the time the angel first appeared unto him; therefore Alma did rejoice exceedingly to see his brethren;*

> *and what added more to his joy, they were still his brethren in the Lord;*

Now we will start to look at a formula here. Number one:

> *yea, and they had waxed strong in the knowledge of the truth;*

This is a prerequisite. You have to have a strong knowledge of the truth. Number two:

> *for they were men of a sound understanding*

Ponder that. What do you think that means? Number three:

> *and they had searched the scriptures diligently, that they might know the word of God.*

These are some prerequisites. Now look at the first words in verse 3:

> *But this is not all;*

Notice the semicolon. Those three things in verse 2 are absolutely necessary in order to tap into what verse 3 is going to teach us. *"But this is not all;"* and here's number four, another part of the formula:

> *they had given themselves to much prayer, and fasting;*

So, there are four steps; the strong knowledge of the truth, they were men of a sound understanding, they searched the scriptures diligently, and they fasted and prayed much.

> ***therefore*** [because of all of this] *they had the spirit of prophecy, and the spirit of revelation,*

Because of those four things they had *"the spirit of prophecy, and the spirit of revelation"*:

> *and when they taught, they taught with power and authority of God.*

Now, I'd like us to ask ourselves a question. What is *the spirit of prophecy* and *the spirit of revelation*? It is pure *Book of Mormon* doctrine, especially *the spirit of prophecy*.

I want to work on *the spirit of revelation*, first of all. Let's go and find out what *the spirit of revelation* is. Let's go to *Doctrine and Covenants* 8:2-3. This is the Lord's definition of *the spirit of revelation*. Verse 2,

> *Yea, behold,* ***I will tell you in your mind*** *and* ***in your heart****, by the Holy Ghost, which shall come upon you and which shall dwell in your heart.*

Now, when the Lord speaks to you, He is going to speak to you in a particular way. He's going to speak to your **mind** and to your **heart**. He speaks to your **mind** in the form of *thoughts and impressions*, and He speaks to your **heart** in the form of *feelings*. There is a process involved here that goes from testimony to conversion. When we get a testimony from the Holy Ghost, and He testifies to us that something is true, that testimony is the beginning foundation for something greater. If you sit back and don't move beyond testimony, you probably won't stay active or stay *in* the gospel of Jesus Christ.

Testimony is the beginning. It's centered in the mind. The place you want to go is from the mind to the heart. When your knowledge and foundation moves from testimony in the mind down into the heart, you've moved from testimony to conversion.

Student 5: Why is it that there is a separation between the mind and the heart? It's very strange. It's as if there's a conflict between what's in your head and what's in your core, or the essence of your spirit, what your spirit wants. Why are they both not immediately connected and agreeing with each other?

Mike: Well, they **are** connected, and that's why verse 3 says:

Now, behold, ***this*** *is the spirit of revelation,*

"This" is meaning receiving revelation in your mind through thoughts, and in your heart through feelings. So, it's the process of receiving revelation into the two areas that the Lord speaks to. The most powerful, lasting one is centered in the heart. My feeling is that you can't get a witness that is heart centered/converted, unless you, first of all, obtain a testimony through the power of the Holy Ghost. It's a matter of intensity. This is why so many people who investigate with the missionaries, join the Church, and bear their testimonies at their baptisms and say, "I know that the gospel is true. I know this. I know that." And that's true! They have received a witness of the Holy Ghost. If it doesn't go any further than that, if it doesn't move down into some other things that are deeper and more profound, those people that have just joined the Church that have a witness of the Holy Ghost and a testimony, are not likely to remain in the Church.

Student 4: Verse 4 says:

> *Therefore this is thy gift; apply unto it, and blessed art thou, for it shall deliver you out of the hands of your enemies, when, if it were not so, they would slay you and bring your soul to destruction.*

So, it's a gift. If we apply it in our minds and it gets into our hearts, then it becomes a gift to us.

Mike: Thanks, [student]. All of these things move by degrees, from lesser to greater, from portions to fullnesses, from testimony to conversion, from conversion all the way up to knowledge. It's just degrees of *receiving revelation.* The point is the *Book of Mormon* talks about **two** things. It talks about *the spirit of revelation*, which we have defined here, and then it talks about something in connection with that called *the spirit of prophecy*. In *the spirit of revelation*, we want to seek to become converted. The Lord says that if you are converted, He will heal you. Whenever He talks about conversion, you are going to see the word *heal* there. So, there's a deeper something. Also, when we get into the converted area, we're getting into an area that the scriptures refer to as *the Baptism of Fire and the Holy Ghost*. All of these things are designed to make you "*more sure.*" If we have a little time, I want to talk to you about it tonight. Everything is moving from unstable to **sure**, and this degree of revelation is the same thing. It moves from something foundational to something very significant and profound that *is heart-centered.* The people who are staying in the Church had something happen in the realm of the heart. All of the people who join the Church have had something happen in the realm of the mind. They've had a witness come to them. The Lord says, *"I will tell you in your **mind**."* See, they've had that. It has to go beyond that. Otherwise, you're on very, very shaky ground. It's my feeling that the majority of the people who are going inactive in the Church today have not taken what they started with and moved it into the realm of the heart. That may be that they just don't know any better. They had received something that was so wonderful. This witness of the Holy Ghost to your mind, this testimony, is powerful. It's enough to motivate people when they come out of the world and want to enter into a covenant and bear a testimony. But, it's just the beginning. It's just the start. Satan will try to distract them and say, "Hey, you've got it now. This is all you need to do. You don't need to go any further." And that testimony that you received, will not sustain you in the trials of life that you need to go through in order to obtain wisdom. It won't do it. I think that all of us on the line tonight have had experience with *the spirit of revelation*. It's a more common term than *the spirit of prophecy*. Of the two terms, *the spirit of revelation* is the one that we talk about most often. It's a common subject. *Doctrine and Covenants* 8:3:

> *Now, behold, this is the spirit of revelation; behold this is the spirit by which Moses brought the children of Israel through the Red sea on dry ground.*

What in heaven's name has Moses and the Red Sea got to do with the rest of verse 3 and verse 2? I remember when I read that, I thought, "That's a strange thing. Why does the Lord bring Moses in there and how does *the spirit of revelation* relate to the experience of Moses and the parting of the Red Sea?" Then, I studied that and found out. Notice that the Lord, in verse 2 says, *"Yea, behold, I will* ***tell*** *you in your mind..."* Then you've got to ask the question, **tell** you what? Well, one thing is "I will **tell** you that the Church is true." Is that all? "I will **tell** you that the *Book of Mormon* is true." Is that all? "I will **tell** you that Joseph Smith was a prophet." Is that all? Or, can we develop *the gift of revelation* to where God **tells** us of things that are going to happen in the future, so that when you come to that point you've already seen and already had revealed to you what's going to happen? So, here's the question: before Moses ever stood on the edge of the Red Sea, with the Egyptian army on one side and a million plus people between the Egyptian army and the Red Sea, had God already told him through *the spirit of revelation* what to do at that point? Had there already been a sort of rehearsal? Is this where Moses stands, and he looks at the Children of Israel, and they are in a panic mode because the largest army in the world is bearing down on them and they are in the worst position they could be, with their back to the sea? Moses turns around and doesn't say, "Oh my gosh! What shall I do?" He turns around, holds up his staff and says, "Be still and see the power of God." Now, where in heaven's name did that come from? Where did he get that knowledge from? He already knew what he was going to do before they get down there. He's not panicked, and he's not worried. Everything is in perfect control. The Egyptians looked at Moses and said, "That's a poor general. His back is to the sea." Moses knows exactly what he's going to do. He knows exactly how it's going to happen. He knows exactly the words to say and the actions and ***signs to make*** so that the elements obey him. And how did he do that? Why he had *the spirit of revelation*! So, this can go a whole lot further than what we think about it being just a testimony of the gospel and being converted. This can go further than that. Does that make sense? This is why he mentions Moses in verse 3.

Now, let's go to the second part. The second part is really exciting. Let's go back over again to Alma 17:3. The sons of Mosiah, because of those four things they'd done, *"they had the spirit of prophecy, and the spirit of revelation, and when they taught, they taught with power and the authority of God."*

Now, we talked about *the spirit of revelation*. What is *the spirit of prophecy*? How is prophecy used, observed, and experienced in the Church today? I know how revelation is, right? We talk about that all of the time. But here, the *Book of Mormon* puts these two together; *the spirit of prophecy* and *the spirit of revelation*. They are two separate things. How does prophecy work in the Church of Jesus Christ of Latter-day Saints? Ask yourself that question. How does prophecy work? What is prophecy? What is this? What are we talking about? Well, prophecy is always **future**. Prophecy is not present, and it's not past, so when you are talking about prophecy, it has something to do with the future. So, when you prophesy, you are speaking about something that is going to happen that has not yet happened. Now, what is this? The *Bible* gives us a key. You can say that we can go through the *Book of Mormon* and we see Samuel the Lamanite on the wall saying, "If this people do not repent, I will utterly destroy them." So, there's a **prophet** on the wall **prophesying** of something future. Right? If they have *the spirit of prophecy* that must mean that the sons of Mosiah went out there and they were able to prophesy of future events that had not yet happened. But, you know what? That doesn't really make a lot of sense to me. And then I came across this key that opened things up. Surely that's true. Surely *the spirit of prophecy* is to be able to have the Spirit of the Holy Ghost come upon you and say, "Open your mouth and tell these people about something in the future that's going to happen, that hasn't happened yet." And then surely that's *the spirit of prophecy*.

But, let's go to the book of Revelation in the *Bible* and let me show you something that was just massive for me. This just opened up a whole new realm of understanding and study for me. Revelation chapter 19 and it's just one little verse. In verse 10 we get a little key. And by the way, this is the only verse in the *New Testament* that mentions *the spirit of prophecy*. So, one little verse mentions *the spirit of prophecy* and opens up the whole understanding of the *Book of Mormon*. Now, when we look at the *Book of Mormon*, after we understand this key, you're going to say, "Oh my gosh! There's another puzzle piece. There's a little something for me to seek after on my journey to my Father." This is John the Revelator, and he's speaking to an angelic messenger, and this angel is speaking as though he's the Lord. He's speaking in the first person and even referring to himself as the Lord, the King of Kings. John is a little bit confused. This interview with the angel starts back on chapter 1, and now we're wrapping it up. As the interview with the angel ends, look at verse 10 where John says:

> *And I fell at his feet to worship him.*

Now, here's John the Revelator who falls down to worship an angel and he's confused because this angel is speaking as though he's Christ. Then the angel said:

> *And he said unto me, See thou do it not: I am thy fellowservant, and of thy brethren that have* ***the testimony of Jesus****:*

Now, underline that, and I want you to ask yourself a question. This angel says, "I'm one of you because I *have the testimony of Jesus*." What the heck is that? Look at the rest of the verse:

> *worship God:* ***for the testimony of Jesus is the spirit of prophecy****.*

It's the only verse in the whole scripture, all of the cannon, that tells you what *the spirit of prophecy* is. It is the testimony of Jesus.

Now, we think we know what that means, right? You say, "Oh, well, I have a testimony that Jesus is the Christ. I get up on Fast Sunday and bear testimony that I know that Jesus Christ is the Son of God, the Savior of the World. I have a testimony of Jesus; therefore, according to this, I'm also in possession of *the spirit of prophecy*." But, I'm going to say that doesn't fit because what you see in the *Book of Mormon* with the people who have *the spirit of prophecy* **is not** what the average Latter-day Saint has. The testimony of Jesus, this angel has it. Whatever this is, this angel is in possession of *the testimony of Jesus*.

Now, let's go look at a couple of other scriptures. Let's go back to the *Book of Mormon*, Alma 9:20, and flesh this out a little bit. The way this is understood is that every Latter-day Saint that can stand up and bear testimony of Jesus Christ, in Fast and Testimony meeting or anywhere else, is in possession of *the spirit of prophecy*. That's the way that we would interpret that, right? And I suppose to a very fundamental lesser degree, there's some truth in that, but that is not what the *Book of Mormon* is talking about. In Alma 9 we have a warning that is given by Alma, concerning the Nephite people. Go to verse 20 where he described a people who have been *highly favored* of the Lord. *Highly favored* is something we've talked about in the past. *Highly favored* means that you can go to the Lord and ask for a favor and because of your **status** with Him, He will grant that favor. There have only been a few people in the scriptures that have had this status. Nephi refers to himself as one. The brother of Jared is one. Start to think about this. Look at verse 20:

> *Yea, after having been such a highly favored people of the Lord; yea, after having been favored above every other nation, kindred, tongue, or people;*

And here's how they were favored:

> *after having had* ***all things*** *made known unto them,*

There's your first key:

> *according to their desires, and their faith, and prayers, of that which has been, and which is, and which is to come;*

These Nephite people had obtained a *highly favored* status with the Lord. Now, look at verse 21:

> *Having been visited by the Spirit of God; having conversed with angels, and having been spoken unto by the voice of the Lord; and having* ***the spirit of prophecy,*** *and* ***the spirit of revelation****,*

Notice these were placed right smack in the middle of all of these things,

> *and also many gifts, the gift of speaking with tongues, and the gift of preaching, and the gift of the Holy Ghost, and* ***the gift of translation****;*

Now, brothers and sisters, that "*translation*" is not translating ancient documents.

Student 6: Oh. Oh!

Mike: The *gift of translation* in verse 21 is the gift that Enoch and his people obtained because the Nephites had access to that. The man who's speaking right here, Alma, is going to be translated. Alma goes away, and you can follow it through and can find out that Alma does not experience physical death. Look at verse 23:

> *And now behold I say unto you, that if this people, who have received so many blessings from the hand of the Lord, should transgress contrary to the light and knowledge which they do have, I say unto you that if this be the case, that if they should fall into transgression, it would be far more tolerable for the Lamanites than for them.*

Think back, in the middle of all of that is *the spirit of prophecy and the spirit revelation.* Obviously, not what we're talking about when we get up on Sunday and say, "I'd like to bear my testimony."

So then, what is this thing called ***the testimony of Jesus***? It's one of those hidden little pearls that the Lord hides right in plain sight. It's where Jesus Christ **personally** testifies to **you**, that He is the Christ, the Savior, and you witness that. ***The testimony of Jesus*** is where Jesus comes to you, and *bears testimony to you* of His resurrected, glorified, exalted status. These Nephites had this. It's a whole lot more than the testimony of Jesus that we're talking about in the Church. We're not talking about you receiving a witness that Jesus is the Christ through the power of the Holy Ghost, but you are actually having Jesus Christ look at you face to face and say, "I testify to you the following thing." You receive His testimony. **That's** *the spirit of prophecy*. And that now fits with everything else here. You can now read these other verses, and you can see that when the sons of Mosiah taught, they taught with power and with authority from God. Why? They received a witness of the Savior from His own mouth. He testified to them of His divinity, His resurrection—well, in this case, not a resurrection because he wasn't born yet. But nonetheless, He testified of His divinity and His future ministry and whatever else the Savior wants to testify to you about when you have that experience and receive the testimony of Jesus. Notice how that's hidden, and the Lord very successfully hides one of His greatest pearls in plain sight because of the vernacular that we use in the Church. Day-in-and-day-out, we hear "I have a testimony of Jesus, or I'd like to bear my testimony of Jesus." But in reality, it's something much deeper, much more significant.

Let's look at a couple of other scriptures here for just a minute. Let's go to *Doctrine and Covenants* 11:24, which is one of two that talks about this. Things start to fall into place here. It's like a jigsaw puzzle. These are like huge puzzle pieces. Verse 24:

> *Build upon my rock, which is my gospel;*

He is speaking to Hyrum Smith at this point. Verse 25:

> *Deny not the spirit of revelation, nor the spirit of prophecy,*

There are those two things again:

> *for **wo** unto him that denieth these things;*

*"**Wo**"* is a pretty serious word. But can you see that if what we're talking about is the truth about these things, they are significantly more profound and much deeper than we thought? And if you go against these things, if you deny them, you are in a precarious, serious place. It's like he said back in Alma 9, that if these people should go contrary to the light and truth they have received, it'll be worse for them than any of the Lamanites. Notice that right in the middle of that list of things that made them *highly favored* is this thing called *the spirit of prophecy*,

which the book of Revelation says is the ***testimony of Jesus***. No wonder the sons of Mosiah were so powerful!

Now, go to section 20. In the heading of this section is a little pearl. Section 20 is called the Constitution of the Church. It was originally called the Articles and Covenants of the Church. Look at the top heading where it says, *"Revelation on Church Organization and Government, given through Joseph Smith the Prophet."* Preceding his record of the revelation, the Prophet wrote:

> *We obtained* ***of Him*** *[Jesus Christ] the following,* ***by the spirit of prophecy and revelation****; which not only gave us* ***much information*** *but also pointed out to us the precise day upon which, according to His will and commandment, we should proceed to organize his Church once more here upon the earth.*

See, this is all done before 1830. They received instruction through *the spirit of prophecy*. Notice when he says that we obtained information *"of Him"* and then it's got brackets *[Jesus Christ].* So, Christ is talking to these men and giving them information on precisely what they should do, how to do it, and the date they're to do it. That's called *the spirit of prophecy,* or the testimony of Jesus; pure *Book of Mormon* doctrine. You and I should seek for *the spirit of prophecy* and *the spirit of revelation.* We should seek for it. It all ties in with what we've talked about before. This all talks about having an encounter with Christ. This is talking about having Him reveal to you, personally, in an intimate and personal way, speaking with you through the veil, obtaining promises from Him by the *More Sure Word of Prophecy*, which is your first trip when you go to the veil at the temple. Symbolically, the first time you knock at the veil, that is the *More Sure Word of Prophecy*. You're obtaining promises and information from the Lord by conversing with Him **through** the veil. See, you're not in His presence yet. All of these things are tied into that. When you have an encounter with Jesus, it doesn't have to be in His presence. If you hear His voice say, "[your name], I am Jesus Christ," and you obtain promises, you don't see Him, but you hear His voice, and when He speaks to you, then you've obtained the ***testimony of Jesus,*** which is *the* *spirit of prophecy.* I will tell you also that when you obtain a promise from Him, and information that Joseph was talking about here at the heading in Section 20, where it says that "We obtained information," you can speak of things that are future and yet to come because you have information now, from the source of all light and truth. In that information, you're going to know things that are coming that have not yet happened, and that's prophecy.

Student 1: The visions that Spencer had?

Mike: Absolutely. [student], you're exactly right. Let's go to Jacob chapter 4. Here's one more reference to this so we can get a feeling that this is a whole lot more than a testimony on the first Sunday of the month. These Nephites, even though they kept the Law of Moses, the Law of Moses was dead to them. They kept it because they were commanded to observe the law, but they said, "The law is dead unto us, and we are alive in Christ." That's where we want to be! Now, this is Mike Stroud chapter 14, verse 3: My feeling is that the Church of Jesus Christ of Latter-day Saints is to us, in our day, what the Law of Moses was to the Nephites, in their day. The Church is training wheels. It's designed to take us somewhere else. If we get stuck in that, then the purpose of the Church is not being fulfilled. For example, every member knows that they're not a member of the Church very long before somebody is talking to them about preparing to go to the temple. You're not baptized very long before somebody is saying, "Hey, we need to get you ready to go here," when you've just barely arrived in the Church, and now they're talking about getting you to go somewhere else. What is this? It's because it is the purpose of the Church of Jesus Christ. Think about this, brothers and sisters: the main ordinances that we perform in the Church worldwide, over and over weekly, are Aaronic Priesthood Ordinances, baptism. I just went to a baptism. My little granddaughter was baptized. That's an Aaronic Priesthood Ordinance. Now, of course, the confirmation is Melchizedek. The sacrament is Aaronic Priesthood. It's designed to lift us, point us. What did the law of Moses do? It was pointing them to something higher. It was given to them as a schoolmaster to teach them something, which if they followed these ordinances, these carnal commandments, these rites, and ceremonies, it would lead you to something greater. So, the Nephites came out and said, "We keep the law but it's **dead** to us," And that's their wording, "it's dead, and we are alive in Christ." That's what the Church is trying to do today. It's trying to get us to rise up to something that's much more significant, more profound, more ennobling, more glorifying. We get stuck. So, let's go to Jacob 4:6 and let me show you this:

> *Wherefore, we search the prophets, and we have many revelations* ***and the spirit of prophecy****; and having all these witnesses we obtain a* ***hope****, and our faith becometh unshaken,*

The spirit of prophecy is to take you to a ***hope*** that leads to unshaken faith. One of these nights we need to have a lesson on ***hope*** because what we talk about on ***hope***, usually is not the ***hope*** that these people were talking about. Go back to verse 4:

> *For, for this intent have we written these things, that they may know that we knew of Christ, and we had* ***a hope*** *of his glory many hundred years before his coming; and not only we ourselves had* ***a hop****e of his glory, but also all the holy prophets which were before us.*

Now, go back down to the middle of verse 6:

> *and having all these witnesses we obtain* ***a hope****, and our faith becometh unshaken, insomuch that we truly can command in the name of Jesus and the very trees obey us, or the mountains, or the waves of the sea.*

Do you think that's a testimony on the first Sunday of the month that results in that kind of stuff? Notice in the middle of verse six what it says, *"We have many revelations and the spirit of prophecy,"* which means these people have stood in the presence, heard the voice of God, seen His face, obtained promises, and have power with Him to act in the name of God, as though they were God. That's where these people are. That's a deeper meaning to *the spirit of prophecy* which **is** the *testimony of Jesus*.

Student 5: You know what? I'm thinking about this when I read this. I'm thinking about my own culture. You know, I'm Peruvian, and in my culture, we have our ancestry, the Incas, very, very famously known. There is a city named Machu Picchu. This city is at the very top of a mountain. As far as I've seen on documentaries and research, they have no explanation of how that city could have been built there. How could it have gone all the way to the top of the mountain? They have no evidence or way to find the source of the materials and even how they even put those stones, cut them up in perfect form and shape, and put them on the very top of the mountain. It's literally impossible. And I'm thinking about this gift that these people have in Jacob 4, and I'm thinking I bet these were the builders and they had faith. And they had to do some crazy mountain moving things in order to make those things happen. There is no other explanation. Even my sister, when I talk about this with her, we truly believe that the power they had not only gave them the power to command stones and mountains to move and to go to places or to be divided or cut in pieces, but also to have their own physical strength improve and increase. We hear a story in the *Old Testament* about Samson, the guy who ripped off the gates of a city and carried them on the top of a hill. You know what I'm talking about?

Mike: I do!

Student 5: Yeah, I mean, it's ridiculous. I mean, I think these people were highly blessed, and they had all of those gifts. I believe that could be the source of all those unexplainable cities. They are all now abandoned because eventually, they all gave up, the Nephites did. They just gave in to the devil, unfortunately. It's sad. It's depressing.

Mike: One of these days we're going to have the information and know the answers to these things, aren't we? Well, brothers and sisters, let me summarize again by giving the keys in Alma 9. Alma warns his people that "You know too much! If you turn against what you've received, your future will be utter destruction." Nephi saw it. All the prophets saw it. We have a Nephite people that are extinct by genocidal war. Have you ever wondered why these nations were wiped out? The Israelites weren't wiped out. They had wars, but it wasn't extinction. These people became extinct from the earth. The reason is that they had ***all things*** made known to them. They were visited by the Spirit of God. They conversed with angels. They were spoken to by the voice of the Lord and had *the spirit of prophecy* and *the spirit of revelation*. They had all of the *gifts of the spirit* including the gift of translation, to be taken from the earth and to join the City of Enoch. These Nephites had these gifts active. If you sin against that, you've sinned against such light and knowledge that the greater the light, the greater the condemnation and the Nephites don't exist today because they did turn against that. I like to concentrate on the positive. They obtained this! And they did it under the Law of Moses, which just blows me away! They had the success and obtained what the Law of Moses was designed to do. It never did do it.

Let me show you another thing in 3 Nephi 19. Look at what happened to these people. They had things take place. No wonder they were wiped out. I'm not surprised at all. In chapter 19, you have a sanctification going on among the people where they are physically changed.

You ought to look at what happens in 19. We don't have time tonight, but I call 3 Nephi 19 the Holy of Holies of the *Book of Mormon*. Let's skip what it's talking about and just go to verse 32:

> *And tongue cannot speak the words which he prayed, neither can be written by man the words which he prayed.*
> *[33] And the multitude did hear and do bear record; and their hearts were open and they did understand in their hearts the words which he prayed.*
> *[34] Nevertheless, so great and marvelous were the words which he prayed that they cannot be written, neither can they be uttered my man.*
> *[35] And it came to pass that when Jesus had made an end of praying he came again to the disciples, and said unto them:*

Now, look at this. He's already been among the Jewish Saints, He spent thirty years over in Jerusalem, He's completed His ministry, and look what He says:

> *So great faith have I never seen among all the Jews;*

And that, my friends, includes the First Presidency and the Quorum of the Twelve in the *New Testament*. What's happening here in the *Book of Mormon* **never** happened on the Eastern Continent. Peter, James and John, and the Twelve, never saw what you're reading about in 3 Nephi 19. He said:

> *wherefore I could not show unto them so great miracles, because of their unbelief.*
> *[36] Verily I say unto you, there are* ***none of them***

"Them" includes the First Presidency and the Twelve:

> *that have seen so great things as ye have seen; neither have they heard so great things as ye have heard.*

Now, that's what the Nephites did and look what happened to them. The point is, they did obtain heaven. They did obtain all the promises, and they obtained the fullness of the Melchizedek Priesthood. They had the ministry of angels. They had all of the *gifts of the Spirit*. They had personal encounters with the Lord Jesus Christ and KNEW Christ. They didn't know ABOUT Him; they KNEW Him. The *Book of Mormon*, my friends, is the handbook for us to do the same. What other reason do you think we have this book? Mormon comes out and says, I write these things with the hope *"that ye may learn to be more wise than we have been."* It's a handbook on how to obtain what they obtained, and then be wiser than they were. That's the purpose of the *Book of Mormon*. Tonight's lesson was *The Spirit of Prophecy* and *the Spirit of Revelation*. I hope it has been informative to you and that you have learned some things.

References:
Alma 17:2-3
D&C 8:2-4
Revelation 19:10
Alma 9:20-23
D&C 11:24-25
D&C 20 heading
Jacob 4:4-6
3 Nephi 19:32-36
Mormon 9:31

Chapter Twenty
Podcast 020 Made Sure

Tonight, I want to talk to you about the word ***sure***. It's a word that when we read it in the scriptures, and it's throughout the scriptures in various ways, it should trigger us to pay special attention to what that means. Now, when you think of the word, *sure,* your mind probably goes to the temple. There are some things in the temple that use that word. The word *sure* always ties something in and makes it secure. It secures something. It makes it so that it's stable, immovable, and secure. In some cases, the way Peter uses it in 2 Peter chapter 1, once you are *made sure* then, you cannot fall. In ancient times, when they crucified a person, they drove the nails into their hands based upon the weight of the person being crucified. That's a well-known fact among archeologists in the Middle East that have found ample evidence of Roman crucifixion. They were at best, economically minded. They did not want to spend time, energy, or resources any further than they had to, in the execution of criminals. So, if they could secure a person's body to the cross by using nails in the palm, then they would do that and be completely satisfied with it. However, if they judged that the person's body weight would pull the nail through the palm and the flesh of the hand, then they would go ahead and secure the person's body with nails through the wrist. This ensured that the person's body would not fall off the cross, and so they made that execution, that person's body, *sure* and secure that it could not fall.

An interesting little side-note to this is that President Kimball, in talking about the crucifixion of the Savior, said that they fastened the body of the Savior with nails to His palms and then lifted Him upon the cross. He intimated that they did not put nails in his wrists until He was upon the cross and then went up afterward while He was up there, and secured His body with nails through the wrists. It appears they misjudged the weight of the Savior's body and so, without taking His body down off the cross-piece, had to go up probably with ladders, and fastened it with two more nails in His wrists; thus securing it so that His body would not fall. Now, with that in mind, what we hear about the ancient executions and what's referred to in the temple opens up a whole new pattern of things for us to look at.

Let's go to 2 Peter, chapter 1. We are going to look at some scriptures that use the word *sure* in them. I hope what that will do, is kind of get you focused and looking in a direction that you haven't looked before. You can read all of the verses before, but I want to go to verse 10. Verses 1 through 10 lists the steps to what Peter calls, *[making] your calling and election sure*. Verse 10 is the only place in the scriptures where this term is used:

> *Wherefore the rather, brethren, give diligence to make your* ***calling and election sure****:*

There's another term that uses the word *sure*. Now, the process of having one's *calling and election made sure* is referred to, and you can see it all through the scriptures, but it is not referred to with that terminology. But look at what comes after *giving diligence to making your calling and election sure*:

> *for if ye do these things, ye shall never fall:*

So, there is your key. Anytime that we see the word *sure* and the Lord uses it in specific ways, know that you are secure, that you've obtained something that you can't fall from. And then in verse 11:

> *For so an* ***entrance*** *shall be ministered unto you abundantly into the everlasting kingdom of our Lord and Saviour Jesus Christ.*

That *entrance* is you entering into the presence of the Father and the Son, to sit upon thrones, and to inherit all that They have because you have made your *calling and election sure,* and shall never fall. We have talked about *calling and election* in the past, but we won't go into that right now.

Let's go to another one. Let's go to *Doctrine and Covenants* 131:5. It's another place where this interesting word, *sure*, is used. On May 17th, 1843, the prophet gave a definition and said this:

> *The more **sure** word of prophecy means a man's knowing that he is sealed up unto eternal life, by revelation and the spirit of prophecy, through the power of the Holy Priesthood.*

Now, we talked about *the spirit of prophecy and the spirit of revelation* last week. So, we tie all these keys in and they are like a jigsaw puzzle, that when you put it together, you make this marvelous ceramic that pulls things together and shows you a picture of your pathway back to the Father. When you obtain this *more sure word of prophecy,* you know that you're sealed up to eternal life. You have obtained that promise, and the interesting term is the *more **sure** word.* You can receive the word of prophecy and obtain a promise, but this one makes it *sure*, meaning you cannot fail. You obtain promises from the Lord that ensure—and isn't it interesting that the word *ensure* has within it the word *sure*. It en*sure*s that you have a Heavenly Inheritance with the Father and the Son. We should seek for these things. We should ask the Lord, we should knock, and we should obtain these precious promises that Peter talks about.

Now, let me show you another one. Let's go over to Isaiah. Here's an interesting one. I don't know if you've ever seen this one or not, but it's kind of fascinating. Isaiah knew about these things and spoke about them in kind of a cryptic way. We want to go to Isaiah 22 and start in verse 20**:**

> *And it shall come to pass in that day, that I will call my servant Eliakim the son of Hilkiah:*

Now, look at your footnote 20a:

> *Eliakim shall replace Shebna. Moreover, the symbolic name 'Eliakim' in ensuing verses becomes representative of the Messiah, the Savior, especially v. 23-25. The name means 'God shall cause to arise.'*

So now, from verse 21, we're not talking about the son of a high priest that lived in the day of Isaiah, but we're talking about the Messiah. Notice what Isaiah says:

> *And I will clothe him with thy robe, and strengthen him with thy girdle, and I will commit thy government into his hand: and he shall be a father to the inhabitants of Jerusalem, and to the house of Judah.*

Notice the key words robe and girdle. We're talking temple things here. The robe and the girdle are always symbolic of a monarch who rules and reigns and sits on a throne:

> *[22] And the **key** of the house of David*

Look at your footnote down there, 22a: *Priesthood, Keys; Sealing* power:

> *And the key of the house of David will I lay upon his shoulder; so he shall open, and none shall shut; and he shall shut, and none shall open.*

That has reference to the sealing power. Remember in Matthew 16:19 when the Savior said:

> *And I will give unto thee the keys of the kingdom of heaven: and whatsoever thou shalt bind on earth shall be bound in heaven: and whatsoever thou shalt loose on earth shall be loosed in heaven.*

Here is something to remember: once you obtain this sureness as it pertains to the priesthood, you obtain the power to seal on Earth and in heaven. It goes with it.

Now, back to Isaiah 22, verse 23:

> *And I will fasten him as a nail in a sure place;*

That is a reference to the future crucifixion of the Savior:

> *and he shall be for a glorious throne to his father's house.*
>
> *[24] And they shall hang upon him all the glory of his father's house, the offspring and the issue, all vessels of small quantity, from the vessels of cups, even to all the vessels of flagons.*

Next in 25, whenever you see Isaiah use the term *in that day,* or *at that day,* or *at that time*, it always has reference to the latter days:

> *In that day, saith the Lord of hosts, shall the nail that is fastened in the sure place be removed, and be cut down, and fall; and the burden that was upon it shall be cut off: for the Lord hath spoken it.*

It has reference to the Savior completing His perfect atonement. *"The burden that was upon it,"* is the burden of the sins of all mankind. Through the atonement, the ability of those sins to be erased, cut off, to be removed is complete through Christ's perfect atonement. Notice the wording in verse 23, *"I will fasten him as a nail in a sure place."*

Isn't that wonderful? So, those are some references to that. Here's another one: you'll see the word *assurance*. *Assurance* is another scriptural term, and right smack in the middle of the word *assurance* is the word *sure*. So, the word *sure,* in gospel dynamics, has a very deep and pointed meaning. It is something that all of God's children should seek to obtain through promises, covenants, and endowments, so they can be *made sure* in this life. Here's another mystery: once you have that word used on your behalf while you're in this life, you enter into something that the Lord calls *the rest of the Lord.* You have now obtained promises. There is no question concerning your standing. From God Himself, you have obtained those promises and the assurance that when you leave this world, the telestial mortal world, you will have an inheritance with Christ and the Father in the celestial realms. So, the word *sure* and *assurance, made sure, more sure word*; all of these things point toward a state that the Lord refers to as the *rest of the Lord.* If you want to look at that, Alma 11, 12, and 13 talk a lot about the *rest of the Lord.* It's mentioned in all of the scriptures. Any questions or comments on that? Does that make sense?

Let's go to Ether chapter 12. Let me show you another one. Somebody asked me just this last week, "Is what you are talking about a part of *this*, or is it a part of *that*?" And they were seeing bits and pieces, like a jigsaw puzzle set on a table. All of these terms: the *rest of the Lord, the more sure word of prophecy,* and *calling and election made sure;* all of these things are describing the same place, the same position that you want to obtain. They may be talking about ordinances that need to be performed or something like that. They are all talking about the same kind of a thing. Let's go over to Ether 12:4, and it is talking about *hope*. I want you to notice the words that are used:

> *Wherefore, whoso believeth in God might with* ***surety hope*** *for a better world, yea, even a place at the right hand of God,*

In the Church, when we talk about hope there are two kinds of hope. There's the hope that the world talks about and then there's the *hope* that the scriptures talk about. They are two different things. The hope that the world talks about, really puts what you desire out of your control. In other words, "The Lord willing and if the creek don't rise, and if I'm a good boy and I do this, and I do that, **then maybe** this will happen. I hopc it does." That's not the hope the scriptures talk about. Notice that the *hope* that the scriptures talk about add with it the word *surety;* you "*might with* ***surety*** *hope for a better world yea, even a place at the right hand of God,"*

> *which hope cometh of faith, maketh an* ***anchor*** *to the souls of men, which would make them* ***sure*** *and* ***steadfast****, always abounding in good works, being led to glorify God.*

Now, here we have some keywords, and I would circle them: *surety, anchor, sure,* and *steadfast*.

That is the greatest definition of *hope* anywhere in the scriptures. If you want to define *hope,* then that's your best definition. So, notice what the words are. This *hope* that Moroni is talking about here, he ties in the words *surety, anchor, sure* and *steadfast "always abounding in good works, and being led to glorify God."* **This** *hope* is an *assurance* that you obtain. It's a revelation from God, who gives you a promise of a future inheritance. You obtain from God, a promise of a future inheritance and as a result of that, you obtain this *hope* that Moroni is talking about. Now, it's hard for us to understand sometimes because we have a different paradigm of *hope*. We have *hope* almost tied in with *wish*, and it's not the same thing at all. This thing is there because you have obtained a promise from God that He will not break, which is immutable, and you are now *at rest*. You have no more concern for the welfare of your soul. All of these different things pull together and give you a little different feel for what we're talking about here. Now, everything we've talked about for the last few weeks, about every lesson we've given, are all appendages that tie into this one thing. I had somebody this week that asked me if I would give some lessons on the signs of the last days. I said that I really didn't want to do that. I've taught those all my life by the way, and at one time the signs of the Second Coming were really important to me. But, they are really NOT important to me right now because the things that change the human heart are more important to me than reading the signs of times. Is reading the signs of the times important? Sure, it is. The Lord commands that we do that and to be watchful continually. But I'm more concerned, at this point, with how we can change the human heart to such a degree that that person becomes pure and then qualifies for all of the promises, all of the higher blessings of the gospel and the Melchizedek Priesthood. That's much more important to me. There are a lot of people who read the signs, both in and outside of the Church. You can go to YouTube and put in "the signs of the Second Coming" and "the signs of the last days," and you will see people that are very scripturally knowledgeable, but they do not understand how to access the power of the Atonement of Christ, so that the human heart can be changed and purified, and so you can have your sins remitted. Rather than go there, I'd wanted to continue to focus on these kinds of things. So, there are the thoughts I wanted to give you on *sure* and *hope*. In reality, I don't really have any more tonight, on this Father's Day, other than that right there. That's all I wanted to share with you tonight. Questions or comments?

Student1: I was always under the impression that the crucifixion was mainly done by rope and that only Christ was the one with nails. I don't know where I got that idea.

Mike: Well, the Romans were sure masters of it and they had it down to a fine art, but it was used by all ancient peoples. Can I just tell you that they crucified people sometimes by the thousands at a time? When you see the two thieves portrayed on the side of Christ, they usually want to take the crucifixion and show Christ crucified with nails, but they show the two thieves tied up with ropes. That's not true at all. It was a common form of execution. They have been known to line the sides of roads for miles with crucified persons to emphasize that you don't come out in open rebellion against Rome. Lots of people crucified their people. Can I tell you that crucifixion is the form of death for the Atonement, everywhere in eternity? *Everywhere*. That's the form of death. To be lifted up on a cross and killed in that manner has great symbolism. If you'll look in 3 Nephi 27:14:

> *I had been lifted up upon the cross, that I might draw all men unto me.*

Joseph Smith taught that the Father of Jesus was a Savior and that He died for the sins of a world. If you look at it and you see all saved beings and if you believe in men and women who have been saved and exalted (they are called the Elohim), that has to be done through Atonement sacrifice. There has to be an Atoning One and crucifixion is the way that that's done because of all the symbolisms involved in that form of death. Joseph Smith taught, in the King Follett Discourse, that Jesus said:

> *I do the things I saw my Father do.*

And then Joseph Smith asked:

> *Jesus, what are you going to do?*

And He answers rhetorically:

> *To lay down my life as my Father did, and take it up again. My Father worked out His kingdom with fear and trembling, and I must do the same.*

In another place, Joseph taught that there never was a father that wasn't first a son, and there never was a son that didn't have a father. So, there is a genealogy of Heavenly Parents that go back endlessly. The process for Them to become saved men and women in a celestial world is the exact same process that we're involved in. There is no other way. That's the pathway that all exalted men and women have trod before us, and we're following in their footsteps.

References:

2 Peter 1:10-11
D&C 131:5
Isaiah 22: 20-25
Matthew 16:19
Ether 12:4
3 Nephi 27:14
The King Follett Sermon

Chapter Twenty-One
Podcast 021 Neutralized

Foreordination, let's talk about that. Those are assignments that we receive before we are born, given to us by Heavenly Father on account of our faithfulness in keeping His commandments in the first estate, the premortal life. When it says foreordination, we can take that literally. That means that hands are laid on our heads, and we are ordained to a mission, some assignment that Heavenly Father has given us as we counseled with Him. He trusts us. We've proven our abilities in the premortal life to do certain things, and in His wisdom, He assigns us, during our time on Earth, to use those talents and abilities that we developed there to bless His other children. That assignment is accompanied with an ordination. Hands are laid upon our heads, and we receive from Father in Heaven, blessings, and power for us to fulfill that foreordained mission. Another word that could be used to describe that would be *destiny*. The Prophet Joseph Smith, in the *Lectures on Faith*, said that it is critical for us to know, through revelation, that the path that we're pursuing is acceptable to the Lord. The path that you're pursuing needs to be the one you were foreordained to pursue before you came here. He'll let you know if you are on that path and if the direction you're going at this point is acceptable and if He's pleased with it.

Student 4: What is the reference on that?

Mike: The reference on that is Mike Stroud chapter 13, verse 3. [students laughing]
Student 4: You said *Lectures on Faith.*
Mike: It's in *Lectures on Faith* numbers 4 and 6, on finding out if the path that we're pursuing is acceptable to the Lord, and we need to find that out through revelation. That will help you get a feel for your foreordained mission and calling. Now, the doctrine of *election* means that you were elected before you were born, to fulfill this mission on account of your decisions and the choices you had made before you came here. You obtain a favorability status, a favored status with the Lord, because of who you were and what you did before you came here. Now, here's the bottom line on that election, and it ties in with our premortal life. Some people come into this life with an advantage because of who they were and what they did before they were born. All of these things tie together: election, foreordination, and destiny. The same thing applies in this life, if we do what we're supposed to do, then when we leave this life and go into the next world, we go in with either an advantage or disadvantage. The privileges you enjoy in this life, where you are, who you are, and what you are doing is a direct result of who you were and what you did before you were born. That's the doctrine of *election.* You can look that up in your *Bible dictionary.* It basically says that you come into ***favorable contact*** in this life with the gospel, the priesthood, the ordinances of the temple, with all of those things—and I would include your birth, where you're born, at the time you were born—are all given to you, are all rewards, if you will, for what you did, and how faithful you were in serving the Lord before you came here. Now, we know that's a true principle because we know that after this life, there are some places that are going to be more desirable than others. So, what you do here will determine what kind of blessings you are privileged to enjoy in the next world. Just back that up one estate, and it's the same thing. What you are enjoying here—if you're enjoying the privileges of favored citizenship, if you're born into circumstances where you come into favorable contact with the gospel, the priesthood and all of that—is all tied into who you were and what you did in the world before this one. Does that make sense?

Student 4: Yes!
Student 6: So, if we are a pioneer and we went through all of that, or we came into homes that were not as strong, how does that all fit into this, Mike?
Mike: Well, it's hard to come out and say that if you're in a home where you have been abused, that it was because you didn't do what you should have done before you were born. I'm not saying that because ultimately any experience that appears to be negative, at face value, can end up being one of your greatest blessings. So, I'm just going to say that when it's all said and done, there are people who enjoy favorability status. The *Bible dictionary* says that they come into *favorable contact* with these things. Now, to break that down into individual households and lives is too complicated to do, isn't it? There are just too many ins and outs, but in a general sense, the blessings that you enjoy in this life that give you a favorable condition are the result of who you were and what you did before you came here. That's as far as we can go on that and if you want to look in your *Bible dictionary* under *election,* it says this on the bottom of page 662:

> *An "election of grace" ... has reference to one's situation in mortality; that is, being born at a time, at a place, and in circumstances, where one will come in favorable contact with the gospel. This election took place in the premortal existence.*

It all ties in with *foreordination* and *election of grace*. All of these things are tied in together.

Alma is talking about that in chapter 13. Now, let's go to that for just a minute and see if we can break this down. I remember the first time I read Alma 13. I read it through, and then I said, "What the heck did he just say? What was that **all** about?" Look at your chapter heading in Alma 13:

> *Men are called as high priests because of their exceeding faith and good works—*

Let's stop right there. The high priests that they're talking about here are not the high priests that we have in the stakes of the Church right now. That's the first thing we need to understand. Alma is talking about something completely different here. He is talking about a priesthood order that they enjoyed in their day, which we do not have available to the general membership of the

Church unless you enter the temple. If you never enter the temple as a member of the Church of Jesus Christ of Latter-day Saints, you cannot even begin to touch what Alma is talking about here in chapter 13. That's the priesthood order that's referred to throughout the *Book of Mormon*. So, the high priests we are talking about here are the high priests of what they call *the Holy Order*. Now, we've talked a little bit about this in the past and about institutional priesthood and Patriarchal Priesthood. We've talked about the priesthood that can be received by the laying on of mortal hands and about another order of priesthood that can only be received through immortal hands and so, we're talking about a higher order of the priesthood here. Go back to the chapter heading:

> *Men are called as high priests because of their exceeding faith and good works—They are to teach the commandments—Through righteousness, they are sanctified to enter into the rest of the Lord—*

Now, here's some information to help you out with Alma 13: there is a division in this chapter, and the first nine verses are talking about what takes place in the premortal world. That'll help you! So, in verse 1, it talks about priests who are ordained after *His Holy Order*. We're talking about something that already took place; they were foreordained before they were born. Look at verse 2:

> *And those priests were ordained after the order of his Son, in a manner that thereby the people might know in what manner to look forward to his Son for redemption.*
>
> *[3] And this is the manner after which they were ordained—*

Now, here's your key, watch:

> *being called and prepared from the foundation of the world according to the foreknowledge of God,*

That's foreordination in the premortal world. And here's why it took place: *"on account of their exceeding faith and good works."* There are men and women who excelled in the first estate. And because of their **excellence**, which is where the word excel comes from, and their exceeding faith and good works they received a more desirable ordination and the Lord used them to be the leaders. Abraham said that God saw these noble and great souls. Abraham 3:23:

> *These I will make my rulers;*

So, there's a group of souls that excelled in the premortal life. Go back to Alma 13:3:

> *on account of their exceeding faith and good works; in the first place* [premortal life] *being left to choose good or evil; therefore they having chosen good, and exercising exceedingly great faith, are called with a holy calling* [in the premortal world], *yea, with that holy calling which was prepared with, and according to, a preparatory redemption for such.*

The preparatory redemption is another key that means it's talking about the premortal world because the actual redemption doesn't take place until we get down into the telestial world, where we become spotted with sins and corruption, etc. when we're out of the presence of the Lord. Now, look at verse 4:

> *And thus they have been called to this holy calling on account of their faith* [in the premortal life], *while others would reject the Spirit of God* [in the premortal life] *on account of the hardness of their hearts and the blindness of their minds, while, if it had not been for this* [rejection] *they might have had as great privilege as their brethren.*

There's your excelling; not everybody is the same. Some passed their first estate, like Abraham 3 says, and others failed the first estate. Verse 5:

> *Or in fine, in the first place they were on the same standing with their brethren;*

In other words, they had the same opportunity. All of the sons and daughters of God had the same opportunity. God is not a respecter of persons, and there is in Him, no shadow of changing. But, as it is here, so it was there. Some have chosen to be valiant, to be steadfast, to be immovable, and others were casual in their approach and as a result, did not receive as desirable an election as others. It's the same thing here. All we're doing is repeating, in a mortal state, what took place in an immortal, premortal state. And verse 6 gives the purpose:

> *And thus being called by this holy calling, and ordained unto this high priesthood of the holy order of God, to teach his commandments unto the children of men, that they also* ***might*** *enter into his rest—*

It doesn't say that they did, but that they ***might***. So, the whole purpose here is to prepare people so that they can enter into something called the *rest of the Lord*.

Now, here's the challenge in this world. Men who are ordained to the priesthood in this life were foreordained to that priesthood before they came here. If you hold the Melchizedek Priesthood in this life, you were ordained to that priesthood before you came here. That is the teaching of the Prophet Joseph Smith. Now, you can be foreordained to have that ordination in this life and opt-out, so that you forfeit it, and many do. That's the purpose of this lesson and what I want to talk to you about tonight. We have this foreordination, but you can be effectively *neutralized.* And most of the Melchizedek Priesthood holders in the Church have been effectively *neutralized.* Now, this neutralization comes for a number of reasons. I feel that the number one reason is that we have become casual in our approach to the doctrines of the gospel of Jesus Christ. Lucifer puts us to sleep to the degree that we think that what we know and what we enjoy is all there is. For example, if you were to teach in any class in the Church that there are priesthood ordinations above that which we experience in the Church of Jesus Christ of Latter-day Saints, you would find, almost without exception, that it's unknown and unbelieved. And yet, what I want to propose to you is that what we are seeing in the Church of Jesus Christ of Latter-day Saints is foundational and it is trying to teach us to rise up and obtain something more significant. Everything in the gospel, brothers and sisters, is designed to move you in a transitional way from something lower to something higher, everything. If you can grab hold of that concept or that principle, it really makes a lot of things that we see in the Church and around us in our views make sense. For example, we're continually talking to the members about paying tithing. And we continue to talk about the paying of tithing and about Malachi chapter 3, *"Will a man rob God?"* We talk about

section 119 and we quote all these scriptures, and that's good and appropriate. But, if people could only understand that tithing is a transitional principle that is trying take us to something better, from something less to something greater, from something lower to something higher, then we might find a little different success on the principle, instead of making people feel guilty that they're robbing God.
"Would you rob, or will a man rob God?"
"Oh, my gosh! I don't want to rob God!"
"Well, you're robbing God if you don't pay your tithing."
So, we can shame them and make them feel guilty, so they say, "Well, I don't want to rob God. He's been so good to me," etc. Or, we can teach them that everything they're being taught in the gospel is designed to transition them from where they are to something higher, nobler, more profound, and with greater blessings. Then, that's a different view of things. Does that make sense? It's the same with the priesthood. It's the same with the Church. The Church of Jesus Christ of Latter-day Saints is not the end result. You're looking for membership in a different church, folks. As you joined the Church of Jesus Christ of Latter-day Saints, you are not through; you're just beginning! It's foundational. It's transitional. It's trying to transition you from membership in this organization into membership of the *Church of the Firstborn.* Your next step is membership into the *Church of the Firstborn.* When you came into this church, you came in through a process of investigation. You were given certain things to study, and there were missionaries that instructed you and moved you forward. They gave you challenges and made you promises, taught you principles and taught you how to go to God and get an answer as to the truthfulness of this whole message of the Restoration. Well, you are now involved in investigating the *Church of the Firstborn.* **Everything** that we teach on this podcast is designed to introduce you into the *Church of the Firstborn.* The temple is the beginning of instruction and ordinances into the *Church of the Firstborn.* The Church of Jesus Christ of Latter-day Saints has been referred to as the "Outer Church." We used to have a hymn that we sang that's not in the hymn book anymore called "The Outward Church Below." And we need to be a part of the *Outward Church Below*. Below is the

telestial world; that's the below. And the Outward Church is a physical outward institution that is run by mortal men and women. That's the Outward Church. When you enter the temple, the first ordinance you participate in is the initiatory. The initiatory is an initiation; you are being initiated into something else. You're now leaving the Church of Jesus Christ of Latter-day Saints and being initiated into the *Church of the Firstborn*, which, by the way, is the *Inward Church Above*. You've got the *Outward Church Below* and the *Inward Church Above.* The above is terrestrial. It's the next estate, it's millennial, the third estate. You are now in a mortal, telestial second estate. The next estate is the millennial, terrestrial third estate and the organization of that estate is the *Church of the Firstborn.*

Student 4: My wife and I went to the temple yesterday, and I noticed that most of the temple ceremony is Adam and Eve sinning and being separated from the presence of Elohim, and then eventually from Jehovah, except for when receiving messengers. That particular part took thirty or forty minutes to do. And then we progress to the different stages, and that didn't take long. My thought was that the first telestial part is where all the work has to be done for us to change and not become hard-hearted and fall behind. Does that make sense?

Mike: It does! Good point. So, what you're doing in the *initiatory*, which is a four booth/stage ordinance, and you're going through four booths. Each one of the four booths represent the four estates of probation. The first one is your premortal life, the second booth is mortality, the third booth is the millennial/terrestrial world, and the fourth booth is the Celestial Kingdom where Father dwells. And you are being taught that as you go through. All of this is designed to introduce you to something else. I heard a person say, and you've heard me say this before, that the member of the Church that never makes it to the temple; his membership is frustrated. That's because the purpose of membership in the Church of Jesus Christ of Latter-day Saints is foundational and is designed to transition you into the *Church of the Firstborn.* Brigham Young said that all of the ordinances of the temple are ordinances of the *Church of the Firstborn*, all of the ordinances. So, what you're being instructed in is how to obtain, step by step, through ordinances, the *Church* *of the Firstborn.* When you become a member of the *Church of the Firstborn*, brothers and sisters, you have entered into the *rest of the Lord.* Now, go with me back to Alma 13, and I want you to look at verses 11 and 12 and think about this, okay? Now, in verses 10 through the rest of the chapter, it's talking about mortality. So, verses 1 through 9 are talking about premortal life, and 10 through 31 are talking about this world, this life. Verse 11:

> *Therefore they were called after this holy order and were sanctified, and their garments were washed white through the blood of the Lamb.*

If you want to see that actual process described vividly, read 3 Nephi chapter 19. 3 Nephi 19 is the *Book of Mormon* account of what verse 11 is talking about where it says, *"[they] were sanctified, and their garments were washed white through the blood of the Lamb."* Now, look at verse 12:

> *Now they, after being sanctified by the Holy Ghost, having their garments made white, being pure and spotless before God, could not look upon sin save it were with abhorrence; and there were many, exceedingly great many, who were made pure and entered into the* ***rest of the Lord*** *their God.*

The rest of the Lord is a terrestrial place. You have membership in the *Church of the Firstborn.* You have obtained a higher order of priesthood that we've talked about before. You have had heavenly hands laid upon you. You have obtained promises from God Himself, with His own mouth, calling you by your name, which is your first trip to the veil. When you go to the veil in the temple, you go there twice, but the first time you go is to obtain promises from God. You speak with Him through the veil. You don't see Him, but you hear His voice. And then the second time you go up to the veil, you enter into His presence. The first trip to the veil is *making your calling and election sure*. It's the same as the more *sure word of prophecy,* where you obtain from Him personally, to you intimately, calling you by name and you, hearing His voice, but not seeing His presence, you obtain promises. That effectively brings you into and makes you a member of the *Church of the Firstborn* and opens the door for you to now have the next level, which is called the *Second*

Comforter, where you have a personal encounter with the Lord Jesus Christ, personally. When those things happen, you have obtained membership in the *Church of the Firstborn* and have entered into *the rest of the Lord*.

One of the names of the Holy Ghost and one of the names of Christ is the *Comforter*. They comfort you. I believe Heavenly Father is a *Comforter* also, though it is not referred to in Scripture. The *First Comforter* is the Holy Ghost, and the *Second Comforter* is Jesus Christ Himself. This means that you are no longer in turmoil. You have no more questions concerning your standing. You have obtained promises that give you an inheritance with the Lord and part and portion with Him. At that point, you are at rest concerning your status with Him and your future with Him. You're at rest; there is no more concern. You're comforted, you're consoled, and you are at rest. There's no more turmoil concerning, "What is my standing with God?" Does that make sense to you? Does that sound okay? Now, the Church is trying to bring us up to this level, and at the last general conference, a remarkable thing took place. A talk was given by President Russell M. Nelson. It was the opening address of the priesthood session. I want to read just a couple of things, so just listen to and ponder this. He had several fears, and he lists a few of them. Here is fear number one:

> *I fear there are too many men who have been given the authority of the priesthood but who lack priesthood power because the flow of power has been blocked by sins such as laziness, dishonesty, pride, immorality, or preoccupation with the things of the world.*

Think of the word *neutralized*. I'm going to give you those things again. We don't have priesthood power among the brethren because of *laziness, dishonesty, pride, immorality, or preoccupation with the things of the world*. There's another scripture that ties into this. Section 121:34 says:

> *Behold, there are many called, but few are chosen.*

You've heard that about a thousand times, right? You need to ask yourself some questions, "What does it mean to be called and what does it mean to be chosen?"

> *And why are they not chosen?*

Then, He gives the reason:

> *[35] Because their hearts are set so much upon the things of this world, and they aspire to the honors of men.*

Neutralized! Let me say it again, *"Their hearts are set so much upon the things of this world."* So, we disqualify ourselves from these upper-level blessings for these reasons: your hearts are set upon the things of the world, you aspire for the honors of men, laziness, dishonesty, pride, immorality, and a preoccupation with worldly things. Here's his second fear:

> *I fear there are too many priesthood bearers who have done little or nothing to develop their ability to access the powers of heaven.*

See, there's a difference between being ordained to the priesthood, and having priesthood power. There's only one place, anywhere, where this term *power **in** the priesthood* is mentioned, and that is at the most sacred place, at the most sacred moment, and is at the veil in the temple of the Lord. It's the only place that term is used; *power **in** the priesthood!* So, his second fear is *"too many priesthood bearers who have done little or nothing to develop their ability to access the powers of heaven.*" Third fear:

> *I fear that too many have sadly surrendered their agency to the adversary and are saying by their conduct, "I care more about satisfying my own desires than I do about bearing the Savior's Power to bless others."*

That's fear number three. We surrender our agency. *Neutralized!* So, who *neutralizes* us? We do! We make choices that take away light. Light and truth are the same things. They're not different things. Light is truth and truth is light. Section 88 comes out and says, *"Truth shineth."* Of course it does, because truth is light and it is the food of righteousness. That's what causes us to thrive. Now, fourth fear:

> *I fear, brethren, that some among us may one day wake up and realize what power in the priesthood really is and face the deep regret that they spent far more time seeking power over others or power*

> *at work than learning to exercise fully the power of God.*

This talk is a shift in the direction of the Church. I prophesy, Stroud chapter 26, verse 3 [students laughing], that this is a major shift by prophets and apostles to move us to a place we are not yet and have not been, and as a matter of fact, are losing ground to get there. Now, look at this. I've got it underlined, capitalized, bold, and in red. When he said this, I just almost wanted to jump up off the chair and say, "Hallelujah!" Listen carefully to what President Nelson said after his four fears:

> *I urgently plead with each one of us to live up to our privileges as bearers of the priesthood. In a coming day,*

And I want to testify to you, that day is near!

> *Only those men who have taken their priesthood seriously, by diligently seeking to be taught* ***by the Lord Himself****,*

Now, if you're like me before I was tuned into these things, I would say, "Oh that's nice. Christ will teach me through his prophets, through his apostles, through my bishop, through my stake president, anywhere but Himself." I want you to not wrest that scripture. Don't wrest this! Don't wrestle with it! Take it at face value because that's the way President Nelson wants it to be taken. I know it is!

> *Only those men who have taken their priesthood seriously, by diligently seeking to be taught* ***by the Lord Himself****, will be able to bless, guide, protect, strengthen, and heal others.*

So, if you want to bless, guide, protect, strengthen, and heal others, you have to have an encounter with Christ and be taught by Him:

> *Only a man who has paid the price for priesthood power will be able to bring miracles to those he loves and keep his marriage and family safe, now and throughout eternity.*

Whoa, what a blessing that is! Now, at the end of that same priesthood session, President Monson gets up. I'm telling you there was a shift. The Lord is working through his servants to wake us up and bring us up; wake up and rise up. He tells this story:

> *During World War II, a friend of mine was serving in the South Pacific when his plane was shot down over the ocean. He and the other crew members successfully parachuted from the burning plane, inflated their life rafts, and clung to those rafts for three days.*
>
> *On the third day, they spotted what they knew to be a rescue vessel. It passed them by. The next morning it passed them by again. They began to despair as they realized that this was the last day the rescue vessel would be in the area.*
>
> *Then the Holy Spirit spoke to my friend: "You have the priesthood. Command the rescuers to pick you up."*
>
> *He did as prompted: "In the name of Jesus Christ and by the power of the priesthood, turn about and pick us up."*
>
> *Within a few minutes, the vessel was beside them, helping them on deck. A faithful and worthy bearer of the priesthood, in his extremity, had exercised that priesthood, blessing his life and the lives of others.*

I will tell you, brothers and sisters; we are not going to come up to this level without extreme experiences. You're just not going to do that. Are you willing to do that? Are you willing to pay the price? Are you willing to sacrifice and do whatever is necessary to have power over the elements?

Go with me to Jacob chapter 4 and look at what these Nephites did through this Priesthood Order that they had and that you and I can have. These Nephites were amazing! The message is that we have access to this. There is no reason why we can't have this same thing. The *Holy Order*: you're introduced to it and taught. The beginning teachings of the *Holy Order* take place in the temple. It begins with an ordinance called the *Initiatory.* Now, let's go to verse 5, with Jacob talking about the prophets that lived before him:

> *Behold, they believed in Christ and worshiped the Father in His name, and also we worship the Father in His name. And for this intent we keep the law of Moses, it pointing our souls to him; and for this cause it is sanctified unto us for righteousness,*

I believe the Church of Jesus Christ of Latter-day Saints is to us what the law of Moses was to the Nephites. It's pointing us to something higher. Now, verse 6:

> *Wherefore, we search the prophets, and we have many revelations and the spirit of prophecy; and having all these witnesses we obtain a hope, and our faith becometh unshaken, insomuch that we can truly command in the name of Jesus and the very trees obey us, or the mountains, or the waves of the sea.*

That's where we need to be. Sisters, your job is to help your husband come up to that level of priesthood power. He can't reach this level unless he meets the Lord. And sisters, you are a help-meet, not a help-mate, but a help-meet. And for you and your husband to enjoy this level of priesthood power and blessings, you have to work together. Sisters, help your husband meet the Lord so that he can have that encounter, and you'll be blessed with the riches of eternity as you do that.

Any questions or comments on this thus far? Can you see how easy it is to *neutralize* this whole thing, to stop this?

Students: Yeah.

Mike: Can you see that being casual in your membership is one of the things that *neutralizes* you? Can you see that thinking that you have everything that the Lord has to offer for your membership, *neutralizes* you? Just because you do not hear it in general conference and just because you do not hear it spoken by the Brethren, doesn't mean it's not there. The Brethren speak of the *lesser portion of the word.* Everything you hear in Church, everything you hear in general conference, every manual, every lesson, and every talk is the *lesser portion of the word.* One of the ways you harden the heart is that you assume that what you are hearing is "all there is." If you won't harden your heart, and you ask, seek, and knock for more, the Lord will begin, step-by-step, to present you to the *greater portion of the word,* which He refers to as the *mysteries of God*. Hardening your heart is a *Book of Mormon* term, and is hardly ever used in the *Bible*. Hardening your heart means you've refused to listen to or heed the prompting of the light of Christ, the Holy Spirit. You make a choice to not heed that light. That's hardening your heart. If your heart is hard, then all you will ever have is the *lesser portion*, and what's more, you'll continue to harden your heart so that even the lesser portion will begin to fade. And then, what you do know you'll lose, and you'll come to a state where you know nothing. Alma calls that *"the chains of hell"* in chapter 12.

Good stuff! Now, let's close up tonight's lesson by going over to the *Joseph Smith Translation*, JST. It's right after your *Bible dictionary* and before the gazetteer and the maps. What President Nelson is trying to get us to do is come up and obtain what we're going to read about here, and what we've talked about all evening. You have a *foreordination* and an *election* to these things. Satan wants to *neutralize* that, and he does it through many, many devices. President Nelson mentioned some of those, and we've talked about some of them. I was teaching the Gospel Doctrine class, and I mentioned to the group that if the Savior were to come into our class today and visit us, He would love us and bless us and smile and maybe have a nice little chuckle with us because He's cheerful. He who bids you to be of good cheer is cheerful and has a great sense of humor, and He likes to laugh. But, what He would say is this, "My dear brothers and sisters, let Me get serious with you for just a moment, just for a second. You live way below your privileges and My expectations." That's what He'd say. He would say it in a loving, kind way, but it would prick us to the center, and we would know that it was true. ***Neutralized***—living below our privileges and below the expectations of the Holy Father and His Son—***Neutralized!***

Let's look and see in JST Genesis 14:25-40. This is talking about this higher order that the *Book of Mormon* calls the *Holy Order*. Let's just look at some of the things that they can do there, which are wonderful. We've talked about this before, and this is a covenant and ordination that God makes, notice what it says in 28:

> *It being after the order of the Son of God; which order came,* ***not by man****, nor by the will of man;*

This is not something you obtain from mortal man or an institution. It is not institutional.

> *neither by father nor mother;*

It's not patriarchal. You can't get it by lineage. You can't get it through an institution:

> *neither by beginning of days or end of years;* ***but of God.***

This has to come from Him:

> *[29] And it was delivered unto men* ***by the calling of his own voice,***

Remember we talked about hearing the voice of God? Remember *the more sure word of prophecy*? That's what this is. You receive this through *the calling of His own voice*:

> *according to his own will, unto as many as believed on his name.*

And the Lord says this, *"It will come in Mine own due time, in My own way, and according to My own will."*

Let me stop and share something with you that the Spirit taught me a week-or-so ago. I don't remember if I've taught or shared it with you, but this is potent. I have trouble with patience. I don't know about you, but I have trouble with it. Patience is tough on me. I know about these things, and I want them. Oh, how I want them! And I say the words, "I'm willing to wait patiently." I say those words in my prayer because I know it will come," According to Thine own will, in Thine own way, and in Thine own due time." I can say those words, but inside I'm impatient, and I find myself asking, "Why doesn't He give me these things? He has told me that if I ask in faith, nothing doubting, then He will give me whatever is expedient in Him. Why doesn't He do that?" Here's what the Spirit taught me in answer to that prayer: everything comes in equal opposites. So, if you are asking for a blessing from God that could be measured on a scale of one to ten and let's say the blessing you are seeking for is a five-level blessing; then by eternal law, there has to be a number five opposition from the evil side to the blessings received from God. If you're receiving a blessing at a level five, you can't expect for opposition to be at a two. Nor will it be at a six or seven, but it will be at a five. Heavenly Father wants to give you that five, but here's the question: Can you handle the trial and adversity that always accompanies it, which is also at a five? Are you prepared for that?

And in my case, the Spirit said, "Mike, I've got this blessing for you, but here's the opposite at the same level, and that, My son, you are not ready for."

So, I was willing to say, "Wow, I understand now!" because guess what? Father and Jesus are not in the process of damning, destroying, and losing you. They are in the business of exalting and saving you, but eternal law demands equal time. Now, that was taught by the early Brethren, and you can also see it played out in the first two chapters of the Book of Job. So, you know what? I'm satisfied, and I'm willing to wait because I know I'm being prepared for the opposite of the blessings I seek. And that when the time comes, and the Lord gives me that blessing, it will be because in the wisdom of Him that knoweth all things, I'm ready. And I won't be spiritually destroyed by the experience. Go back to JST Genesis 14, verse 29:

> *And it* [meaning this order which the *Book of Mormon* calls the *Holy Order*] *was delivered unto men by the calling of his own voice...*
> *[30] for God having sworn unto Enoch and to his seed with an oath* ***by himself****;*

Did you catch that? Not an oath through a mortal, but this was an oath direct from God's mouth:

> *that every one being ordained after this order and calling should have power, by faith, to break mountains, to divide the seas,*

Think about the Nephites over in Jacob 4:

> *to dry up waters, to turn them out of their course;*
> *[31] To put at defiance the armies of nations,*

That's one I think we're going to be looking at here before long:

> *to divide the earth, break every band, to stand in the presence of God* [the Second Comforter]; *to do all things according to his will, according to his command, subdue principalities and powers; and this by the will of the Son of God which was from before the foundation of the world.*

Those are the things you can accomplish that God has in store for you if you will seek for them. And they begin by an *initiatory* ordinance in the temple. All of this begins that day you enter the temple and receive an initiation. Into what? The *Church of the Firstborn*. Do you have membership in it? No, but by the time you do have a membership, you can do these things. These things accompany membership in the *Church of the Firstborn*. Now, look at the last verse;

> *[32] And men having this faith, coming up unto this order of God, were translated, and taken up into heaven.*

If you've never read anything else in the JST, this one in Genesis 14 is enough. These are the excerpts that are too lengthy to be included in the footnotes.

Now, brothers and sisters, what's the purpose of all this? The purpose of all this is to inspire us to seek for something higher. It's always kind of the core of our lessons, isn't it? I just spoke at a funeral of a dear sister that I have known for years. She died at 88. Our last conversation was that you leave this life with an advantage. We've talked about this. It's all about advantages and disadvantages. The more of an advantage you can attain to while you're in mortality, within the veil, in a fallen world called hell, then the greater will be your glory and progress in the world to come. We have to seek for everything that we can and never be satisfied with less, never.

Again. Let me just close by quoting this one thing by President Nelson:

> *I urgently plead with each one of us to live up to our privileges as bearers of the priesthood. In a coming day, only those men who have taken their priesthood seriously, by diligently seeking to be taught by the Lord Himself, will be able to bless, guide, protect, strengthen, and heal others. Only a man who has paid the price for priesthood power will be able to bring miracles to those he loves and keep his marriage and family safe, now and throughout eternity.*

And one of the last things he said was on how we do this. I thought I'd throw this one in because this is really neat. He gives a bunch of ways; study the scriptures, go to the temple, and then he said this:

> *And if you* ***truly*** *want more priesthood power, you will cherish and care for your wife, embracing both her* ***and her counsel****.*

Whoohoo, isn't that good?

Student 6: That's good!

Student 1: I love it!

Mike: [laughing] I thought you ladies would like that. Well, brothers and sisters, I love you, and I hope that's helpful to you tonight. Tonight's lesson is called *Neutralized*, and I think you'll like the avatar that Margie has put up. She has got this great avatar. I love the gospel, and I am so grateful. I leaned over to my wife today in the middle of Sacrament meeting. I felt angels close. We sang a song called *Dearest Children, God is Near You*, and as I sang the second verse, I felt angels close. I leaned over to my wife, and I said, "I am so grateful for the things that I know." And I say this in the name of Jesus, our Savior, and the Messiah, amen.

References:

Abraham 3:23
Alma 13:02-12
President Monson: April 2016 Priesthood Session of General Conference
Jacob 4:5-6
President Nelson: April 2016 Priesthood Session of General Conference
JST Genesis 14:25-40
Book of Job 1 and 2 (showing principle of Satan being allowed equal time)

Chapter Twenty-Two

Podcast 022 The Remnant

Last week's lesson was called *Neutralized*, and I was surprised by how many comments we had on it; probably as many comments as we've had on any discussion at all. One of the comments came from back East on foreordination and neutralization, and how we can have our foreordained mission neutralized through the various strategies, snares, and traps of the adversary, and through the use of our own agency, to where we just become satisfied with less. I think that is probably the biggest form of neutralization in priesthood power and in gospel growth there is. We just become satisfied. We become complacent. And that gives new meaning to the temple part where Adam is asleep, and the Lord says, "Awake and arise." That's what we need to do and never be satisfied with less.

I spoke at a funeral this last week for a lady who died, who was a good friend of mine. We recorded the funeral sermon, and I'm going to go ahead and put it up on Pod-o-matic, as a podcast (See introduction). This was a woman who was never satisfied with mediocrity, as far as the gospel goes. She was always searching. It got her in trouble quite a few times. I've known her for twenty-five years. But, because of her searching nature and never being satisfied with the gospel status quo, so to speak, it got her in trouble, and many people accused her of being faithless because of her inquisitive nature. She grew up in an environment of scientific thought. Her husband was a scientist, and he left the Church because he could not justify gospel knowledge with scientific doctrine. He couldn't do it. That affected this lady quite a bit, and she struggled with the place of science and faith in this world her whole life. But, the thing I appreciated about her was that she was always seeking for more. That's what we need to do.

The big problem from the day of the Restoration on to this day is that we have a universe of information and knowledge available to us that we're failing to access and take advantage of. There is a whole universe of knowledge out there. There is something in us, in this fallen world, that wherever we are with our knowledge, we think that we have enough. The *Book of Mormon* seems to talk about this, and it goes over into the nature of scriptures. When people have a certain volume of knowledge, such as the *Bible*, it is a major challenge for God's children in the telestial world to accept that there could be more than that. We just become so locked in and resistant to change, that it damns us. It takes the whisperings of the Spirit and sometimes to be shaken up out of our complacency, our spiritual doldrums, in order for us to come to the knowledge that what we've got is only a thumbnail and there's so much more available there. And then, once we find out what's available out there, we're hesitant to move on it because, a lot of times, what's available goes against existing traditions and existing paradigms.

I was telling a man this week that God hides His greatest secrets in contradictions and paradoxes, and that for you to access these secrets, i.e. the *mysteries of Godliness*, it's going to cause some discomfort. You're going to have to be uncomfortable because, many times, these things come to you in direct opposition to what you hold to be absolute truth. We've talked about this—this knowledge of Godly things, of what's truth and what's half-truth—and it's a real tricky thing in this world. Joseph Smith struggled with these kinds of things. I'm going to refer you to a few little quotes by the Prophet Joseph Smith here. He said this:

> *It is my meditation all the day, and more than my meat and drink, to know how I shall make the Saints of God comprehend the visions that roll like an overflowing, surge before my mind. Oh!*

> *How I would delight to bring before you the things which you never thought of! I am glad I have the privilege of communicating to you some things which, if grasped closely, will be a help to you when earthquakes bellow, the clouds gather, and the storms are ready to burst upon you like peals of thunder. Lay hold of these things and let not your knees or joints tremble, nor your hearts faint.*

Did you catch that? The information that Joseph wanted to give the Saints was of such a nature that the majority of them would have their knees tremble, their hearts faint, and would barely be able to grasp and embrace it, if at all. He also said this:

> *I desire the learning and wisdom of heaven alone. I have not the least idea if Christ should come to the earth and preach such rough things as He preached to the Jews, that this generation would reject Him for being so rough.*

That's an interesting statement. One more:

> *The great thing for us to know is to comprehend what God did institute before the foundation of this world. Who knows it?*
>
> *Had I inspiration, revelation, and lungs to communicate what my soul has contemplated in times past, there is not a soul in this congregation but would go to their homes and shut their mouths in everlasting silence on religion till they had learned something...*
>
> *Why be so certain that you comprehend the things of God when all things with you are so uncertain? You are welcome to all the knowledge and intelligence I can impart to you...*
>
> *The sound saluted my ears, "Ye are come to Mount Zion... What would it profit us to come unto the spirits of just men, but to learn and come up to a standard of their knowledge?"*

He tried to teach us, through everything he did, how to come up and obtain what he obtained, and by and large, the Saints rejected it as a whole. So, what are we going to do to be different from that? We have to be open and willing to be uncomfortable to embrace greater truth because it will make you uncomfortable. Some of the things that Joseph taught were of such a nature that he would look at general authorities sitting on the stand in general conference and point to them and say, "If I were to reveal to you what God has shown me, you would try to take my life." Interestingly enough, some of those people that he pointed to actually did conspire to take the Prophet's life and were some of the main people that were the cause his death at Carthage; stake presidents and general authorities. Interesting stuff. All he was trying to do was to bring to them what God had revealed to him.

So, that's an interesting thing, and I don't know that we have progressed much beyond that in 2016. As we've mentioned in the past, we are a lot like the children of Israel were in the days of Moses. Moses wanted to bring them all up to have a personal encounter with God. This was a selected, separate, called out group from the world because they had already been called out of Egypt. But, because of the hardness of their hearts and the traditions that they had embraced during the time that they were in Egypt, the vast majority of the people could not take the leap. So, as a result, they lost the opportunity for the Melchizedek Priesthood, the fullness of the priesthood, and the doctrine of translation. Moses wanted to bring his people up to have the experience that Enoch and his people had had and that Melchizedek and his people had had, but they couldn't make the leap. Joseph Smith wanted to do the same thing, and those Saints failed in the attempt.

Now, we're living in a day when we are going to have the opportunity, one more time, to embrace these things. A small portion of the Latter-day Saints, only a small group from within the congregation of the Latter-day Saints will embrace it.

Student 1: How do you know that?

Mike: The Brethren have talked about it in many general conference addresses. Now, let's go over to the *Old Testament* for just a minute, the book of Joel. You can find it on page 1136; Joel chapter 2 and I want to go to verse 28. This is a famous scripture that has been quoted in many general conferences by many general authorities and is talking about our day, these latter-days, where the Lord will pour out his spirit upon all flesh. But, as we sometimes do, we emphasize one scripture and don't look at the scriptures that precede it or that follow it to get a deeper understanding. See, verse 28 is a scripture we all know:

> *And it shall come to pass* ***afterward,***

That's an *Old Testament* way of saying, "In the last days." Whenever you read in *the Old Testament* a prophet saying, "And it shall come to pass *at that day* or *in those days,*" and sometimes it even comes out and says, *"in the last days,* or *in the latter-day,"* then you know they are talking about these latter-days. But, here Joel says, *"afterward"* and that is an indicator that we are here in the latter-days:

> *that I will pour out my spirit upon all flesh; and your sons and your daughters shall prophesy, your old men shall dream dreams, your young men shall see visions:*

And that was quoted as recently as Brother Packer a few conferences ago, and he said that scripture was being fulfilled and we live in the day of that fulfillment. In fact, every prophet that quotes that scripture now says that this is our day and that sons and daughters and young men and old men are receiving the gifts of revelations, dreams, and visions in our day like never before. Verse 29:

> *And also upon the servants and upon the handmaids* ***in those days*** *will I pour out my spirit.*

The next verse is a giveaway so that we know what period of time he's talking about. Verse 30:

> *And I will shew wonders in the heavens and in the earth, blood, and fire, and pillars of smoke.*
> *[31] The sun shall be turned into darkness, and the moon into blood,* ***before the great and terrible day of the Lord come.***

It's pretty clear now that we're talking about events just prior to the Second Coming. I believe that the fulfillment of verse 30 is already upon us and is going to escalate where it says, *"Wonders in the heavens and in the earth, blood, and fire, and pillars of smoke."* I think that's happening and it's going to be escalating to where it'll be startling. It'll be stunning. Now, verse 32 is the verse we never quote, and verse 32 is the one I want to talk to you about. Keep that in mind and tie it in with the previous verses. So, we're talking about the day just before the coming of Christ, *the great and terrible day of the Lord,*

> *And it shall come to pass, that whosoever shall call on the name of the Lord shall be delivered:*

That's a great promise especially in a day of destruction and turmoil and cataclysmic catastrophe after catastrophe. It's nice to know that there is deliverance.

Now, Mount Zion in the *Old Testament* has reference to America and the New Jerusalem, and here the old Jerusalem over in the state of Israel is also referenced:

> *for in mount Zion and in Jerusalem shall be deliverance,*

So, you're going to see deliverance come from two world capitals that will have the beginning of their establishment in the days just prior to the Second Coming. And then, those two world capitals will continue to function in perfection on into the millennial, terrestrial, third estate world:

> *as the Lord hath said, and in* ***the remnant*** *whom the Lord shall call.*

This is the only place where that *remnant* is mentioned in connection with the New Jerusalem and Mount Zion on the American continent, and Jerusalem in Israel. That *remnant* is being organized and moved upon by the Spirit now. That *remnant* is coming from the congregations of the Latter-day Saints.

Student 7: Hey Mike, I've got a question, is that okay?

Mike: Go ahead, speak up.

Student 7: Okay, so looking at this list here, deliverance will be found among Zion, in Jerusalem, and then it also appears that this *remnant* will also be able to offer deliverance as a refuge.

Mike: Exactly. So, you've got deliverance found in three places/groups of individuals. Mount Zion is centered on the children of Joseph, Ephraim, and Manasseh; the deliverance in Jerusalem is centered among the Jews, and the early Brethren talked about the *remnant* coming from among the Latter-day Saints. The *remnant* is a preparatory group that begins to establish the cause of Zion before the actual real-estate, and the city of New Jerusalem has its foundations laid. I believe that *remnant* is being called, marshaled, and organized right now. Some of the interests that this *remnant* has, for example, are doctrines such as having your *calling and election made sure*, the *more sure word of prophecy*, the *Second Comforter*, the *ministration of angels*, the ministry of *just men made perfect*, and the *spirits of the just* that Joseph was talking about in that last quote. They're interested in these things because the Spirit rests upon them and they are gathering all the knowledge they can about these lofty doctrines. This knowledge will place them in a position where, without man-made weapons, they will be able to withstand the onslaught of evil that is coming our way, which will engulf and consume the majority of the population in the telestial world. These are men and women who have power over the elements. These are men and women who can call down fire from heaven. These are men and women who can cause themselves, and those they love, to be transported without limitations of time and space.

Student 1: So, you say women. How will we do that? We don't have the priesthood.

Mike: I didn't say priesthood was required here.

Student 1: I just assumed that if we had such power, it would be with the priesthood.

Mike: The priesthood is designed for men to help them do things that women already, by nature, have as part of them. All of the higher blessings of the gospel that we mentioned, all of those terms we just referred to, are available to individual women. The priesthood is not required. Men need the priesthood to help them to learn the obedience necessary to sacrifice and to do what women already do by nature. The key to all of this is sacrifice. Go to section 97 in the *Doctrine and Covenants*. You've heard me draw a distinction in the past between the natures of men and women. It is a big deal! The temple also helps us understand this in the initiatory blessings that are administered to women. The blessings are different than the wording of the covenants and blessings available to men. Section 97:8:

> *Verily I say unto you, all among them who know their hearts are honest, and are broken, and their spirits contrite, and are willing to observe their covenants* ***by sacrifice****—yea, every sacrifice*

> *which I, the Lord, shall command—they are accepted of me.*

Now, you're not going to observe to keep your covenants by sacrifice unless you have the prior ingredients of that scriptural list in place. For example, you need to be honest, your heart needs to be broken, and your spirit contrite. You need to be in that state of grace. Go to 3 Nephi chapter 9. Don't you find it interesting that before the Lord appeared to the Nephites, He talked to them? In this chapter, we are ending a dispensation, several dispensations of blood sacrifice, animal sacrifices, and in verse 19 He says:

> *And ye shall offer up unto me no more the shedding of blood;*

For four thousand years that was the sacrifice that was acceptable to God from his covenant people. So, all those people who were killing those animals, brothers and sisters, had all been baptized by immersion for the remission of sins, all of them. Adam, the first man, was baptized and all of them had hands laid upon their heads and received the gift of the Holy Ghost. They had obtained a priesthood order which came, at least down to Moses, genealogically through the lineage of their fathers. It's called the *patriarchal order*. We've talked about it before. It wasn't the same order. Now, look at what he says here:

> *And ye shall offer up unto me no more the shedding of blood; yea, your sacrifices and your burnt offerings shall be done away, for I will accept none of your sacrifices and your burnt offerings.*

Up until this point, it was acceptable. Now, here we go; here's the shift in the paradigm. Look at your date at the bottom of the page, 34 AD. Christ has already resurrected from the dead. He is about to appear to these people.

> *[20] And ye shall offer for a sacrifice unto me a broken heart and a contrite spirit. And whoso cometh unto me with a broken heart and contrite spirit, him will I baptize with fire and with the Holy Ghost, even as the Lamanites,*

That's the new sacrifice. So, this *remnant* is a group of people who've risen up and obtained a personal encounter with God.

They had experienced all of these things that we've talked about in all of our lessons. They now have power with God to act as though they were God, and He honors that. They can speak a word, and the elements obey. They call down fire and consume their enemies. This is my opinion, but this *remnant* is a group of people that are being prepared right now. It's a quiet thing and is not something that's getting any publicity. That group of people is designed to pave the way for all of the events that are coming up. They're going to be able to help rescue and protect people. It is that group of people that President Nelson talked about when he said:

> *I urgently plead with each one of us to live up to our privileges as bearers of the priesthood. In a coming day, only those men who have taken their priesthood seriously, by diligently seeking to be taught by the Lord, Himself, will be able to* ***bless, guide, protect, strengthen, and heal others****. Only a man who has paid the price for priesthood power will be able to* ***bring miracles*** *to those he loves and keep his marriage and family safe, now and throughout eternity.*

That is the group we're talking about. That is the *remnant*. Of course, this was addressed to men in a priesthood meeting, but I tell you that women, by nature, already have that. Their whole lives are full of sacrifice, and men's are not. Man inherently cares for himself, looks out for himself, and is very self-centered. Women aren't. Everything a woman does is a sacrifice for somebody else. She loses her own identity when she marries a man, takes his name, and loses hers. From that point on, there is never a moment, but what she doesn't sacrifice for her husband and children. Even her monthly, physical cycle represents the shedding of blood, which is symbolically sacrificial of her very nature because anciently all covenants were made by the shedding of blood. And the shedding of blood is always symbolic of sacrifice.

So, it's all very fascinating, and this is the place to where this *remnant* is rising. We have to be able to access the powers of heaven. In times of crisis, we have to be able to raise our arms to the square and be so favored of God because of what we have attained, by obedience and diligence, that he will honor it. And whatever you speak, first it will be given to you by the Spirit, and second, because of that, it will take place.

Student 1: I have a question.

Mike: Okay?

Student 1: The group that is following Denver Snuffer, they think they're that group?

Mike: Well, there may be some of them that are.

Student 1: How could they? How could they since they are apostatizing? Don't you believe that they're apostatizing?

Mike: I don't know. I know some of those people, and I know that they are honorable people and their hearts are in the right place. I don't know what the Lord is going to do there, but I do know some of them personally, and they are fine, good people and they have strong faith. Whether or not they have been deceived, and whether their doctrine is false, that is something between them and the Lord.

One of our listeners asked a question this last week about those *noble and great ones* that God said He would make His rulers, over in Abraham 3. And his feeling was that the *noble and great ones* are those who are in leadership positions in the Church. He was asking about that. And my feeling is that Church leadership positions have nothing to do with that group of people called the *remnant*. It's true that Church leaders can be a part of that, but to think that for you to be considered *noble and great,* you have to hold some Church leadership position, well, that reeks of being a *respecter of persons*. God tells us that He is no respecter of persons, but he that keeps the commandments is favored of God. So, what I'm saying is that we may be surprised at what God is doing. We have a tendency to think that we understand everything He is doing and that we have a pretty good handle on how He works, and I think we're in for some real surprises in the day that's coming.

I've read Spencer's book *Visions of Glory* several times, and I hold it personally as a true record given to this man for his benefit. But in it, he saw women who were translated, and their husbands weren't. In this group, that Joel calls the *remnant*, were people who had obtained power over the elements, over time and space, which were the favorites of heaven, that could call down the blessings of heaven and the powers of heaven, and in some cases, there were women translated before the men. In one case, there was even a translated woman, who was in charge of a group of people who were making their way back to the Jackson County area, via Canada, and she used her power to annihilate a group of mobsters that were bent on killing everybody in the company. She simply just used the power of heaven, as a translated being, to do that. So, what we're trying to do is rise up to that position of excellence. Let me read to you a statement out of the sixth *Lecture on Faith,* that kind of talks about what's necessary for us to become a part of this group. I want to be a part of this group. I unabashedly tell you that I want to be a part of this group. Interestingly enough, Lecture six is called The Law of Sacrifice. He says:

> *[W]e next proceed to treat the knowledge which persons must have that the course of life which they pursue is according to the will of God, in order that they may be enabled to exercise faith in him unto life and salvation.*

Now, I'm going to skip a couple of paragraphs. It talks about the necessity of knowing, and not merely believing that you are in good standing with God. This whole section is designed to help you come to a knowledge, an absolute knowledge, using the words *sure* and *assurance*. In fact, in paragraph three, it says:

> *Having the assurance that they were pursuing a course which was agreeable to the will of God... **knowing** (not merely believing) that when this earthly house of this tabernacle was dissolved, they had a building of God, a house "not made with hands, eternal in the heavens" (2 Cor 5:1).*

I want to read the fourth paragraph to you. All of this built around the idea that how we come to this level of power is through sacrifice:

> *Such was, and always will be, the situation of the saints of God, that unless they have **an actual knowledge** that the course they are pursuing is according to the will of God, they will grow weary in their minds and faint;*

Now, the circumstances of the world are going to be such. They're going to be so pressing and so stressful, that unless you have this peace about you, which only comes with you having obtained a personal promise from God himself, by his own mouth, you just won't be able to withstand the pressures of everything as the world implodes. You won't be able to do it. Then it goes on to say:

> *for such has been, and always will be, the opposition in the hearts of unbelievers and those that know not God, against* ***the pure and unadulterated religion of heaven*** *(the only thing which ensures eternal life),*

What we want to do is to obtain that religion. The Church of Jesus Christ of Latter-day Saints is the platform to help us come up and obtain that religion. That religion has its core membership in the *Church of the Firstborn* and all of these people who are the *remnant* that Joel is talking about, have membership in the *Church of the Firstborn*. We've talked about that a little bit.

Student 6: What page is that, Mike?

Mike: It's on the law of sacrifice, Lecture six, in the *Lectures on Faith*. It goes on to say:

> *that they will persecute to the uttermost all that worship God according to his revelations, receive the truth in the love of it, and submit themselves to be guided and directed by his will, and drive them to such extremities that nothing short of an* ***actual knowledge of their being the favorites of heaven, and of their having embraced that order of things***

Now, think about everything we've talked about for the last 20 weeks:

> *which God has established for the redemption of man,*

Unless you get to that point, Joseph says that nothing but **that**:

> *will enable them to exercise that confidence in him necessary for them to overcome the world, and obtain that crown of glory which is laid up for them that fear God.*

And then this famous quote in section 7:

> *Let us here observe, that* ***a religion that does not require the sacrifice of all things, never has power sufficient to produce the faith necessary unto life and salvation****.*

That's where we need to go, and those things are describing the *remnant* that God will use to deliver people in the latter-days. Ultimately that *remnant* will include or be part of, the group of men and women that the scriptures refer to as the 144,000.

Go over to section 77 and let me show you other criteria necessary in order to be a part of the *remnant*, which Joel talks about. We've mentioned that the foundations of moving up to this include ordinations in earthly institutions and under the hands of mortals. We've talked about that, right? So, all of this is preceded by membership in The Church of Jesus Christ of Latter-day Saints and is absolutely necessary. Nobody in our day will obtain any of this, short of membership in this church. I mean, it is the prerequisite for it and is the platform. However, if you stay on that platform and go no further, the highest you can come to is the level of the upper telestial/lower terrestrial being. It definitely won't take you any higher than that. But, let's go over to question 11 in section 77. This is the question and answer section of *the Doctrine and Covenants*, where the people asked the Prophet Joseph questions, and he gave answers. Here is the question:

> *What are we to understand by the* ***sealing*** *the one hundred and forty-four thousand,*

Remember reading how John the Revelator said that they were **sealed** in their foreheads? That is God's code-speak for obtaining the fullness the Melchizedek priesthood and having your *calling and election made sure*, being sealed up unto eternal life. That's what that means. Having the mark of God in their forehead, that's a gospel codeword for being sealed up unto eternal life. This is the answer to question 11:

> *We are to understand that those who are sealed are high priests,*

Now, first of all, let's say that it's not a high priest in The Church of Jesus Christ of Latter-day Saints. This high priest is in a higher *Patriarchal order* that you receive from God Himself, and they are high priests ordained unto the *Holy Order of God*.

This is not the institutional Melchizedek Priesthood that we see functioning in Church today. The institutional Melchizedek Priesthood that we see in the Church today is preparatory and necessary for this order in our day. Anciently, it wasn't because there wasn't even an institution. There was no platform institution like The Church of Jesus Christ of Latter-day Saints, for the first thousand years of man's history. It goes on and says that the high priests are:

> *ordained unto the holy order of God, to administer the everlasting gospel; for they are they who are ordained out of every nation, kindred, tongue, and people,* ***by the angels***

Notice that *"by the angels"* is not an ordination by mortal hands. This is not an ordination that comes down through priesthood quorum, or a record kept of it in the Church records or ministered under the authority of the president of the Church. This is something new. This is the *remnant*, and they are ordained by the angels:

> *to whom is given power over the nations of the earth,*

And here's what the *remnant* is going to do:

> *to bring as many as will come to the church of the Firstborn.*

See, last week we drew a little parallel. When we come into The Church of Jesus Christ of Latter-day Saints in our day, there is a process: we meet with the missionaries, and the missionaries teach us, they instruct us, and we learn certain things. We take those things we are taught to God in prayer and study, with a sincere heart, with real intent, having faith in Christ, and we ask the Father in the name of Christ if these are true. We receive a witness and enter into a covenant through baptism, and become a member of The Church of Jesus Christ of Latter-day Saints. See, that's the process. All of us, when we first went to the temple, we began a new process of investigation. We are now investigating a higher church, and there's a process involved. Whereas, the elders and sisters were messengers of the lower church; angels, the spirits of *just men made perfect*, and heavenly messengers are the missionaries, so to speak, of the *Church of the Firstborn*. And so, you're involved in a process now, seeking entrance into and membership in the *Church of the Firstborn*.

When you get that you become a part of the *remnant* that Joel is talking about.

I want to mention that the *remnant* is going to be active **before** the New Jerusalem is established in America and **before** the dedicated temple is built in the old Jerusalem, where the *Old Testament* says the Messiah will come. So, the *remnant* is a preliminary group that's preparing the way for everything that will take place in the millennial area. It is a... what do we want to call it? What would you call that when a small group goes out first and prepares the way? They're not very big. There aren't many in it, number wise. It's a vanguard.

Student 6: Is this part of the 144,000 we are talking about, or is it something different?

Mike: I think that these people are going to be a part of that group, but they will precede it. You're going to see that these are members of the Church; mortal men and women who step up and obtain a level of excellence that the gospel offers, before the actual administration of the 144,000. The 144,000's ministry takes place, as the world has sunk into anarchy and total chaos. One of the main ministries of the 144,000 is rescuing the covenant members of God's kingdom, who are now isolated and trapped in various nations, with no way to escape outside of heavenly means. These are the people that the 144,000 bring to mount Zion, the New Jerusalem. They come singing songs of praise, and there's a reason why they sing songs of praise. Their situation was so utterly hopeless that without angelic administration and intervention of the 144,000, there is no way they could escape their trapped condition in their native nations without the intervention of the special translated men and women. The *remnant* precedes and prepares for that. I testify to you that the *remnant* is being prepared now.

Student 6: So, they are translated beings that are going to help them? Is that what you're saying, Mike?

Mike: If they are not, they will be. Translation is a gift that accompanies all of these upper-level blessings, knowledge, and covenants. But, it comes in the due time of the Lord, as He needs them. I really, really, really desire, with all my heart's righteous desire, to be a part of this *remnant*. And I think that it's not by chance that people are studying these things. The fact that you have an interest in them is an indicator that you have received and hearkened to a call. If you find yourself dwelling on topics such as Zion, obtaining the promise of eternal life, higher orders of priesthood, obtaining promises from God, etc.—if all of these resonate with you, it's because that is your future. My feeling, my friends, is that these things would not resonate with you unless your foreordination were to obtain them while still in the flesh. I believe the reason that it resonates with you, the reason you become intrigued, and in my case, almost obsessed with some things is because that was a foreordination before you came here and you now are hearkening unto the call. It is unfolding before you and the obtaining of these things and becoming that person is on the horizon. Otherwise, you would not have those feelings. What, I'm trying to say is that the feelings are indicators of the fulfillment of what's coming.

Student 4: Mike?

Mike: Yes?

Student 4: Spencer said, "The greater our righteousness and the more "one" our alignment was with heaven, the more latitude we had in using these gifts. In the beginning, the point was to bring us to flawless obedience, perfect trust, and spiritual purity. Once accomplished, the purpose of everything we received was to enable us to serve God, and to beautify and enrich our lives."

Mike: Great quote.

Student 6: So, it's going to be important then, to understand the discernment of spirits, so that we can overcome. That's the whole reason. It is the full aspect of receiving all these other blessings so that we can overcome the evil influence in our lives. And that's what I see anyway. Is that what you see?

Mike: That's so well put. I couldn't say it any better than that. Well put. The whole idea is to obtain knowledge and power in this life, so that in the next world, if you go into the spirit world or if you find yourself in eternity bypassing the spirit world, you'll have power over the evil that exists there because you exercised and had experience in overcoming evil here.

Student 3: Oh, I love that! That's beautiful!

Mike: Now, remember that God is God because He has more knowledge than we do. Remember when Joseph Smith said, "A man is saved no faster than he gets knowledge." It is knowledge that exalts, and it is knowledge that gives you dominion over evil spirits and over the dark side.

Student 3: Right.

Mike: Here is the full quote by Joseph Smith:

> *A man is saved no faster than he gets knowledge, for if he does not get knowledge, he will be brought into captivity by some evil power in the other world, as evil spirits will have more knowledge, and consequently more power than many men who are on the earth.*

That's a sobering quote.

So, in the world we came from, in the world we're in, and in the worlds, we're going to, there has to be opposite evil to good, and that evil always seeks to captivate and destroy you—always! What we're learning in these experiences in this life, in the schoolroom called the telestial world, among other things is that we're trying to obtain knowledge that gives us power and dominion over evil enemies that now, and in the future, will still strive to enslave us. God and the Elohim sit in the places they do because they have **knowledge** that places them beyond the power of evil that exists throughout all eternity. It's also the thing that makes them happy. That's why they are so happy.

Student 1: Are you saying that when we reach eternal life, we still have opposition?

Mike: Oh, there is always opposition in eternity, always. There is never anywhere in eternity, anywhere, where there isn't opposition.

Student 1: But, I just figured that it would be all done with when we got out of this world of strife.

Mike: You are done. Just because opposition exists doesn't mean that it has power over you. It just exists. It has to be there. You have to ask yourself the question: the devil that we talk about in this world, who is introduced into the Garden of Eden, how did he become a devil? At one time that person was a prince of light. So, how did this person, who is a prince of light, fall and become a devil?

Student 6: I've wondered that.

Mike: Well, the answer is that there are older devils and there is resurrected evil that exists. We know that. For example, we know that Cain will resurrect and became a Satan, have a resurrected body and will rule and reign in eternity. But, we're taught by the Brethren that those that never had bodies, that were never born and that were never resurrected, go backward until their spiritual identity is dissolved back into native intelligence.

Student 1: That's what I thought because you mentioned that once. So, if they dissolve—

Mike: But, you have two groups, [student]. You have those who have never been born, hence never die, hence never resurrect; and then you have sons of perdition, who are born, die, and resurrect. Those are sons of perdition. Cain is a son of perdition.

Student 1: Will they not be dissolved eventually?

Mike: *The Pearl of Great Price* teaches that Cain will rule over the Lucifer because he has a resurrected body. What did Lehi say in Nephi 2:11? There have to be opposites in **all** things.

Student 6: And throughout eternity?

Mike: That is correct!

Student 6: [laughing, sigh] Okay!

Student 1: We thought we just have to endure here.

Mike: What you're going to do is reach a point where you enter into the *rest of the Lord.* Evil has no power. Think about the temple endowment. There is a point where Satan is cast out of their midst. Right? There's a process there where he has no more power over you. That does not mean he stops tempting you. That doesn't necessarily mean that he stops trying. It just means his efforts are futile as far as it comes to you. Do you think that Satan stops trying to capture prophets and apostles who have risen to a certain spiritual excellence, just because they are prophets and apostles?

Student 6: No.

Mike: But the point is that just because people come to that certain point in their progress, doesn't mean the opposition of the adversary stops. They're just not as effective, or they are not effective at all. They just don't have the effectiveness anymore because you have gained knowledge and experience that gives you supremacy over evil.

Student 1: So, eventually you have more power because you are righteous.

Mike: That's because you've changed, not that he doesn't try, not that he ceases to exist. It is just that he can't get you because you have been made pure.
Student 6: So, how do we relate this to Heavenly Father and Heavenly Mother?
Mike: In what way? Do you mean, does Satan still try? Does evil still try?
Student 6: Yeah,
Mike: I don't know. But, I know that if they do, it doesn't work because they have achieved this level where they are in a state of happiness. They confront it. Look in the temple:

> "What are you doing here?" Those are Gods speaking!
> Satan says, "Oh, I'm doing here what was done on other worlds."
> Then God asks, "What is that?"

See that confrontation that they come up against? It's still there. If you look into the first chapters of Job, Lucifer comes before God, and God asks:

> "What have you been doing?"
> Lucifer says, "I've been going to and fro in the earth, and up and down in it."

1 Peter 5:8 says he is:

> *as a roaring lion, walketh about, seeking whom he may devour:*
> Then God asks Lucifer, "Have you considered my servant Job?"

Do you see this interaction? They, the gods, bump up against this. It's there, and it always exists. They're always bumping into evil, and it just exists. If you're a God, and you have children in a state of probation on a telestial world, and there is evil opposition on that world, and those children of yours look to you for redemption and salvation, do you think you're not going to bump up against evil as your plan for their redemption unfolds, even though you're resurrected? You're always going to have something to do with evil because it provides the necessary opposition for growth for your children, in order for your children to become Gods.
Student 1: Then why do we say Christ will gain the victory?

Mike: The victory comes not because evil ceases to exist and is banished into outer darkness. The victory comes in that you have obtained knowledge and power over evil so that it does not affect you. **You** control **it**. You can either allow it, or you can banish it from your presence. You have that power. That's what we're learning to do in this estate and in the various estates of progression. We are learning how to come to a point of supremacy where we can control that. Christ first put the devil and all of the evil works of the devil under His feet, and the last enemy He overcame was death, and that's just not physical death, but that's spiritual death. Do you want to talk about God encountering evil? Go to *Doctrine and Covenants* 88:6 and referring to Christ it says:

> *He that ascended on high, as also he descended below all things, in that he comprehended all things, that he might be in all and through all things, the light of truth;*

To descend below all things as a God means that you go even below the deepest darkest abyss of perdition. He went down below all of that.

Student 1: I can kind of see that. I guess I have to put the puzzle together.

Mike: So, the point is this: you are changed through the gospel of Jesus Christ. You're made pure, you're spotless, you're sanctified, and through that process, evil has no effect on you. Are you going to come up against it? Absolutely, because it exists, **and has to exist,** in order for there to be progression in eternity. There has to be evil. There has to be opposition.

Student 4: They are taking out our general authorities. They're infiltrating our bishops and stake presidents, our leaders, and they are trying to infiltrate us! So, it's always going to be there. And, as you said, we have to have more power.

Mike: The evil you'll come up against in the future, as you obtain the status of God, will originate within your own family unit. How's that for coming up against it?

Student 1: You've got family doing it?

Mike: Sure! Lucifer is a child of our Father in Heaven. That evil originated within His family unit. Now, if the pattern is the same, you're going to have, in your spirit families, when you become a

Mother and a Father in Heaven, a certain number of your children that are going to rebel against light and truth. That's the pattern. And those people will rebel and be cast out of your presence and provide opposition for the rest of your family members as they move into the schoolroom, called the telestial world, and begin their lessons in mortality. The people that oppose us, brothers and sisters, are not strangers. They are our brothers.

Student 6: I don't know if I like this. [laughing]

Student 1: Me too!

Mike: The point is that each one of us is trying to come to a point where we rise above this and gain supremacy over it. The priesthood is given to men to help them do that. One of the reasons for priesthood is that men need the priesthood to help them learn how to sacrifice. It is not in our nature to want to sacrifice. It **is** in a woman's nature, but it is not in a man's. The priesthood is there to help us learn how to sacrifice.

Student 6: I think something like that will also help us to see, if we look at our lives, years ago: where were we? How did we understand the adversary? Did we understand him? How much did we under-putt? And then, look at our lives now and see how much we understand, and how much we have put him under and have overcome. And so, maybe that is what we really can look at and see that progression happen, and see that is what is going to happen in years to come, as we overcome and receive more power, as we're obedient and trust our God in these things.

Mike: Well, [student], you and I have had some private talks over the last year or so. I can still remember walking through the park in New Jersey, on a young Single Adults activity, and you and I were talking about some things that you were learning. You were very excited about it. It was new! I remember sitting under a big oak tree and just marveling at how you are grasping these things. I want you to think back now, over the last year. Think about the knowledge that you've gained that gives you power that you didn't have just a year and a half ago. Just think about that.

Student 6: That brings so much gratitude to my heart.

Mike: And then now, multiply that every year that we're in this place and you take that when you go into the spirit world. There is a reason why people are in paradise, and there's a reason why people in the spirit world are in that other holding place. The reason people are in paradise is because they have obtained knowledge and experience that gives them power over evil spirits that exist in that world. Those evil spirits can't touch them. That's a paradise, and the reason it's a paradise is that they are above and free and have supremacy and ascendency over the evil that exists in that world. If you haven't gained that knowledge and experience in this life, you find yourself subject to those evil spirits when you go there. In which case, those in paradise will come over and try to teach you the gospel and change your heart and get you to repent. But, if you can do that here, you'll find yourself in paradise and those spirits that are over there, who are evil, who want you to be miserable, have no power over you. They have congregations over there, and they meet in meetings, and the devils try to deceive them. You'll go over there, and if those evil spirits try to bar up the way, either as a man or woman, in the name of Jesus Christ, you can command them to disperse and they will. Now, if you don't have that power there, then you'll find yourself among them.

Student 6: But Mike, it has got to be different from here because you have people that are doing the same thing you're trying to do. The influence around you is greater, in yourself, and in those around you. And so, isn't it true that as we build up in our existence and progression, that it will be like-minded people around us who will be striving, and the Spirit will be stronger, even around us, as well as inside of us?

Mike: Well, that's the pattern. What you are doing now is looking at patterns and the patterns that you see in this life, help you understand what took place in the world before you came here, and what's going to happen in the world that you're going to. You are doing that. Patterns unfold mysteries. It's a wonderful way to do that.

Well, it's past time. It's been an hour and ten minutes. I don't even know what we'll call this lesson. I have no idea what to call this lesson. Nonetheless, I hope it was interesting and helpful to you.

References:

History of the Church, 5:362; from a discourse given by Joseph Smith on Apr. 16, 1843, in Nauvoo, Illinois; reported by Wilford Woodruff and Willard Richards The Purpose of the Gathering of Israel, Joseph Smith, June 11, 1843; History of the Church, 5:423-427
History of the Church, 5:529–30; from a discourse given by Joseph Smith on Aug. 13, 1843, in Nauvoo, Illinois; reported by Willard Richards.
Joel 2:28-32
D&C 97:8
3 Nephi 9:19-20
President Nelson: April 2016 Priesthood Session "The Price of Pricsthood Power"
Joseph Smith Lectures on Faith 6
D&C 88:6

Chapter Twenty-Three
Podcast 023 The Terrestrial World

Let's go to section 76 in the *Doctrine and Covenants*. I would like to discuss with you the great terrestrial world. We're in a telestial world right now. The telestial world is a hell-place, and by hell, I mean a place of restriction. One of the main restrictions is the veil. When you get into the terrestrial and celestial worlds you don't have that veil, so by definition, a hell-place is a place where there are some pretty serious restrictions, the veil being one. Another restriction is that it's a place where devils and unclean spirits reside and have interaction with mortals. They provide the opposition necessary for our progression on the path back to the Father. So, I'd like to chat a little bit with you about *the world to come*. Now, section 76 gives us just a little glimpse, and we'll come back to that in a minute. I want to quote a verse for you out of section 130. It says this:

> *[18] Whatever principle of intelligence we attain unto in this life* [in this telestial world], *it will rise with us in the resurrection* [that's some future time down the road].
>
> *[19] And if a person gains more knowledge and intelligence in this life through his diligence and obedience than another, he will have so much* ***the advantage in the world to come***.

That's a great scripture. The older I get and the more I learn about the gospel, the more significance that scripture has. We've talked previously about having an advantage in the world to come. Now, there's always a judgment at the end of each estate, always! Wherever we are—whether in a first estate, a second estate, or a third estate—by the end of each estate, when you pass through that judgment, you want to enter the world to come, the next world, with an advantage. Now, you did that when you left the first estate and came here. And you enjoyed tremendous advantages in this life, and we can list many of those. We won't, but it comes as a result of who you were, what you did, and where you were in the previous estate. That same thing applies here. The world to come is not the spirit world. It could be for many people, but the spirit world (after death) is still a telestial state. It is true that there are some people in the spirit world who have attained a terrestrial level and those people are in a state of Paradise. But it's not the same terrestrial world that we're talking about that's ushered in by Christ at His Second Coming. That's the one we want to talk about tonight. So, what we do in this world, what we're doing right now, is either going to allow us to move into this next estate, this next world, advantaged or disadvantaged. The disadvantage disqualifies you from even being there. You won't make it. If you don't pass the judgment of the telestial world, you can't enter into the terrestrial world. So, we're going to refer to the terrestrial world as *the third estate*. Even though that's not scriptural, it is. I want you to know that it is a probationary estate.

Most of the members of the Church, when we talk about being in a probationary estate, will almost exclusively limit that to the telestial world we're in now. But, the estate before we came here, the premortal life, was also a probationary estate. It's possible, brothers and sisters, to be in a probationary estate that is veiled and to be in a probationary estate that is unveiled. You're in a probationary, veiled estate right now, the telestial world. All telestial worlds are veiled, probationary places. The estate before we came here was also a probationary estate, but it was unveiled. You were in the presence of God. And yet, one-third of the hosts of heaven, a third-part (not a third percent, a third-part), failed to pass that probationary test. In this world, if you don't achieve a level that qualifies you for a Terrestrial Kingdom, you will have failed the second estate. Those who fail the second estate, mortality, fail to rise above a telestial level. They fail it. And so, their disadvantage is that they are not allowed to enter the great terrestrial, millennial third estate. They can't do it. And they die in the Second Coming, and their spirits remain in a hell-place, in the spirit world, for 1,000 years. They're still in school. They're still in session. They did not pass the course. Comments or thoughts on that?

Student 6: So, you're saying that the terrestrial is after we leave here and it's not in Paradise? Is that what you're talking about?

Mike: That's what I'm saying. Now, people's spirits who have lived on this earth and died, that have been redeemed from the Fall, that merit a paradise-state in the spirit world, have attained a terrestrial level of spirituality. Okay? Now, they're not in the terrestrial world. You and I need to rise above this world and attain unto a terrestrial status. We'll talk about what that is, what qualifies a person for the terrestrial status. But, those who don't do that cannot enter into either paradise in the spirit world or are not qualified to enter into the terrestrial world that will be ushered in at the Second Coming of Christ. So, there's a great burning that takes place, the great cleansing of fire. Joseph Smith said, *"Noah came before the flood. I have come before the fire."* When Christ appears in glory with the Enochian Saints, the city of Enoch that comes down, they will appear in fire, and the glory of their appearance will cleanse the earth of everything that is telestial. Everything that's telestial: animals, buildings, anything that partakes of that world, will end. This is why we're told that at the Second Coming, the terrestrial world will usher in a new heaven and a new earth and all old things will become new.

Student 6: So, our gardens and our trees, all that will go away.

Mike: All of that goes away.

Student 6: That's sad. [laughing]

Mike: Well, what we mean when we say, "goes away," is that it's just changed back into another status. The people, their bodies die in the fire, and their spirits go into the spirit world into a telestial place, not Paradise, but a telestial place where their education continues. Hopefully, they will be able to better themselves and improve themselves during that thousand-year period that their spirits are held there, and when they come out have advantages that they didn't have when they went in. The whole idea is to help God's children based on wherever they are, which comes as a result of their choices, to move up. Always moving up, always pulling them up higher, so they can enjoy greater light, truth, and privileges. Comment?

Student 4: I like what Spencer says about how our diet changes. How the gardens are MORE beautiful. The food and the things are more desirable there than they are in this world.

Mike: Yes, you get a real good feel of the terrestrial world through Spencer's book, *Visions of Glory*. So, let's talk for just a minute about translation. The Prophet Joseph Smith said that the doctrine of translation is a doctrine that belongs to a terrestrial order. So, take people like John the Revelator, the Three Nephites, Alma, Phillip, Moses, other various characters, and all of those people in the past who have obtained translation; they now abide by the order of a terrestrial level. So, translation is not celestial; it's terrestrial. We always want to jump from rung two on the ladder, to rung six. We have a tendency to want to do that. I've done this, so I know what they will answer, but if I were to ask people what the world to come is, and I mention *Doctrine and Covenants* 130:18-19, almost without exception they will answer, "The celestial world." A few will say, "The spirit world," but the majority will say, "The celestial world." So, we're going from a telestial second estate and wanting to jump to a celestial fourth estate, and we drop out the third terrestrial order altogether in our thinking. The world to come is that *thousand years millennial, terrestrial third estate*. You want to be there, brothers and sisters because there are lessons to be learned, experiences to have, and wisdom to be gained in this estate that prepares you for the celestial. I don't believe that anyone can enter into a celestial glory and bypass the terrestrial, millennial world. I think it's a sequence. I think it's a rung on the ladder and to miss that would severely limit you and give you great disadvantages in eternity. So, it's a step-by-step process, and that's the world that's coming.

Student 6: So, what you are saying then is that the only way to have a terrestrial experience is during the Millennium, or while we're here?

Mike: The terrestrial experience, the terrestrial world, the world to come is the Millennium, but you can have a terrestrial experience, as an individual person, while still living in the telestial world. In fact, that's desirable. Now, it's desirable that we rise up and that we obtain that level of spirituality and privilege, while we're still in the telestial world. Will the majority do that? Absolutely not! Because to do that means that you become Zion. Zion is terrestrial. The concept of Zion does not belong in the telestial world. What we try to do in the telestial world is to establish Zion. Every great patriarch that's ever lived, from Adam on down, has tried to do that. Some have had some success. Enoch is probably one of the greatest successful Zion establishers, and another one is Melchizedek. But Jesus, Himself, was not able to establish a Zion society. Obviously, he had people within his discipleship that attained it individually because we know that Phillip was translated. And there were people there, according to Paul in the book of the Hebrews that had obtained the *Church of the Firstborn*. So, ancient saints obtained the *Church of the Firstborn*. The *Church of the Firstborn* is a terrestrial order. Does that answer that?

Student: Yes, but at the same time, I have another question. I thought Zion was more of a celestial glory, I mean a celestial order, but you are saying that it's not a celestial order, it's a terrestrial order?

Mike: It is a terrestrial order, but that's not to say that Zion does not exist in the Celestial Kingdom because the government of the Celestial Kingdom is Zion. What we're trying to do is to move people into this society a step at a time. It's not something you can jump into, obviously. So, if we can do everything we can to start to obtain a Zion society while in the telestial world, it's going to give us huge advantages when we enter into the terrestrial world, which is a Zion order. The Millennium, during the terrestrial world, will be the great Zion that the scriptures talk about. Isaiah's talking about that. You're going to see that it's the Zion of the scriptures, and it has its first real establishment, society-wide, for a lengthy period of time in the Millennium. In this world it's been tried, it's been experimented with, it's had limited success with individuals. The closest we've ever come to a Zion society is Melchizedek. Joseph Smith tried it and absolutely could not bring it to pass; Brigham Young tried it;

Adam tried it. And so, it's very, very difficult to do in the telestial world, but it is something we're commanded to do.
Student 4: Wilford Woodruff wanted it also.
Mike: All of the prophets wanted it! Absolutely! There have been a lot of individuals who have obtained that status.
Student 4: There's a book, I don't know the title, but Wilford Woodruff looked for it all the time. He was trying for it, but I don't think he knew how to get the people to see it. He had the same problem as everyone else. He knew about it before people could see it.
Mike: What do you think the number one impediment to Zion is? What's the biggest obstacle?
Student 6: Self-pride? Selfishness?
Mike: That's certainly one of them, but the scriptures identified *the mainspring of all corruption*. This is in section 123:7 in the *Doctrine and Covenants*. And *the mainspring of all corruption* that causes the whole earth to groan under its iniquity is, according to the Lord, the "creeds [false traditions] of the fathers" that are passed on to the children who inherit the father's lies. That's the main impediment. That's what stops Zion. Okay? Interesting, huh? Now, brothers and sisters let me just move a little bit further here and let's just talk about what is required for you to be a Zion person. In section 76, the Lord gives us some statements on that and tells us what it's all about. As you move up in kingdoms from telestial, terrestrial, to celestial, it's obvious; the populations decrease as you move up. So, in other words, the inhabitants of the telestial world are going to be more than the inhabitants of the terrestrial world and the terrestrial more than the celestial, etc., etc. Look at verse 71:

> *And again, we saw the terrestrial world, and behold and lo, these are they who are of the terrestrial, whose glory differs from that of the church of the Firstborn who have received the fullness of the Father, even as that of the moon differs from the sun in the firmament.*

Now, here we go with the qualifications:

> *[72] These are they who died without law;*

Who do you think that is? Are we talking about children here? Children dying without law? So, let's take a little child, from birth to age eight, and he dies somewhere within that period of time. Are they considered among these in verse 72; the first thing that describes the terrestrial people, they are those that died without law? Are they children?

Student 1: Some of us say yes, and some of us say no.

Mike: Ok, so little children who die prematurely; what does the scripture tell us? They are alive in Christ and inherit what glory?

Student 6: The celestial glory.

Mike: The celestial glory. So then, if we are talking about verse 72, the terrestrial world, we are not talking about children when we refer to those who die without law. So, we have to be talking about adults, or people who are accountable. Now, it's very interesting; the Lord takes a group He calls the *heathen nations*. Let's talk about them first of all. Go back to section 45 in the *Doctrine and Covenants*. This is not something we talk about very often. Section 45, verse 54. These are people that inherit a terrestrial world:

> *And then shall the heathen nations be redeemed, and they that knew no law shall have part in the first resurrection;*

Now, the *first resurrection* is broken into two parts. There's the celestial part of the *first resurrection*, and there's the terrestrial part of the *first resurrection*. All persons who will resurrect with celestial bodies and all persons who resurrect with terrestrial bodies have part in the *first resurrection*. Some of the prophets have referred to the celestial being *the morning of the first resurrection*. I read Joseph Fielding Smith and B. H. Roberts today, and the terrestrial was referred to as *the afternoon of the first resurrection*. It's not scriptural, but the Brethren have called it that. And notice what it says, *"that they shall have part in the first resurrection;"* these are those that are terrestrial because obviously you cannot go to the celestial kingdom and be ignorant of law. It says these people die and they didn't know law:

> *and it shall be tolerable for them.*

Now, let's break down this heathen deal a little bit. Who are the *heathen nations*? What the heck is that? Any idea?

Students 4: They don't believe?

Student 6: They have no understanding.

Student 4: They have traditions of their fathers.

Mike: Are heathens the same as inactive Christians?
Student 1: No.
Mike: Ok, so, by definition, heathens are people who worship idols. They do not worship the living God. The word heathen comes from the word *heath*, and it means living in the country. They're not city dwellers. They're country dwellers. And the **-en** at the end of *heathen* comes from *pagan*. So, *heathen* and *pagan* are related. *Pagan* comes from the word *pagas,* which means village. So, these are village-country dwellers. That's interesting, something interesting to ponder there. The further away you get from the land, the further away you get from the country and into the city-dwelling metropolitan areas, the less likely you are to be spiritually inclined. You'll notice at the beginning of the world, Adam had certain sons, in particular, Cain, that went off and built cities. It's interesting that those that reject the Patriarchal Priesthood and the revelations of God went and established themselves in cities. The cities, even anciently, became the places where iniquity and wickedness thrived. Don't you find it interesting that all of the ancient fathers, all of the patriarchs, the antediluvians, they were all pastoral? They were all out in the country. And don't you find it interesting in our day that there is a desire for city-dwellers to be in the country? City-dwellers, innately inside them, long to be out in the country, out in the woods, out in the forest. There's something about that. The more we lose touch with the earth, the more likely we are to be deceived and seduced by evil spirits. There's something about remaining close to the earth. There's something about putting your bare toes in the grass and your fingers in the dirt.
Student 1: And yet, in the *Book of Mormon,* you read often that they build cities.
Mike: They built cities and as you'll find out, when you look at them, that where they built them, that's where they had their problems. The cities are where apostasy developed and persecution developed, until eventually, in 3 Nephi chapters 8, 9, and 10, the Lord has a long list of huge cities that were annihilated. Interesting stuff.

It's interesting that the name *heathen* means country dwellers in villages, but the definition of a *heathen* is those that worship idols. Another term that is used for *heathens* is the *gentiles.* So, when Paul takes the gospel to the gentile world in Corinth, Ephesus, Thessalonica, and different places, the biggest thing he contended with there was the worship of false idols and false gods.

So, here we go brothers and sisters, the *heathen nations* are terrestrial people. They'll inherit a Terrestrial Kingdom, and it shall be *"**tolerable** for them."* I just find that such a fascinating word, *tolerable*. The only place that I can find in the scriptures where the Lord uses the word *tolerable* is with the *heathen nations* that live and die without law and inherit a terrestrial world in the future.

Let's go back to section 76:73:

> *And also they who are the spirits of men kept in prison, whom the Son visited, and preached the gospel unto them, that they might be judged according to men in the flesh;*

Now, verse 74 is the key to that group. Notice you have a semicolon at the end of verse 73 and it continues to a period in verse 74. These people were the antediluvians. These are the wicked that Noah preached the gospel to and they rejected it and were still in that hell-place, that restricted place, when Christ went to Paradise, organized His ministers, and sent them to preach the gospel to these men and women. Look at verse 74:

> *Who received not the testimony of Jesus in the flesh, but afterwards received it* [in the spirit world].

Okay, here's another group of terrestrial people. So, let's talk about that for just a minute. We'll just glance over that. If a person, in this life, has what the Brethren call "a reasonable opportunity" to accept the gospel and they reject it, and go into the spirit world and accept the gospel there, they are inheritors of the terrestrial world, but not the celestial. I would assume that "a reasonable opportunity" has been interpreted as they felt the Spirit and the Holy Ghost bore testimony to them that the message they heard that was true, but they rejected it. They died without having made covenants or accepting that message.

Student 6: Yeah, so they had an opportunity here, but rejected it. They went to the next world and accepted it there, but they are

not able to get into or are not ready for celestial glory. Is that what you're saying?
Mike: That's right. If you reject the gospel here and accept it afterward in the spirit world, your place of habitation is a terrestrial order. These are people who accept the gospel in the spirit world but heard it in life and rejected it. Now, you have to have some stipulations there. Of course, the Lord is going to judge the person whether they had "a reasonable opportunity," you see? I mean we can't say the missionaries had a bad day, or this person slammed the door, and that was their chance. That doesn't fit. So, there has to be "a reasonable opportunity." There has to be some discussion. I believe there has to be a witness of the Holy Ghost born to those people, where they know that it's true, and then the cares of the world—remember the parable of the sower—the cares of the world choke them out, and they just can't make the decision. But they die and accept it in the spirit world, a terrestrial order. They belong in this group. Verse 75:

> *These are they who are honorable men* [and women] *of the earth, who were blinded by the craftiness of men.*

The key word there is ***honorable***. So, a minimum requirement of being terrestrial then is being ***honorable***. Can I just tell you right now that no covenants or ordinances are required for the terrestrial world.
Student 6: For the terrestrial world?
Mike: That's correct. All of the ordinances, all of the covenants that you and I participate in, are design only for the celestial world. There are no covenants or ordinances required for the terrestrial or the telestial world. Now, taking this a step further, everything we do in the Church of Jesus Christ of Latter-day Saints is designed to move the people, not to a telestial, nor a terrestrial, but to a celestial world. But, you can't make the leap from telestial to a celestial, even though everything is designed to get you there. You have to go in increments, climbing the ladder Joseph talked about, starting with the first rung and proceeding on, here a little there a little, precept upon precept, line upon line. See, that's how that goes.

You can see another minimum requirement of the terrestrial world by reading who the telestial people are. The main sin in the telestial world is sexual immorality. Now, look around us. We're in the telestial world. Can you see that as a fact? Is sexual immorality a problem in the world? Is it a problem in the Church? It is a problem in the telestial world, so for you to go to the terrestrial world, you have to be ***honorable***, and you need to be ***morally clean***. Those are your minimum requirements right there.

Student 4: Can you explain why the word are is used so many times, but in the verses before it was *shall*? Why is it so important to have *are* versus *shall*?

Mike: Well, *are* is in the present and *shall* is in the future. So, when it is describing these people in the terrestrial world, what we are seeing over and over is *those who are—, who are—, who are—, who are—,* etc., etc. When you get into the celestial world, you are going to see a whole list of *those who are—,* followed by a whole list of *they who shall—.* But, we'll talk about that another time.

You don't have to be a Mormon, brothers and sisters, to repent and obtain a **forgiveness** of sins. To obtain a **remission** of sins you need to enter into a covenant. But a **forgiveness** of sins is available to every man and woman who comes unto Christ, repents, and calls upon His name. Margie and I attended the Assembly of God church today. We went down to see our friend, who is an emeritus pastor speaking there and we spent two hours with those folks. As I listened to the sermons of those people who praise the Lord and talked about their experiences coming from a sinful past to a delivered present, there is no question in my mind that they have been forgiven of their sins. No question because the Spirit bore testimony to me of that.

You don't have to be a Mormon to know that adultery is wrong. It's the seventh commandment of the Ten Commandments. You don't have to be a Mormon to love Christ and call on His name and be taught by the Spirit how to repent and receive a forgiveness of their sins. If you have committed adultery or fornication or any sexual immorality, you need to have repented of that and been forgiven of it, to qualify for a terrestrial world. It's not limited to members of this church. Now, we won't go into it tonight, but a **remission** of sins is something different. A **remission** of sins can only come as a result of baptism and the gift of the Holy Ghost. **Remission** is not only forgiveness but also a healing experience, where not only are the sins forgiven, but all of the effects of them are removed. That's another lesson; we won't go into that tonight. But, suffice it to say that you must be ***morally clean*** and ***honorable*** to enter the terrestrial world, which means then that there will be millions of people in the terrestrial, millennial third estate who are not members of the Church. And there will be millions of members of the Church who will not make it there. Where much is given much is required. He who sins against the greater light receives the greater condemnation.

Now, let's go back to section 76 again:

> *There are they who receive of his glory, but not of his fulness.*

Those who enjoy the fullness of Christ will have to inherit what glory, terrestrial? Christ sits on the right hand of the Father in glory. So, if you want to have the fullness of Christ's glory where are you going to have to be?

Student 1: Celestial.

Mike: Yes, you're going to be in the celestial world. These are they who receive of the presence of the Son, but not the fullness of the Father. Christ ministers to the terrestrial world. Those of you, who go to the temple, know that there are four booths. The second booth is the telestial mortality world; the world we're in. It is a water-based world. When you enter the third booth, you are entering the millennial, terrestrial world. It is a fire-based world. The temple worker who is in the third booth represents the Savior, who ministers in the terrestrial, millennial third estate. The fourth booth is the celestial world, and that booth has a person in it, and that person represents the Holy Father. These four booths represent the four estates of our movement back to Heavenly Father, step by step. So, the person in the fourth booth is the Father, the person in the third booth is the Son, the person in the second booth, the telestial world, represents the Holy Ghost, and the first booth is your premortal life. Most people think there are only three booths and that the first one you go into is a waiting room. It's not a waiting room. You pass through a veil to get to that first booth. You are in an estate and that estate you are in, in that first booth, represents your first estate, which is the premortal life where you are an organized spirit son or daughter. When you pass through that second veil, that is the veil of birth, and you are entering the telestial world, and it is water-based. Anyway, there are some fun things to think about there.

The terrestrial world to come in the Millennium is not the Terrestrial Kingdom. It's the terrestrial world. Let me give you a little mystery to ponder. In the temple, it talks about creating earths and organizing worlds. There's a difference between an earth and a world. In Matthew chapter 24, the disciples came to Christ as He sat upon the Mount of Olives, and they wanted to know about His Second Coming. It also talks about this in *Doctrine and Covenants* 45, but it's the Joseph Smith translation that we want to go to for this. JST Matthew 1:4:

> *And what is the sign of thy coming, and the end of the world,* ***or the destruction of the wicked****, which is the end of the world?*

Now, they talked about the word *world*, not meaning a planet, but *world* meaning a population or group of people. It is clear in these verses that the destruction of the world represents the destruction of the wicked or the burning off of telestial persons at the Second Coming of Christ. So, that's an interesting little thing to think about there right now. When we talk about populations, and we talk about earths and planets, it may be a different thing. The terrestrial world is the phase that this earth is going through that we call the Thousand Year Millennium. That's the terrestrial world. At some future time, there will need to be a planet organized and placed in a terrestrial order so that resurrected terrestrial beings can reside on that world. That's called the Terrestrial Kingdom. The terrestrial world is a phase of this earth's progression because we know the destiny of this world. This earth that we're on right now, Mother Earth's destiny is not to be a Terrestrial Kingdom, but its destiny is to be crowned and become a Celestial Kingdom. So, right now it's a telestial world getting ready to move into a terrestrial world, and eventually, will be crowned and become a Celestial Kingdom. Then the Telestial Kingdom and the Terrestrial Kingdom will have to be organized planets separate from this world that we're on right now. Do you understand what I'm saying? Separate from it and placed in a telestial or terrestrial order, so that resurrected beings of that order can inhabit that kingdom. And they are Kingdoms because they are presided over by kings.

Student 6: So, when the judgment comes and we are given the kingdom that we are prepared for, and let's say I am to go to the Terrestrial Kingdom, is there hope for me to move up after that, or is that where I spend eternity?

Mike: That is a great question. Go with me over to section 76. The authorities of the Church quote section 76, verse 112. Here it talks about the people in these various places. Let's go to verse 111 first:

> *For they shall be judged according to their works, and every man shall receive according to his own works, his own dominion, in the **mansions** which are prepared**;***

Semicolon, now we don't pay enough attention to these semicolons.

> *[112] And they* [those who are in these mansions] *shall be servants of the Most High; but where God and Christ dwell they cannot come, worlds without end.*

Now, we quote that scripture to show that once you resurrect and inherit a kingdom of glory/life, whether it's telestial or terrestrial that you can progress within that kingdom, right? But, you can't go from kingdom to kingdom. Isn't that what we teach? Let me read something to you, and I will put it up on my handouts. This is by Hyrum Smith:

> *Hyrum Smith (Assistant President of the Church, Church Patriarch, Member of the Quorum of the Twelve) August 1, 1843—Those of the Terrestrial Glory either advance to the Celestial or recede to the Telestial [or] else the moon could not be a type (a symbol of that kingdom), for it (the moon) waxes and wanes.*

Those are the words we use to describe the wane. So, he said that you either progress forward from the terrestrial or recede back. Now, this is interesting here, and I've got a dozen quotes I'll put up for you. The interesting thing is that it does not talk about progressing from the Telestial up. Let me give you one more here. This is by Franklin D. Richards, a member of the quorum of the twelve. This is May 17, 1884. This is the end of the quote:

> *Thus the people of God will go forward. They will go forward, like unto the new moon, increasing in knowledge and brightness and glory, until they come to a fullness of celestial glory.*

Interesting quotes. B. H. Roberts, he took that verse in section 76, verse 112 where it says, "*where God and Christ dwell they cannot come, worlds without end,*" and said this:

> *But if it be granted that such a thing is possible,* [in other words progression from kingdoms] *they who are at the first entered into the celestial glory—having before them the privilege also of eternal progress—have been moving onward, so that the relative distance between them and those who have fought their way up from lesser glories may be as great when the latter* [those who are coming up] *have come into the degrees of celestial glory in which the righteous at first stood, as it was at commencement. Thus: Those whose faith and works are such only as to enable them to inherit a telestial glory, may arrive at last where those whose works in this life were such as to enable them to entrance into the celestial kingdom—**they may arrive where these were, but never where they are**.*

Isn't that an interesting thing there!

Student 6: So, what I understand this to say then is that we may be able to move up from kingdom to kingdom, but let's say, for instance, that my mother, brother, sister, and father are in the Celestial Kingdom. I could come up, but I won't be with them. I could come up to that kingdom, but do you see what I'm saying? Is that what you got out of that?

Mike: It says, "*where God and Christ dwell they cannot come, worlds without end.*" Well, that means that if everybody is moving up and progressing, you can be where they've been, but not where they are because they continue moving up also. That's what these guys were teaching. Here's another thing in section 76. It talks about how those of the celestial world minister to those in the terrestrial world. This is section 76:86-89. Those in the terrestrial world minister to those in the telestial world. Those in higher worlds have an assignment as messengers to administer to those in lower worlds. My question is, to what end are we administering to them for if it's not to allow them to progress and to come up? What's the purpose of going down? It doesn't make sense to me. What are you doing just to go down just to visit and say, "How's the weather today in the telestial world?"

Student 6: But here's my question, Mike. If my brother is in the Celestial Kingdom, we're in the Terrestrial, and we work ourselves up to the Celestial, wouldn't we be with them? Why wouldn't we be with them if we have that same glory? Did I make that clear?

Mike: Well, to answer your question let me read to you one last statement by the First Presidency. This is the Secretary to the First Presidency in a letter in 1952, and again in 1965:

> *The brethren direct me to say the Church has never announced a definite doctrine upon this point. Some of the brethren have held the view that it was possible in the course of progression to advance from one glory to another, invoking the principle of eternal progression; others of the brethren have taken the opposite view. But as stated, the Church has never announced a definite doctrine on this point.*

So, brothers and sisters, what it boils down to is that the Lord has given us a thumbnail, section 76, but has on purpose withheld details. Now, these details are what we call the *mysteries of Godliness*, and they are to be revealed to the saints. We can know the answers to all of this. There's not a question that we have on any of this that you can't know the answer to, but you have to take it to God in prayer and obtain divine revelation concerning it. Now, once you are told that you may also find yourself under restraint to not move it forward. Brigham Young said that when you have revealed to you something that's true that has not been canonized by the Church, you put it on the shelf and hold that and not publicly teach that until the Church makes it public. The point is, however, that the Lord can and will reveal to us things that have not been revealed and are not publicly taught by the Church. In fact, He encourages us to go after these things. And then when you obtain these pearls, if you are close enough to the Spirit, the Lord will direct you, if, when, and to whom you are to share these pearls. Does that make sense?

Student 6: Yeah, thanks very much!

Mike: This week as I was pondering this, I read a scripture in Matthew chapter 25. Let me show you what the Spirit taught me. I just rejoiced in this. It was so fun! I had been pondering the terrestrial world. Matthew chapter 25. This is the famous one you know:

> *Inasmuch as ye have done it unto one of the least of these my brethren, ye have done it unto me.*

Right? It also has the *parable of the talents*. Now, I want you to go to Matthew 25, and as he comes back, he receives an accounting from the people. I'd like to go to verse 21, and He repeats it again in verse 23. To the servant who had doubled their talents:

> *His lord said unto him, Well done, thou good and faithful servant: thou hast been faithful over a few things, I will make thee ruler over many things: enter thou into the joy of thy lord.*

The thought that I had on that was that it's in the telestial world where we are given the opportunity to be faithful over a few things. You, in the telestial world, who go and receive your endowments are anointed to become kings and queens, priests and priestesses, to rule and reign in the House of Israel. We have to be anointed to do that. Now, because you've been anointed to do that doesn't mean that you **are** a king or a queen, a priest or a priestess. You have simply been anointed to become such. This verse right here, where you are faithful over a few things, is your responsibility in the telestial world. If you pass that and the Lord says, *"Well done, thou good and faithful servant,"* in the terrestrial, millennial world you will have Him say, *"I will make thee ruler over many things: enter thou into the joy of thy Lord."* I believe that verse 21 and 23 are talking about the sequence of moving from telestial/mortal to terrestrial/translated. In the first place, you don't automatically rule over kingdoms. You don't automatically become king and queen. Every king or queen, before they obtain that was a prince or a princess. Princes and princesses don't rule over kingdoms. They rule over something called *principalities,* which is an apprentice kingdom. It's a smaller dominion. It's where you're learning how to become a king and a queen, while you're still a prince or a princess. And it's my feeling that that takes place in the terrestrial, millennial world. That's where we're going to start to rule and reign.

Student 6: Wow!

Mike: And if you prove faithful to the principality and dominion that you're given—the beginning of your kingly reigning—then you can advance to a higher a kingdom, where you will then be a king and a queen, where you will then rule over those who worship you and look to you for salvation, redemption, and exaltation.

We're out of time, and we'll pick this up again in the next lesson, but I wanted to share with you what the main purpose of the millennial, terrestrial world is. We teach in the Church that the main purpose is missionary work and work for the dead. And those are definitely millennial works; they are definitely! What I would like to present to you is that the main purpose of the terrestrial, millennial world is to beget life. And the other thing I want to share with you to think about is that if in the millennial world you're in the presence of God, then the third estate is an unveiled estate and yet, it is probationary. Wherever you have *probationary*, then it means there is the possibility of falling and failing. Brothers and sisters, we know that the millennial world is probationary because we know that at the end of the millennial world Satan is loosed, there is a huge battle and many fall. By definition, that is a probationary world.

I want to talk to you next week, about begetting life in the terrestrial, millennial world. I want to talk to you about what the sin is at the end of the Millennium that causes Lucifer to be loosed and many to fall from grace. What is the sin? What happens there? How can that be when the majority in the Millennium grow up without sin unto salvation, Satan has no power, and God wipes away all tears? What happens at the end of the Millennium to change that glorious state? Those are the things we are going to talk about next week. Is that okay?

Student 6: That sounds great!

Mike: So, the next time you go to the temple, ponder some of those things when you participate in initiatories, or for that matter in the endowment, and you move from the telestial to the terrestrial. I want you to think about that. Moving from booth two to booth three is the same as moving from the telestial room to the terrestrial room in the endowment ceremony. Ponder these things. Think about the persons who officiate in those rooms and the things we talked about. See if the Spirit will teach you something and you can have a fun time the next time you go to the temple and participate in that sacred ordinance.

References:
D&C 130:18-19
D&C 76:71-72
D&C 45:54
D&C 76:73-76 and 111-112
Matthew 25:21-23
B H Roberts

Progression from Kingdom to Kingdom (Quotes)

Hyrum Smith (Assistant President of the Church, Church Patriarch, Member of the Quorum of the Twelve)

Reference: August 1, 1843, transcribed by Franklin D. Richards; *Words of the Prophet*, pg. 24; CHO Ms/d/4409/Misc Minutes Collection

Hiram [Smith] said Aug 1st [18]43 Those of the Terrestrial Glory either advance to the Celestial or recede to the Telestial [or] else the moon could not be a type [viz. a symbol of that kingdom]. [for] it [the moon] "waxes & wanes." Also that br George will be quickened by celestial glory having been ministered to by one of that Kingdom.

Franklin D. Richards (Member of the Quorum of the Twelve)

Reference: *Journal of Discourses*, Volume 25:236, May 17, 1884

The Savior tells us that the terrestrial glory, or kingdom, is likened unto the glory of the moon, which is not of the brightness of the sun, neither of the smallness nor dimness of the stars. But those others who have no part in marrying or giving of marriage in the last resurrection, they become as stars, and even differ from each other in glory; but those in the terrestrial kingdom are those who will come forth at the time when Enoch comes back, when the Savior comes again to dwell upon the earth; when Father Abraham will be there with the Urim and Thummim to look after every son and daughter of his race; to make known all things that are needed to be known, and with them enter into their promised inheritance. ***Thus the people of God will go forward. They will go forward, like unto the new moon, increasing in knowledge and brightness and glory, until they come to a fullness of celestial glory.***

Brigham Young (Prophet)

Reference: *Journal of Wilford Woodruff*, 5 Aug 1855

I attended the Prayer Circle in the evening ... In conversing upon various principles President Young said none would inherit this Earth when it became celestial and translated into the presence of God but those who would be crowned as Gods and able to endure the fullness of the presence of God, ***except they would be permitted to take with them some servants for whom they would be held responsible***. All others would have to inherit another kingdom, even that kingdom agreeing with the law which they had kept. ***He said they would eventually have the privilege of proving themselves worthy and advancing to a celestial kingdom, but it would be a slow progress.***

Wilford Woodruff (Member of the Quorum of the Twelve)

Reference: *Journal of Discourses*, Volume 6:120, December 6, 1857

If there was a point where man in his progression could not proceed any further, the very idea would throw a gloom over

every intelligent creature. God himself is increasing and progressing in knowledge, power, and dominion, and will do so, worlds without end. It is just so with us. We are in probation, which is a school of experience.

Lorenzo Snow (Member of the Quorum of the Twelve)

Reference: *Collected Discourses* 3:364-65; General Conference Address, 6 October 1893

God has fulfilled His promises to us, and our prospects are grand and glorious. Yes, in the next life we will have our wives, and our sons and daughters. If we do not get them all at once, we will have them some time, for every knee shall bow and ever tongue shall confess that Jesus is the Christ. You that are mourning about your children straying away will have your sons and your daughters. ***If you succeed in passing through these trials and afflictions and receive a resurrection, you will, by the power of the Priesthood, work and labor, as the Son of God has, until you get all your sons and daughters in the path of exaltation and glory. This is just as sure as that the sun rose this morning over yonder mountains.*** Therefore, mourn not because all your sons and daughters do not follow in the path that you have marked out to them, or give heed to your counsels. ***Inasmuch as we succeed in securing eternal glory, and stand as saviors, and as kings and priests to our God, we will save our posterity.*** When Jesus went through that terrible torture on the cross, He saw what would be accomplished by it; He saw that His brethren and sisters - the sons and daughters of God - would be gathered in, with but few exceptions - those who committed the unpardonable sin. That sacrifice of the divine Being was effectual to destroy the powers of Satan. ***I believe that every man and woman who comes into this life and passes through it, that life will be a success in the end. It may not be in this life.*** It was not with the antediluvians. They passed through troubles and afflictions; 2,500 years after that, when Jesus went to preach to them, the dead heard the voice of the Son of God and they lived. They found after all that it was a very good thing that they had conformed to the will of God in leaving the spiritual life and passing through this world.

J. Reuben Clark (First Councilor in the First Presidency to President McKay)

Reference: *Church News*, 23 April 1960, p. 3

I am not a strict constructionalist, believing that we seal our eternal progress by what we do here. It is my belief that God will save all of His children that he can: and while, if we live unrighteously here, we shall not go to the other side in the same status, so to speak, as those who lived righteously; nevertheless, the unrighteous will have their chance, and in the eons of the eternities that are to follow, they, too, may climb to the destinies to which they who are righteous and serve God, have climbed to those eternities that are to come.

James E. Talmage (Educator, Member of the Quorum of the Twelve)

Reference: *Articles of Faith* (book)

Articles of Faith, James E. Talmage (1st Edition, 1899, pp. 420-421)

It is reasonable to believe, in the absence of direct revelation by which alone absolute knowledge of the matter could be acquired, that, in accordance with God's plan of eternal progression, advancement from grade to grade within any kingdom, and from kingdom to kingdom, will be provided for. But if the recipients of a lower glory be enabled to advance, surely the intelligences of higher rank will not be stopped in their progress; and thus we may conclude, that degrees and grades will ever characterize the kingdoms of our God. Eternity is progressive; perfection is relative; the essential feature of God's living purpose is its associated power of eternal increase.

B.H. Roberts (Member of the First Quorum of the Seventy)

Reference: *New Witnesses for God*, Volume 1; pp. 391-392

These are the great divisions of glory in the world to come, but there are subdivisions or degrees. Of the telestial glory it is written: "And the glory of the telestial is one, even as the glory of the stars is one, for as one star differs from another star in glory, even so differs one from another in glory in the telestial world" [D&C 76:98]. From this it is evident that there are different degrees of glory within the celestial and the telestial glories; and though we have no direct authority for the statement, it seems but reasonable to conclude that there are different degrees of glory in the terrestrial world also. It appears but rational that it should be so, since the degrees of worthiness in men are almost infinite in their variety; and as every man is to be judged according to his works, it will require a corresponding infinity of degrees in glory to mete out to every man that reward of which he is worthy, and that also which his intelligence will enable him to enjoy.

The question of advancement within the great divisions of glory celestial, terrestrial, and telestial; as also the question of advancement from one sphere of glory to another remains to be considered.. In the revelation from which we have summarized what has been written here, in respect to the different degrees of glory, it is said that those of the terrestrial glory will be ministered unto by those of the celestial; and those of the telestial will be ministered unto by those of the terrestrial - that is, those of the higher glory minister to those of a lesser glory. ***I can conceive of no reason for all this administration of the higher to the lower, unless it be for the purpose of advancing our Father's children along the lines of eternal progression.*** Whether or not in the great future, full of so many possibilities now hidden from us, they of the lesser glories after education and advancement within those spheres may at last emerge from them and make their way to the higher degrees of glory until at last they attain to the highest, is not revealed in the revelations of God, and any statement made on the subject must partake more or less of the nature of conjecture. But if it be granted that such a thing is possible, they who at the first entered into the celestial glory - having before them the privilege also of eternal progress - have been moving onward, so that the relative distance between them and those who have fought their way up from the lesser glories may be as great ***when the latter have come into the degrees of celestial glory in which the righteous at first stood,*** as it was at the commencement. Thus: ***Those whose faith and works are such only as to enable them to inherit a telestial glory, may arrive at last where those whose works in this life were such as to enable them to entrance into the celestial kingdom - they may arrive where these were, but never where they are.***

B.H. Roberts (Member of the First Quorum of the Seventy)

Reference: *Outlines of Ecclesiastical History*, pp. 416-17

20. But if it be granted that such a thing is possible, they who at the first entered into the celestial glory-having before them the privilege also of eternal progress-have been moving onward, so that the relative distance between them and those who have fought their way up from the lesser glories, may be as great when the latter have come into the degrees of celestial glory in which the righteous at first stood, as it was at the commencement; and thus between them is an impassable gulf which time cannot destroy. Thus: those whose faith and works are such only as to entitle them to inherit a telestial glory, may arrive at last where those whose works in this life were such as to entitle them to entrance into the celestial kingdom-they may arrive where these were, but never where they are. But if it be granted that the chief fact about ***Intelligences is that they have power to add fact to fact and thus build up knowledge, and through knowledge have wisdom, and thus make progress; and if to such intelligences there is granted eternal life-immortality -then it is useless to postulate any limitations for them; for in the passing of even a few thousands of millions of years, even if progress be very slow-there will come a time when these intelligences-men and women of even the telestial glory-may become very acceptable characters, and very important personages.***

B.H. Roberts (Member of the First Quorum of the Seventy)

Reference: *Collected Discourses*, Volume 5, June 21, 1896

And it shall be preached until every soul shall hear, and it shall continue to work with those who are the offspring of God until every knee shall bow, and every tongue shall confess. Salvation, in some order of its many degrees, shall meet the soul of every man and every woman, bringing them unto that exaltation that their souls are capable of receiving, and saving them unto the uttermost-not all alike, any more than men are all alike here, no more than conditions are all alike here; but as the stars differ from each other in brightness or glory, so shall the rewards of men differ in the world which is to come, even "according to their works." But no man shall be left out of the mercy and the grace of God, except only those who do violence unto it, after having once received it; for the crime of high treason against God, and a repudiation of the plan of life and salvation after having received it, merits such punishment and such destruction as is known only to God. But the remainder of the children of God shall find rest in some one of the many divisions of glory that are to be found in the kingdom of God, and shall find peace and glory equal to the development that they have made or are capable of making with the grand opportunities that will be presented to them, ***until progress shall be made from glory to glory, until every soul shall contain all that it is possible for it to receive, even endless progression. For God has decreed that those of the celestial glory, that is after the resurrection, shall minister to those of the terrestrial glory, and those of the terrestrial glory shall minister to them of the telestial glory; and I can conceive no reason why there should be this continual ministration of the higher to the lower glory but for the purpose of exalting all to a higher plane of glory, in the direction of the eternal progression which God has opened to the children of men. This explanation Mormonism makes possible to these facts that we see before us, and which are otherwise inexplicable.***

Secretary to the First Presidency in a 1952 letter; and again in 1965

The brethren direct me to say that the Church has never announced a definite doctrine upon this point. Some of the brethren have held the view that it was possible in the course of progression to advance from one glory to another, invoking the principle of eternal progression; others of the brethren have taken the opposite view. But as stated, the Church has never announced a definite doctrine on this point.

Chapter Twenty-Four

Podcast 024 The Terrestrial World part 2

Well, brothers and sisters, tonight we are going to try to complete our discussion on the terrestrial world. Last week, we mentioned that there is a difference between the terrestrial world and the Terrestrial Kingdom. I got some feedback this week that this was not a clearly understood. Whenever we talk about *worlds*, we're going to talk about populations or organizations of people, groups of people. When we talk about the *Earth* or *Kingdom*, we're going to talk about the physical planet. So, the Terrestrial Kingdom is a planet that will be or has already been organized. It is not this earth. The Terrestrial Kingdom, where terrestrial, resurrected beings at some future time will reside, is not this earth. It will be another planet. The terrestrial world will be this earth in its next estate which is the terrestrial, millennial third estate. We already know from scripture that this earth is an obedient earth. Let's go to section 88 and let me show you a little scripture here. It's kind of fascinating. We've read it many times, but we just skip over it. We don't look into it. Let's see what it says. *Doctrine and Covenants* 88:21 is talking about this earth and its progress back into the presence of the Father:

> *And they who are not sanctified through the law which I have given unto you, even the law of Christ, must inherit another kingdom, even that of a terrestrial kingdom, or that of a telestial kingdom.*

If you can't keep the law of the celestial world, you're going to end up in a different place. Now, in verse 25:

> *And again, verily I say unto you,* ***the earth abideth the law of a celestial kingdom****, for it filleth the measure of its creation,* ***and transgresseth not the law***—

Interesting statement.

> *[26] Wherefore, it shall be sanctified* [this earth]; *yea, notwithstanding it shall die* [at the end of the millennium], *it shall be quickened again* [brought back to life] *and shall abide the power by which it is quickened, and the righteous shall inherit it* [a celestial world].

So, the controversy, the question we had last week was, "What are you talking about Brother Stroud, when you say terrestrial world and Terrestrial Kingdom?" When we talk about the terrestrial world, we are talking about this earth that we are on now, as it moves from this estate into its next estate, which is a terrestrial world, not a Terrestrial Kingdom. The Terrestrial Kingdom will be another planet that resurrected, terrestrial beings who don't qualify for a Celestial Kingdom will dwell on. Whether that planet has already been created and is simply waiting for inhabitants, I don't know, but it will not be this earth. This earth is going to go all the way to its destiny. The Lord says, to *"filleth the measure of its creation,"* and notice that it says it "*transgresseth not the law.*" That's an indicator that there are some earths that are not obedient, otherwise, how can a planet transgress the law? Our planet doesn't do it. With that, you can assume that there are some planets that when they're told to do something, are not as obedient as ours is and therefore, do not fulfill the measure of their creation. So, I hope that explains that little controversy that we had some questions on this week. Some people were asking about that, and I probably didn't make it very clear.

Worlds: when you talk about worlds, and I won't say all of the time, but more often than not, you're not talking about the physical geographical position or place, as much as you are talking about populations, groups of people, and societies. So, that's another little key that we picked up, and you can get that from the Joseph Smith Translation at the bottom of Matthew chapter 24. His disciples said, *"Tell us... [concerning] thy coming, and the end of the world?"* and then Joseph Smith adds in the JST at the bottom, *"or the destruction of the wicked, which is the end of the world?"* In his JST translation, Joseph uses the word *world* to talk about a population of wicked men and women who will be destroyed at His Second Coming. That's an interesting little insight. It gives us some pause to think about when the scriptures say in Moses 1:33:

> *And worlds without number have I created; ...and by the Son I created them, which is mine Only Begotten."*

That gives us a whole different insight. Is he talking about planets or is he talking about the organization of societies upon these planets, which is a great, ponderable thought?

Let's go back to the terrestrial world. Tonight, I'm going to use some things from the temple to help us learn more about the terrestrial world. I have a twelve-page handout for you for tonight's class that I call "Teachings Concerning the Terrestrial Glory." I'd like to just pick up on a couple of things here before we move into some of the things we talked about at the end of last week's class. For example, we teach that every person on the earth will have an opportunity to hear the gospel and either accept it or reject it. I taught that as a missionary, I taught it in seminary, and that's not quite correct. There are whole groups of people that will be judged according to what they **would have** done. They never will, in this life or after this life, have the opportunity to hear the gospel of Jesus Christ and either accept it or reject it. Now, this fits in with what we are talking about regarding the terrestrial world. In *Doctrine and Covenants* 137:5-8, Joseph Smith sees family members and others in the Celestial Kingdom. One of them he saw was his brother, Alvin, who died November 19, 1823, and this revelation was given January 21, 1836. He sees his brother Alvin in the Celestial Kingdom:

> *[6] And marveled how it was that he had obtained an inheritance in that kingdom, seeing that he had departed this life before the Lord had set his hand to gather Israel the second*

time, and had not been baptized for the remission of sins.

Look up in verse 5. Look who else he sees:

and my father and my mother;

They were both alive in Kirtland, Ohio at the time this vision was given. He sees them in the Celestial Kingdom. And so, he's wondering about Alvin in verse 7. How is he in the Celestial Kingdom when he never heard the gospel? He never had a baptism. This was before baptism for the dead was done. We don't have that introduced until the late 1830's or early 1840's:

[7] Thus came the voice of the Lord unto me, saying: All who have died without a knowledge of this gospel, [never had it preached to them] ***who would have received it*** *if they had been permitted to tarry, shall be heirs of the celestial kingdom of God;*

[8] Also all that shall die henceforth without a knowledge of it, ***who would have received it*** *with all their hearts, shall be heirs of that kingdom;*

Remember last week; we said that people who go to the terrestrial world are people who have what the prophets call *"a reasonable opportunity"* to hear the gospel in this life. It's presented to them, and they reject it, for whatever reason, they reject it, and then they die. And they go into the spirit world, and afterward, they accept the gospel in the spirit world. Then section 76 says that their inheritance is that of a Terrestrial Kingdom.

So, these groups of people we're talking about in section 137 are people who, if they had heard it in life, would have accepted it, would have embraced it, would have been valued in it, and would have been assigned a celestial glory. But they didn't hear it in this life, and they become heirs of a celestial world because God knows they would have accepted it if they'd had a chance. So, this doctrine that we teach, that every person will have an opportunity to hear the gospel and either accept it or reject it is not quite correct.

You've also got that whole group of heathen people we talked about last week, the heathen nation, people who worship idols. God simply says that they will inhabit a terrestrial world because they died without law and then He comes out and says that it will be *tolerable* for them. How can we justify this fact that there are whole groups of people in mortality that are never going to have an opportunity to hear the gospel preached to them and will inherit a terrestrial world? How can we justify that with the missionary work where we say we will preach the gospel to **everybody** and everybody is going to have an opportunity to hear it and/or reject it? It has to go back to what we call the *doctrine of election*. It has to go back to the first estate, the pre-mortal life. There were people in the premortal life that, just like here, choose to be casual. If you want to know what took place there, then look at what's taking place here. You have all different classes of people and attitudes and activity and participation. You have people who did not want to be a part of anything going on there and simply withdrew. Classes were being held to be instructed on things they needed to know when they came to the new earth, and some of those people ditched the classes. Instead of being where they should have been, they found themselves where they shouldn't be; just like now. Nothing has changed. As a result of all of these attitudes and all of these different levels of valiancy and apathy and complacency, everything you see on the earth today, you saw in the premortal world. It was all there. As a result of that, when it comes time to come to Earth, some come with great advantages and others come less advantaged. That helps us understand this. It may appear that all of these people who are going to end up in a terrestrial world had no choice on this, but let me read to you a couple of statements by some of the Brethren. This is Joseph Fielding Smith in *Doctrines of Salvation*, and he said this:

> *There were those who were less intelligent and evidently less fit for the exaltation offered to the faithful, yet these also were entitled to salvation from death and the torment of the damned.*

We are talking now about people who are going to end up in a terrestrial world. Notice the key words, less intelligent and evidently less fit. Then President Smith comes out and says:

> *The more progressive and intelligent spirits were not sent to the tribes among the degraded heathen. ...Children born under such*

> *circumstances could not be exalted, yet the Lord in His mercy had decreed to them to do the very best that could be done.*

Watch this. This is your center key, brothers and sisters, to this whole deal:

> ***Not having knowledge of the things of God**, they were to be judged without law and assigned to a place after the resurrection **that would be suited to them** without the fulness promised to the faithful.*

Why did they not have knowledge of the things of God? Because they choose to be in places where they should not have been and as a result, forfeited that knowledge and without that knowledge, you cannot come into this world with an otherwise, advantageous position. Does that make sense?

So, everything in this world that seems to be unfair or inequitable really isn't if you look at phase one or estate one. Everything that is happening in this world today, everything—advantages and disadvantages that appear to be so, coming into favorable contact with the gospel, the temple, priesthood, all of the blessing and ordinances of the gospel—are a direct result of who you were and what you did before you came here. Those people who are not going to have contact, it will be because of choices made before they were born, and the scriptures seem to indicate that there are whole groups of these people. This is what Melvin Ballard, a member of the Quorum of the Twelve said:

> *I wish to say to you that those who died without law, meaning the pagan [/heathen] nations, for lack of faithfulness, for lack of devotion, in the former life, **are obtaining all they are entitled to**. I don't mean to say that all of them will be barred from the entrance of the highest glory. Anyone of them who repents and complies with the conditions might also obtain celestial glory, **but the great bulk of them shall only obtain terrestrial glory**.*

What I'm trying to teach us is that as this world winds up its telestial phase and gets ready to move into the terrestrial world, what we're doing or not doing right now is going to determine what will be in eternity when we leave this world; just like what you did before you came here is determining the favorability, advantages or disadvantages you have here. That's what I wanted to teach on that. Any comments or thoughts?

Let's go to the terrestrial world as the temple talks about it. Everything I could find that had significant doctrine on the terrestrial world, I've included in this twelve-page handout that will be with this lesson. But to really get a feeling or a deeper sense of the terrestrial world, we need to look at the symbolism of the temple and what the temple is trying to teach us about that world. You must ask yourself certain questions. You have to understand that the terrestrial world is a Zion society. The church in the terrestrial world is the *Church of the Firstborn*. The Church of Jesus Christ of Latter-day Saints is the stepping stone to get you into the temple where you are initiated into the ordinances of the *Church of the Firstborn*. Not everybody in the terrestrial, millennial world is going to be covenant people. There are going to be many, many people that have made no covenants with the Lord. As a matter of fact, we said last week that no covenants are required in order to be in the terrestrial world. But, if you're a Latter-day Saint and you've made covenants, and you've been introduced into the *Church of the Firstborn* ordinances through the endowment, and have been faithful on that, then you'll have membership in that church in the terrestrial world. It'll be a different operation.

Now, let me just share with you a couple of things. Last week, I made the statement that the terrestrial, millennial world is a probationary non-veiled place. Your premortal life was a probationary place. Obviously, *a third* failed completely and others were less valiant to one degree or another, so it was a probationary place. The premortal life was unveiled. That's why the *third-part* who are devils on this earth, are such because they sinned against God **in His presence**. The second estate is a probationary estate that is veiled. **All** telestial worlds are veiled estates. Telestial worlds are the schoolhouses where the children of the Gods (the Fathers and the Mothers) come to learn the lessons necessary to come up and become like their Parents. They are all veiled, probationary estates. The millennial world is an **un**veiled, probationary estate. Christ is there. Holy Beings are there, and you see them and have an interaction with them. So, the veil of mortality doesn't exist in the terrestrial world. This means the terrestrial, millennial world is a third estate. It's a necessary step that cannot be skipped if you are moving from one place to another and progressing on your journey back to the Father. But, like your first estate, it being in an **unveiled, probationary estate**, if you sin in that estate, the consequences are much more severe than otherwise, because you sin against God **in a God's presence**.

Now, we know that the Millennium is a place of peace. There are no wars, at least for most of the Millennium. There is no funeral death. There is no need for police departments. There are no soldiers. God will wipe away all tears. The animosity of man and animal and enmity disappears. The lion plays with an ox. The child plays with poisonous serpents. You've heard all of Isaiah's prophecies. There is none to hurt in His holy mountain. Satan is bound. The scriptures tell us that he is bound for two reasons. The Book of Revelations says he has a seal placed upon him and the *Book of Mormon* says he is bound because of the righteousness of the saints. But, for the majority of time in the millennial third estate, Satan has no power. It says that children grow up without sin unto salvation. And yet, at the end of the Millennium, we're told that Satan is loosed to gather his hosts one more time and there is a great war and many fall. So, what is the sin of the terrestrial, millennial third estate that causes people to fall? If you sin in that third estate, you forfeit eternal life, which *Doctrine and Covenants* 14:7 says is:

> *the greatest of all the gifts of God.*

If you pass the third estate judgment, you obtain eternal life. Now, there's a difference between *eternal life* and *eternal lives*. But that's not tonight's lesson. That's something for another time. So, what's the sin that causes this failure for people who made it this far? They're now at the end of their third estate, they've passed the pre-mortal life, they've passed mortality, and now they commit a sin in the third estate, and for them, that ends their progression. At that point, they have forfeited eternal life. I would submit to you that the sin is sexual immorality. Now, where do I get that from? I have to go to the temple to figure this out. But, what I want to share with you are things that I've learned at this point. This is Brother Stroud, Elder Stroud, Brother Mike, chapter 15 verse 6. This is my own personal insight. Nothing is written on this, but I will just present it to you with that in mind.

In the temple ceremony, you progress from room to room. You find yourself in the lone and dreary world, which is the telestial world, the world we're in now. That was after Adam and Eve were cast out of the Garden. It's the second estate, mortality. Then you move from that room in the temple that we call the world room or the telestial room, and you go up. Every little temple has a slight incline. Even the newer temples have a little ramp that may only be an inch tall. But, for you to go from telestial to the terrestrial room, symbolically there is a movement up, even if it's just a little one to two-inch ramp. In the Salt Lake Temple, you move up a full story and go from the first floor to the second floor, still moving up. Now, in each of these rooms, we make covenants. In the telestial room, the covenant we make is the covenant to obey something called the *Law of the Gospel*. I pondered a long time as to what the *Law of the Gospel* was, and I decided and came to find out, that the *Law of the Gospel* is that law that is found in the *Bible*. It can be found in the *New Testament* in the Sermon on the Mount. It can be found in the *Book of Mormon* at the Sermon at the Temple Bountiful. It is the Ten Commandments and Beatitudes. It is *"love thy neighbor as thyself"* and *"do unto others as you would have them do unto you."* The *Law of the Gospel* is the law in the telestial world that teaches you how to interact successfully with others of God's children. It is **a human interaction law**.

Also with that law, there is a charge that is connected. I want to go to the last words of that charge that says that you will *"avoid every other unholy and impure practice."* That charge in the telestial world, "every other unholy and impure practice" **includes** all sexual immorality. *"**Every other** unholy and impure practice."* That includes sexual immorality, homosexuality, transvestism, transgender, and any LGBT. ***All*** of that stuff is included in *"every other unholy and impure practice,"* and you enter into that covenant in the telestial world. And by the way, you're officiating in the Aaronic Priesthood in that world. Think about it now. Go back. There's a difference between being ordained to the Aaronic or Melchizedek Priesthood and officiating in the ordinances thereof. That's something for you to ponder. But, when you take upon yourself the covenant to obey the *Law of the Gospel* and that charge, you are officiating in the ordinances of the Aaronic Priesthood. Now, before you enter into the terrestrial world, you take upon yourself Melchizedek Priesthood, and you don't officiate in the Melchizedek Priesthood until you're in the terrestrial world. Isn't that interesting?

Now, keep in mind that the terrestrial world is the millennial third estate. It's the world to come. It's the one we're on the edge of. It's the one that the world is physically in upheaval over right now, preparing to move from this place in this solar system, one-third of the distance back to the center of this galaxy where this earth was when it was in the Garden of Eden state. That's your tenth Article of Faith. This *"earth will be renewed and receive its paradisiacal glory."* Paradisiacal is another word for millennial, translated, terrestrial state. Now, when you move into the terrestrial world, i.e. the terrestrial room in the temple, the first covenant you make is a covenant to be morally clean. We need to be asking these questions, brothers and sisters. The temple endowment can't teach us much unless we go in there with an inquisitive mind. You go in there with Heavenly Father, saying your prayers, "Father, help me to see things that I can ask you about and receive revelation for." Just being able to see these things in itself is a revelation, let alone having a revelation to explain what it means. Ask for that going in.

My question is this: why do we make a covenant of chastity (which has to do with sexual relations between men and women) in the terrestrial world when we already included sexual cleanliness in the *Law of the Gospel* in the telestial world? Why are we doing that a second time? Now, I will tell you also, that everything that goes along with the temple endowment—each sign, token and name—accompanies a specific law and covenant. So, you're making a covenant of chastity in the terrestrial world. Remember, brothers and sisters, that's the millennial world where Christ dwells. You wouldn't make a covenant of chastity in that world if it weren't possible for you to fail that covenant. There is no need. Also, look closely and ask yourself questions about the signs and tokens. I can't talk about that here, but they will teach you and give you the information you need to know about, what you're doing here and what you need to do to prepare to transition to the next world. All of these things are circumscribed in the one whole. There is not one truth up in one corner that's unrelated to a truth in another corner. It's just that one is found in one corner and the other is in the other. They all belong to the same whole. Our job, in a world where things have been placed in chaos because of the Fall, is to take these pieces and pull them together for our benefit and our progress.

It's because of what I see in the temple and what we just talked about, that I believe two things: First, that the great purpose of the millennial world is to beget life. Now, the life that's being begotten in the millennial world is not the same as begetting life in the telestial world, but you are still bringing forth life. The babies that are born in the terrestrial, millennial world are different than the babies that are born in the telestial, mortal state. But, they come about in the same way because the prophets have taught that life is begotten in only one way in all eternity. There is no other way, and it's the way that we are familiar with: with a man and a woman. There is no other way in all eternity, that life is begotten.

I'm going to give you my opinion here; this is Mike Stroud chapter 6, verse 3. Have you ever wondered what happened in the United States since 1976, Roe vs. Wade? What happens to the 60 million babies that were aborted? And that's just in the United States! I was in the mission presidency in Mongolia, and my job was to interview women for baptism. One of the questions we ask in the baptismal interview of every woman is if she has ever had an abortion performed. I don't believe there was one person that I interviewed, as a counselor in the mission presidency, not one woman that had not had one abortion. Some of them had had multiple abortions in Mongolia. Worldwide, it's happening to these people. I'm not talking about natural miscarriage that takes place within the first trimester, which is a natural occurrence. I'm talking about after the spirit enters the body, and Brigham Young said that when a woman feels the movement of life, what they call a quickening, that's the spirit entering the body. They talk about that taking place around the beginning of the second trimester which is the beginning of the fourth month. And now we have late term and partial birth abortions, and millions of people who had obtained bodies from God are killed and never have a chance to experience mortal life. It's my opinion that the great millennial world is the place for those children to be born again, to have parentage that loves them and wants them and that no child will be forfeited the opportunity of growing up and experiencing a physical body, from babyhood on up through adulthood. In the millennial world, we know that everyone lives to the age of a tree. Well, that could be anywhere from 100 years minimum to 1,000 years because trees live to be different ages. There are redwood trees that are 1,000 years old. The point is that birth and the beginning of life is going to be, what I believe (and this is Mike Stroud) the number one purpose of the great, millennial world.

Second, with that said then, if that's the number one purpose in the millennial world, then the number one sin that would cause people to forfeit eternal life in the presence of God, would be immorality. Hence, we make a covenant when we enter into the terrestrial, millennial world, that we will have no sexual relations with anyone, but our husband or wife. Any thoughts on that or feelings?

Student 6: That's very interesting!

Mike: It's something to think about.

Student 6: Yes, it is.

Mike: And, you can see why that sin would be so serious. If you violate the law of chastity in this life what do you forfeit? Remember the minimum requirement to inherit a terrestrial world was two things. Number one, you had to be honorable; and number two, you had to be morally clean. Irrespective of your religious upbringing or what your creed or anything you believe, each one of us has a light inside of us, the light of Christ, that teaches that husbands and wives should be faithful to each other and you shouldn't kill another human being, at the bare minimum. Whether you have the law given to you or not, the light of Christ teaches those things at a fundamental level. The sanctity of life and the importance of fidelity between husbands and wives—even Stone Age cultures had a feeling for those two things. So, if you violate the law of chastity as a part of the *Law of the Gospel* and the charge that goes along with it at the Aaronic Priesthood level, you forfeit the world to come, which is the terrestrial, millennial world. Then for those who enter the terrestrial, millennial world and make covenants at the Melchizedek Priesthood level (a higher law because you are in the presence of God) and you violate the law of chastity, you forfeit the next world for you. You will not go into the celestial world, and you will lose eternal life.

Student 4: Genealogy looks like a pretty important thing.

Mike: Absolutely. It's not to say that missionary work, genealogy work, and the work for the dead are not also huge important aspects of the millennial world. I agree with that completely. I think we're going to need the millennial world just to straighten up the mess we've made of genealogical records in this world.

Student 4: That's why it will take a thousand years!

Mike: I'm not taking anything away from that. I'm just adding possibly another dimension. There's been nothing revealed on this. This is simply from pondering and deducing what we see in the temple endowment, why we're doing certain things there, and how things fit. I believe, brothers and sisters, that the temple endowment is a template, a road map. It's giving detailed instruction, in symbolic, allegorical form, on how to successfully complete each stage of our journey back to the Father.

Student 4: Think of those two children in Japan. Think of all the murders that are taking place in those countries.

Mike: I believe that no child will forfeit an experience to have that. The Lord says in section 137 that all children who die before the age of accountability will be heirs and will be saved in the Celestial Kingdom. You see, brothers and sisters, being saved in the Celestial Kingdom is **not** desirable. I know that sounds strange, but salvation without exaltation is damnation. And you are saved in the telestial world, you are saved in the terrestrial world, and you can be saved in the celestial world, but if you're not **exalted** in the celestial world, if you don't have eternal life and the opportunity to have eternal lives then you're in a damned state. It's possible for you to be in the celestial world and be restricted. And restriction, by definition, is the definition of Hell. It's not fiery brimstone and devils and pitchforks and all that garbage of Hollywood. It just means you're under restriction. And you are operating at a disadvantage.

Now, let me just say one more thing as we move on here. In the temple, we hear this phrase, "If any of you desire to withdraw rather than to accept these obligations of your own free will and choice, you may now make it known by raising your hand." We don't think about that, but I believe that that statement is made to every person, in every estate as they move forward, especially as we move into higher estates of existence, higher estates of learning and schooling. I believe that persons are given a chance to stop and say, "I don't desire to move forward or to choose to move forward at a risk." Because every time you progress forward, there's a risk that you can fail what you are about to enter into. For example, in Hebrews, it talks about those who defer the resurrection. This is an interesting thing. Paul teaches that people who have qualified for one level of salvation who could say, "I want to claim what I have merited," can defer that and say, "I don't want to claim what I have merited because I want to hope for something better and more." Do you follow what I'm saying there? So, all along the road, agency plays a vital role in our individual paths. Let me just show you an example in Hebrews chapter 11. The whole 11th chapter is 40 verses long, and it's talking about great persons in the scriptures who exhibited fantastic faith: Joseph, Moses, Abraham and on and on and on. Verse 32 is talking about some of the faithful people mentioned in the *Old Testament*:

> *And what shall I more say? for the time would fail me to tell of Gedeon, and of Barak, and of Samson, and of Jephthae; of David also, and Samuel, and of the prophets:*

For the first 31 verses, he's listed Isaiah and name after name after name of great faithful men and women. Now, look what he says in verse 33, talking about all of these great, faithful people, he says:

> *Who through faith subdued kingdoms, wrought righteousness, **obtained promises**,*

We've talked about obtaining promises. You've got to put all of this in this life now, all in this life. None of this is talking about after death:

> *stopped the mouths of lions,*
> *[34] Quenched the violence of fire, escaped the edge of the sword, out of weakness were made strong, waxed valiant in fight, turned to flight the armies of the aliens.*

Look at all of these things these tremendous people did through faith who had obtained promises. What's the promise? They had their *calling and elections made sure.* They were sealed up to eternal life. They had obtained promises and because of the promises and because they were *made sure*, accompanying that was power to do all these things through the power principle of faith. They'd already passed the action side of faith and were now operating on the power side of faith:

> *[35] Women received their dead raised to life again: and others were tortured, not accepting deliverance;*

Now, stop right there. That means all along the way, all these things we've talked about, turning armies to flight, stopping the mouths of lions, and the fire and all of this stuff; they had the power to be delivered. At any moment, they could have been delivered and stopped that, but it says, *"not accepting deliverance."* They choose not to be delivered but to stay in these fiery trials. Why?

> *That they might obtain a* ***better*** *resurrection:*

Not **A** resurrection, but a **better** resurrection. Now, look at the next scripture, talking about a second group:

> *[36] And others* [a whole new group now] *had trial of cruel mockings and scourgings, yea, moreover of bonds and imprisonment:*
> *[37] They were stoned, they were sawn asunder, were tempted, were slain with the sword: they wandered about in sheepskins and goatskins; being destitute, afflicted, tormented;*
> *[38] (Of whom the world was not worthy:)*

These were wonderful men and women.

> *they wandered in deserts, and in mountains, and in dens and caves of the earth.*
> *[39] And these all, having obtained a good report through faith,* ***received not the promise****:*

The second group did not obtain the promises that the first group did. Now, go to the bottom, Joseph Smith Translation:

> *[40] God having provided some better things for them through their sufferings, for without sufferings they could not be made perfect.*

This group was not as progressed as the first group. They're on their way. They have power, but they have not obtained promises and power over the elements and over life and death. The first group could call down fire from heaven. The second group doesn't have that ability, but they endure in faithfulness, knowing that if they do they can become part of the first group. The first group is what Moroni calls in Moroni chapter 7, *chosen vessels*. And then, Moroni says all the rest of us are referred to as *the residue*. So, you have two groups in Moroni chapter 7, the *chosen vessels* and *the residue*. The *chosen vessels* have power over time and space. They are translated beings. The elements obey them. They speak as though they are God. They have higher orders of the priesthood, and when they have special experiences, they testify to *the residue* of these special experiences. They cast their pearls. For what purpose? Moroni says so that *the residue* may have faith to come up and become part of the *chosen vessels*.

Student 6: So, you are saying that the second group said they wanted to stay and suffer. But I'm wondering why they didn't want the same power to release all of these things from them?

Mike: The second group did not have an option of not accepting deliverance. That was not given to them.

Student 6: Oh, I see.

Mike: The second group is in a state of progress coming up to the first group. The second group had not obtained the promises. They are in the process of progressing to that. So, Paul is telling us about two groups. When you get to the second group, you can choose to defer where you are and move forward hoping for something better. Or, "If any of you do not want to move forward…" you can choose-out at that point and obtain **a**

resurrection from the dead that's fitting for the place where you chose to be comfortable. Does that make sense?
Student 6: Yes, it does.
Mike: But, these people know that there is more available. "If any of you desire to withdraw rather than accept these obligations…" So, at every step, once you pass a judgment, once you have successfully completed a particular portion of your path, all you've done is completed **that** class. There's another class. You're given a choice at that point, "Do you want to stay where you are, or do you want to move forward? If you move forward, the blessings are greater, as also are the challenges and the risk. Some people will just say, "You know what? I'm happy where I am. I'm pleased where I am. I don't think I want to go forward." You'll see a lot people like that in the Millennium, who will have an opportunity to enter into covenants with the saints of God and join their society, who will say, "We like being in your society, but we don't want to be a part of you." And that is in the presence of God, knowing that Christ reigns among His saints and that the power of God is seen, in power and great glory among those who've entered into the covenant. Keep in mind that all of these people that are there, at least at the beginning of the Millennium that are not born into the Millennium at least at the beginning, are coming out of great tribulation. The end of the telestial world is going to be such a horrendous, hellacious experience that these people are going to be glad for law and order. But, they won't want to give up the traditions of their fathers, as children who have inherited lies. And that will stop their progression and they will choose-out, just like we do now brothers and sisters. Everything in this world that you see is a pattern for the coming world.

Well, that's an hour. It's been fun to be with you tonight. I hope that completes our discussion. I'm going to include in your handouts on this lesson a twelve-page document called, "The Teachings Concerning the Terrestrial Glory." This is what the Brethren have said. Oh, by the way, one other experience: I was in church today, and during the Sacrament meeting, the Spirit taught me something that I would like to share with you. The spirit taught me that at this point, right now, July 17, 2016, we are in this world where we were in the premortal life just before the third-part, the sons of perdition were cast out. We are in the same type of situation. The conflict is the same. The controversy is the same. The opportunities to stand up are the same. We are reliving again, what you and I have already been through. This is nothing new, and the controversy, the traps, the snares, the lies, and the deceptions are everything that was used to deceive those in the premortal life, and here we are again. We are about to make a transition. The only difference is that you are experiencing it with a physical body.

In closing, I'd like to read a quote to you by the prophet Joseph Smith:

> *It is the privilege of the children of God to come to God and get revelation...*
> *Salvation cannot come without revelation; it is in vain for anyone to minister without it. ...No man can be a minister of Jesus Christ except he has a testimony of Jesus; and this is the spirit of prophecy.*

Our whole purpose is to rise up, and within our stewardship, become prophets and prophetesses. The Church is trying to point us in the direction where every knowledge and every mystery that exists in eternity, can be revealed to us individually. You have access to that if you will become experienced and more perfect in receiving personal revelation. I share that will you tonight, in the name of Jesus Christ, amen.

References:

D&C 88:21
Moses 1:33
D&C 137:5-8
Joseph Fielding Smith *Doctrines of Salvation*
Melvin Ballard
D&C 14:7
Hebrews 11:32-36
History of the Church, 3:389–90; from a discourse given by Joseph Smith about July 1839 in Commerce, Illinois; reported by Willard Richards.

Teachings Concerning the Terrestrial Glory

D&C 76:

71 And again, we saw the terrestrial world, and behold and lo, these are they who are of the terrestrial, whose glory differs from that of the church of the Firstborn who have received the fulness of the Father, even as that of the moon differs from the sun in the firmament.
72 Behold, these are they who died without law;
73 And also they who are the spirits of men kept in prison, whom the Son visited, and preached the gospel unto them, that they might be judged according to men in the flesh;
74 Who received not the testimony of Jesus in the flesh, but afterwards received it.
75 These are they who are honorable men of the earth, who were blinded by the craftiness of men.
76 These are they who receive of his glory, but not of his fulness.
77 These are they who receive of the presence of the Son, but not of the fulness of the Father.
78 Wherefore, they are bodies terrestrial, and not bodies celestial, and differ in glory as the moon differs from the sun.
79 These are they who are not valiant in the testimony of Jesus; wherefore, they obtain not the crown over the kingdom of our God.
80 And now this is the end of the vision which we saw of the terrestrial, that the Lord commanded us to write while we were yet in the Spirit.
97 And the glory of the terrestrial is one, even as the glory of the moon is one.

Joseph Smith - Poetic Version of D&C 76

53 Again I beheld the terrestrial world, In the order and glory of Jesus, go on; 'Twas not as the church of the first born of God, But shone in its place, as the moon to the sun.
54 Behold, these are they that have died without law; The heathen of ages that never had hope, And those of the region and shadow of death, The spirits in prison, that light has brought up.
55 To spirits in prison the Savior once preach'd, And taught them the gospel, with powers afresh; And then were the living baptiz'd for their dead, That they might be judg'd as if men in the flesh.
56 These are they that are hontrable men of the earth; Who were blinded and dup'd by the cunning of men: They receiv'd not the truth of the Savior at first; But did, when they heard it in prison, again.
57 Not valiant for truth, they obtain'd not the crown, But are of that glory that's typ'd by the moon:
They are they, that come into the presence of Christ, But not to the fulness of God, on his throne.
[Times and Seasons 4:82-85]

Terrestrial Resurrection: Part of the Resurrection of the Just

Joseph Fielding Smith

This other class, which will also have right to the first resurrection, are those who are not members of the Church of the Firstborn, but who have led honorable lives, although they refused to accept the fulness of the gospel. Also in this class will be numbered those who died without law and hence are not under condemnation for a violation of the commandments of the Lord. The promise is made to them of redemption from death in the following words: *"And then shall the heathen nations be redeemed, and they that knew no law shall have part in the first resurrection; and it shall be tolerable for them."* [D. & C. 45:54] These, too, shall partake of the mercies of the Lord and shall receive the reuniting of spirit and body inseparably, thus becoming immortal, but not with the fulness of the glory of God. (Doctrines of Salvation, Vol.2, p.297)

Bruce R. McConkie

Resurrection of life, the first resurrection. Those coming forth in the morning of this resurrection do so with celestial bodies and shall inherit a celestial glory; these are they who are Christ's the firstfruits. Those coming forth **in the afternoon** of this resurrection do so with terrestrial bodies and consequently shall inherit that kingdom; they are described as being Christ's at this coming. All who have been resurrected so far have received celestial bodies; the coming forth of terrestrial beings does not commence until after the Second Coming. (D. & C. 76:50-80; 88:95-99.) [Doctrinal New Testament Commentary, 1:196]

Many in the World Live a Terrestrial Law

John Taylor

One thing we do know; one thing is clearly told us, and that is if we are not governed by the celestial law and cannot abide a celestial law, we cannot inherit a celestial kingdom. What is it to obey a celestial law? Where does the celestial law come from to begin with? From the heavens. Very well. What have the people here to do with it generally -- that is, outsiders? Nothing. They do not say they have had any revelation. They have had no principle of that kind unfolded to them. They are living under what might be termed a terrestrial law; and many of them, I think, under the circumstances, do quite as well as we do under our circumstances. We profess to be moving on a more elevated plane than they are. We profess to have come out from the world; to have separated from the ungodly. We profess to be under the guidance of apostles and prophets, pastors and teachers, etc., and to be living under the inspiration of the Most High. They do not profess anything of the kind. (The Gospel Kingdom, pp.327-328)

These Are They Who Died Without Law
D&C 76:72
Joseph Smith
54. Behold, these are they that have died without law; **The heathen** of ages that never had hope, (Poetic Version)

Joseph Fielding Smith
• Through the mission of Jesus Christ a law has been given, the law of the gospel, and that law is binding upon all those who hear it, who come in contact with it; and provision has been made so that those who are without the law or who have not heard the name of Christ, who are ignorant of the plan of salvation, because the gospel has never reached them in any form, shall not be under the same restrictions and condemnation as will those who have received that law. And they who **are without the law, Christ redeems through his blood, and does not require of them that which he requires of me and of you.** (Doctrines of Salvation, 2:29)
• We read in the Book of Abraham that the Lord revealed that in the world of spirits some of the intelligences were greater than others, and these he made his rulers. Contrariwise **there were those who were less intelligent and evidently less fit for the exaltation offered to the faithful, yet these also were entitled to salvation from death and the torment of the damned**. The Lord therefore had a place for these, thus showing his great mercy for all.

We learn from the word of the Lord to Moses that the Lord selected a place for the children of Israel, even before they were born, thus he indicated the number of spirits who were assigned to become the descendants of Jacob (Deut. 32:8-9). We may well believe that **the Lord also parceled out the surface of the earth for all other peoples. Some of these places were evidently designed for inhabitants who had lost interest in or touch with the plan of salvation. We may well believe that the Lord did not permit the more progressive and more worthy spirits to come to the families of the ungodly and the less progressive peoples of the earth.**

It was the privilege **of this less progressive** class, however, to come to the earth, and it was essential for them to receive the blessings of morality. On this topic, however, there is very little revealed, but we may feel certain that it was **essential that the more progressive and intelligent spirits were not sent to the tribes among the degraded heathen.** These people naturally sank under such circumstances into a condition of ignorance and spiritual darkness. **Children born under such circumstances could not be exalted, yet the Lord in his mercy had decreed to them to do the very best that could be done. Not having knowledge of the things of God, they were to be judged without law and assigned to a place after the resurrection that would be suited to them without the fulness promised to the faithful.**

President Brigham Young, by revelation, received a clear view of this truth and has spoken of those who are without law and understanding in the following words:
"When God revealed to Joseph Smith and Sidney Rigdon that there was a place prepared for all, according to the light they had received and their rejection of evil and practice of good it was a great trial to many, and some apostatized because God was not going to send to everlasting punishment heathens and infants, but had a place of salvation in due time for all, and would bless the honest and virtuous and truthful, whether they belonged to any church or not. It was a new doctrine to this generation, and many stumbled at it." (Journal of Discourses 16:42) [Answers to Gospel Questions, 4:11-13]

Melvin J. Ballard

Now, I wish to say to you that those who died without law, meaning the pagan nations, for lack of faithfulness, for lack of devotion, in the former life**, are obtaining all that they are entitled to.** I don't mean to say that all of them will be barred from entrance into the highest glory. Anyone of them who repents and complies with the conditions might also obtain celestial glory, but **the great bulk of them shall only obtain the terrestrial glory.** (Three Degrees of Glory, p.25

Bruce R. McConkie

Those destined to inherit the terrestrial kingdom are: **(1) those who died "without law" -- those heathen and pagan people who do not hear the gospel in this life, and who would not accept it with all their hearts should they hear it; (2) those who hear and reject the gospel in this life and then accept it in the spirit world; (3) those "who are honorable men of the earth, who [are] blinded by the craftiness of men"; and (4) those who are lukewarm members of the true church and who have testimonies, but who are not true and faithful in all things.** (See D&C 76:71-80.) [A New Witness for the Articles of Faith, p.146]

Orson F. Whitney

There is another class mentioned in sacred writ, for whom, in the language of the Book of Mormon, ***"baptism availeth nothing."*** The "heathen nations," who "died without law," are to be "redeemed without law,' and shall "have part in the first resurrection." These, however, are not heirs celestial. Theirs is "the glory of the terrestrial" in **the great Kingdom of the Future**. (Saturday Night Thoughts, p. 246)

Who Received Not the Testimony of Jesus In the Flesh, but Afterwards Received It D&C 76:73-74

Joseph Fielding Smith

Into this kingdom will go all **those who have lived clean lives, but were not willing to receive the gospel**; also those who have lived clean lives but who, notwithstanding their membership in the Church, were not valiant, and those who refused to receive the gospel when they lived on the earth, but in the spirit world accepted the testimony of Jesus. **All who enter this kingdom must be of that class who have been morally clean.** (Answers to Gospel Questions, Vol.2, p.209)

Spencer W. Kimball

Through the scriptures we have a fairly clear picture of the fate of the people of Noah's day who, like many people today, ignored the testimonies of written scripture and of living prophets. Luke records the words of the Savior: And as it was in the days of Noe, so shall it be also in the days of the Son of man. They did eat, they drank, they married wives, they were given in marriage, until the day that Noe entered into the ark, and the flood came, and destroyed them all. (Luke 17:26-27.) **They were drowned in their sins.** Their marriages were for time. They reveled in worldliness. They were possibly like many in the world today who place no curb upon their eating, drinking and licentiousness. Their ignoring the laws of God and the warning of the prophets continued until the very day when Noah and his family entered the ark. Then it was too late. **Too late!** What finality in that phrase! Following their eternal history, we find Peter telling of them more than two millennia later: For Christ also hath once suffered for sins, the just for the unjust, that he might bring us to God, being put to death in the flesh, but quickened by the Spirit: By which also he went and preached unto the spirits in prison; Which sometime were disobedient, when once the longsuffering of God waited in the days of Noah, while the ark was a preparing, wherein few, that is, eight souls were saved by water. (1 Pet. 3:18-20.)

At last, they had a chance in the spirit world to hear the voice of missionaries and prophets again. But **so** late! What sad words! Nearly a further two millennia passed into history and we hear of them again in modern revelation. Of the vision given to Joseph Smith and Sidney Rigdon in 1832, the Prophet writes: And again, we saw the terrestrial world, and behold and lo, these are they who are of the terrestrial. ... *They who are the spirits of men kept in prison, whom the Son visited, and preached the gospel unto them, that they might be judged according to men in the flesh; Who received not the testimony of Jesus in the flesh, but afterwards received it.* (D&C 76:71, 73-74.)

Too late! The terrestrial for them! It could have been the celestial, and it could have been exaltation! But they procrastinated the day of their preparation. The same lamentable cry of "Too late!" will apply to many of today's Church members who did not heed the warning but who proceeded -- sometimes carelessly, sometimes defiantly -- to bind themselves through mortality to those who could not or would not prepare for the blessings which were in reserve for them.The Lord's program is unchangeable. His laws are immutable. They will not be modified. Your opinion or mine does not alter the laws. Many in the world, and even some in the Church, seem to think that eventually the Lord will be merciful and **give them the unearned blessing**. But the Lord cannot be merciful at the expense of justice. (The Miracle of Forgiveness, pp.248-249) < style="font-family: arial;">

Bruce R. McConkie

• Those who lived in the days of Noah shall again hear the truth, for they, too, are among *"the spirits of men kept in prison, whom the Son visited, and preached the gospel unto them, that they might be judged according to men in the flesh; Who received not the testimony of Jesus in the flesh, but afterwards received it."* (D&C 76:71-80.) Theirs, however, shall be a terrestrial inheritance, and not a celestial, because they rejected the gospel in this life and then received it in the spirit world. (The Mortal Messiah, 4:242)

• In what is probably the greatest of all recorded visions, given February 16, 1832, the Prophet saw that those to whom Noah offered the gospel and who were then destroyed in the flood, assuming they repent and accept the gospel in their spirit prison, shall not obtain celestial rest. Theirs is an everlasting terrestrial inheritance because they rejected the truth when it was offered to them in mortality. ("A New Commandment: Save Thyself and Thy Kindred!" Ensign, Aug. 1976, 9)

• Those who have a fair and just opportunity to accept the gospel in this life and who do not do it, but who then do accept it when they hear it in the spirit world will go not to the celestial, but to the terrestrial kingdom. This includes those to whom Noah preached. *"These are they who are the spirits of men kept in prison, whom the Son visited, and preached the gospel unto them, that they might be judged according to men in the flesh; Who received not the testimony of Jesus in the flesh, but afterwards received it."* (D. & C. 76:72-74.) [Mormon Doctrine, p.686]

Melvin J. Ballard

This revelation clearly informs us that any man or woman, not only those in the days of Noah, who heard the Gospel and rejected it, but in this day any man or woman **who has had a good chance to have heard the Gospel to receive it and embrace it and enjoy its**
blessings and privileges, who lived during their life in absolute indifference to these things, ignoring it, and neglected it, **need not hope or anticipate that when they are dead the work can be done for them and they gain celestial glory. Don't you Latter-day Saints get the notion that a man or woman can live in defiance or total indifference, having had a good chance -- not a casual chance or opportunity -- and when they die you can go and do the work for that individual and have them receive every blessing that the faithful ones are entitled to. If that becomes the doctrine of the Church we will be worse than the Catholics who believe that you can pray a man out of purgatory.** But they charge for it and we don't, so we would be more foolish than they. (Three Degrees of Glory, p.26) <>

These are They Who are Honorable Men of the Earth

D&C 76:75

Joseph Fielding Smith

•If he is willing **to abide by only a portion of the law, and rejects the covenants** which govern in the celestial kingdom, notwithstanding he is honest, virtuous, and truthful, he shall be assigned to the terrestrial kingdom where other honorable men shall be found. (Doctrines of Salvation, 2:28)

• Into the terrestrial will go all those who are honorable, who have been morally clean, but who would not receive the Gospel; also those who die without law. (The Way to Perfection, pp.205-206)

• Into this kingdom will go all those who have lived clean lives, but were not willing to receive the gospel; also those who have lived clean lives but who, notwithstanding their membership in the Church, were not valiant, and those who refused to receive the gospel when they lived on the earth, but in the spirit world accepted the testimony of Jesus. All who enter this kingdom must be of that class who have been morally clean. (Answers to Gospel Questions, Vol.2, p.209)

• They who enter into the terrestrial kingdom, the one higher than the telestial, are the honorable men--the honest, the virtuous, those who have been clean, and yet would not receive the gospel. There will be some others also who will go into that kingdom, but in a general sense **these people will be the honest and honorable, who could not or would not see or receive the gospel of Jesus Christ, therefore they are assigned to the terrestrial kingdom.** (Conference Report, April 1942, p. 27)

Spencer W. Kimball

Those who have been decent and upright and who have lived respectable and good lives will go to a terrestrial kingdom whose glory is as the moon. ("An Eternal Hope in Christ," Ensign, Nov. 1978, p. 72; The Teachings of Spencer W. Kimball, p.48)

George Q. Cannon

Terrestrial glory may be all right for honorable Gentiles, who have not faith enough to believe the Gospel and who do right according to the best knowledge they have; (Conference Report, April 1900, p. 55.)

James E. Talmage

Into the Terrestrial order shall enter those who have failed to lay hold on the privileges of eternal life while in the flesh; "honorable men of the earth" perhaps, according to human standard, yet blinded "by the craftiness" of false teachers, false philosophy, science falsely so called. These shall inherit glory, but not a fulness thereof. (The Vitality of Mormonism, p.287)

Neal A. Maxwell

It must be made clear that those whom the Lord calls the honorable men and women of the earth are not being lumped in with the less than honorable. **The honorable may be blinded by busyness, caught up in other causes, or preoccupied with trivia,** but they do not mock the saints of God nor revile. (Things As They Really Are, p.13)

Alvin R. Dyer

Many noble and great bodies will possess the terrestrial kingdom.... These, for the most part, will be men who, during earth-life existence, sought the excellence of men; and some who gave of their time, talents and endeavors to the ways of man-made ideals of culture, science, and education, but thought not to include God and his ways in their search for a complete life. They received more of the spirit of the world and of the wisdom which men teach.... neglecting that spirit which is of God. (Who Am I, pp. 55253.)

Not Valiant in the Testimony

D&C 76:79

Spencer W. Kimball

The terrestrial kingdom will not be enjoyed by the very wicked, for they shall obtain only the telestial. Neither will the terrestrial be given to the valiant, the faithful, the perfected, for they will go into the celestial kingdom prepared for those who live the celestial laws. But into the terrestrial will go those who do not measure up to the celestial. Speaking of one category of terrestrial people, the Lord says: *"These are they who are not valiant in the testimony of Jesus; wherefore, they obtain not the crown over the kingdom of our God."* (D&C 76:79.) The "unvaliant" Latter-day Saint will find himself there. (The Teachings of Spencer W. Kimball, p.48)

Joseph Fielding Smith

"These are they who are not valiant in the testimony of Jesus; wherefore, they obtain not the crown over the kingdom of our God." These enter into the terrestrial glory. Who are they? All who refuse to receive the fulness of the truth, or abide by the principles and ordinances of the everlasting gospel. They may have received a testimony; they may be able to testify that they know that Jesus is the Christ; but in their lives they have refused to accept ordinances which are essential to entrance into the celestial kingdom. They have refused to live the gospel, when they knew it to be true; or have been blinded by tradition; or for other cause have not been willing to walk in the

light. In this class we could properly place those who refuse to take upon them the name of Christ, even though they belong to the Church; and those who are not willing when called to go forth and preach to a perverse world "Jesus Christ, and him crucified." They may live clean lives; they may be honest, industrious, good citizens, and all that; but they are not willing to assume any portion of the labor which devolves upon members of the Church, in carrying on the great work of redemption of mankind. We have known members of the Church who have gone out in the world and have mingled with those not of our faith, and these members were ashamed to have it known that they were Latter-day Saints. Such persons certainly are not valiant in the testimony of Jesus. The Lord has said: *"Whosoever therefore shall be ashamed of me and of my words in this adulterous and sinful generation; of him also shall the Son of man be ashamed, when he cometh in the glory of his Father with the holy angels"* (Mark 8:38). [Doctrines of Salvation, 2:29

Ezra Taft Benson

Concerning those who will receive the terrestrial, or lesser, kingdom, the Lord said, *"These are they who are not valiant in the testimony of Jesus; wherefore, they obtain not the crown over the kingdom of our God."* (D&C 76:79; italics added.) **Not to be valiant in one's testimony is a tragedy of eternal consequence.** These are members who know this latter-day work is true, but who fail to endure to the end. Some may even hold temple recommends, but do not magnify their callings in the Church. Without valor, they do not take an affirmative stand for the kingdom of God. Some seek the praise, adulation, and honors of men; others attempt to conceal their sins; and a few criticize those who preside over them. Considering some of the challenges which the Church faces currently, and which it will continue to face in the future, three statements of former Church leaders come to mind. President Joseph F. Smith said, ***"There are at least three dangers that threaten the Church within, ... they are flattery of prominent men in the world, false educational ideas, and sexual impurity."*** (Gospel Doctrine, 5th ed., Salt Lake City: Deseret Book Co., 1939, pp. 312-13.) These three dangers are of greater concern today than when they were identified by President Smith. A second statement was a prophecy by Heber C. Kimball, counselor to President Brigham Young. Speaking to members of the Church who had [page 64] come to the Salt Lake Valley, he declared: ***"To meet the difficulties that are coming, it will be necessary for you to have a knowledge of the truth of this work for yourselves. The difficulties will be of such a character that the man or woman who does not possess this personal knowledge or witness will fall. If you have not got the testimony, live right and call upon the Lord and cease not till you obtain it. If you do not you will not stand. ... "The time will come when no man nor woman will be able to endure on borrowed light. Each will have to be guided by the light within himself. ... "If you don't have it you will not stand; therefore seek for the testimony of Jesus and cleave to it, that when the trying time comes you may not stumble and fall."*** (Orson F. Whitney, Life of Heber C. Kimball, Salt Lake City: Bookcraft,

1967, p. 450.) The third statement is from President Harold B. Lee, my boyhood companion and friend, and eleventh President of the Church: *"We have some tight places to go before the Lord is through with this church and the world in this dispensation, which is the last dispensation, which shall usher in the coming of the Lord. The gospel was restored to prepare a people ready to receive him. The power of Satan will increase; we see it in evidence on every hand. There will be inroads within the Church. ... We will see those who profess membership but secretly are plotting and trying to lead people not to follow the leadership that the Lord has set up to preside in this church. "Now the only safety we have as members of this church is to do exactly what the Lord said to the Church in that day when the Church was organized. We must learn to give heed to the words and commandments that the Lord shall give through his prophet, 'as he receiveth them, walking in all holiness before me; ... as if from mine own mouth, in all patience and faith.' (D&C 21:4-5.) There will be some things that take patience and faith. You may not like what comes from the authority of the Church. ... But if you listen to these things, as if from the mouth of the Lord himself, with patience and faith, the promise is that 'the gates of hell shall not prevail against you; yea, and the Lord God will disperse the powers of darkness from before you, and cause the heavens to shake for your good, and his name's glory.' (D&C 21:6.)"* (In Conference Report, Oct. 1970, p. 152.) Now, it seems to me that we have within those three prophetic statements the counsel we need, the counsel that is necessary to stay valiant in our testimony of Jesus and of the work of His church in these troubled times. ["Valiant in the Testimony of Jesus," Ensign, May 1982, pp. 63-64]

Bruce R. McConkie

Now what does it mean to be valiant in the testimony of Jesus? It is to be courageous and bold; to use all our strength, energy, and ability in the warfare with the world; to fight the good fight of faith. "Be strong and of a good courage," the Lord commanded Joshua, and then specified that this strength and courage consisted of meditating upon and observing to do all that is written in the law of the Lord. (See Josh. 1:6-9.) The great cornerstone of valiance in the cause of righteousness is obedience to the whole law of the whole gospel. To be valiant in the testimony of Jesus is to *"come unto Christ, and be perfected in him"*; it is to deny ourselves *"of all ungodliness,"* and *"love God"* with all our *"might, mind and strength."* (Moro. 10:32.) To be valiant in the testimony of Jesus is to believe in Christ and his gospel with unshakable conviction. It is to know of the verity and divinity of the Lord's work on earth. But this is not all. It is more than believing and knowing. We must be doers of the word and not hearers only. It is more than lip service; it is not simply confessing with the mouth the divine Sonship of the Savior. It is obedience and conformity and personal righteousness. "Not every one that saith unto me, Lord, Lord, shall enter into the kingdom of heaven; but he that doeth the will of my Father which is in heaven." (Matt. 7:21.) To be valiant in the testimony of Jesus is to *"press forward with a steadfastness in Christ, having a perfect brightness of hope, and a love of God and of all men."* It is to *"endure to the end."* (2 Ne. 31:20.) It is to live our religion, to practice what we preach, to keep the commandments. It is the manifestation of "pure religion" in the lives of men; it is visiting "the fatherless and widows in their affliction" and keeping ourselves *"unspotted from the world."* (James 1:27.) To be valiant in the testimony of Jesus is to bridle our passions, control our appetites, and rise above carnal and evil things. It is to overcome the world as did he who is our prototype and who himself was the most valiant of all our Father's children. It is to be morally clean, to pay our tithes and offerings, to honor the Sabbath day, to pray with full purpose of heart, to lay our all upon the altar if called upon to do so. To be valiant in the testimony of Jesus is to take the Lord's side on every issue. It is to vote as he would vote. It is to think what he thinks, to believe what he believes, to say what he would say and do what he would do in the same situation. It is to have the mind of Christ and be one with him as he is one with his Father. Our doctrine is clear; its application sometimes seems to be more difficult. Perhaps some personal introspection might be helpful. For instance: Am I valiant in the testimony of Jesus if my chief interest and concern in life is laying up in store the treasures of the earth, rather than the building up of the kingdom? Am I valiant if I have more of this world's goods than my just needs and wants require and I do not draw from my surplus to support missionary work, build temples, and care for the needy? Am I valiant if my approach to the Church and its doctrines is intellectual only, if I am more concerned with having a religious dialogue on this or that point than I am on gaining a personal spiritual experience? Am I valiant if I am deeply concerned about the Church's stand on who can or who cannot receive the priesthood and think it is time for a new revelation on this doctrine? Am I valiant if I use a boat, live in a country home, or engage in some other recreational pursuit on weekends that takes me away from my spiritual responsibilities? Am I valiant if I engage in gambling, play cards, go to pornographic movies, shop on Sunday, wear immodest clothes, or do any of the things that are the accepted way of life among worldly people? If we are to gain salvation, we must put first in our lives the things of God's kingdom. With us it must be the kingdom of God or nothing. We have come out of darkness; ours is the marvelous light of Christ. We must walk in the light. ("Be Valiant in the Fight of Faith," Ensign, Nov. 1974, p. 35)

Baptism Not Necessary for Salvation in Terrestrial Kingdom

Joseph Smith

Every man lives for himself. Adam was made to open the way of the world, and for dressing the garden. Noah was born to save seed of everything, when the earth was washed of its wickedness by the flood; and the Son of God came into the world to redeem it from the fall. But except a man be born again, he cannot see the kingdom of God. This eternal truth settles the question of all men's religion. A man may be saved, after the judgment, in the terrestrial kingdom, or in the telestial kingdom, but he can never see the celestial kingdom of God, without being born of water and the Spirit. He may receive a glory like unto the moon, [i.e., of which the light of the moon is typical], or a star, [i.e., of which the light of the stars is typical], but he can never come unto Mount Zion, and unto the city of the living God, the heavenly Jerusalem, and to an innumerable company of angels; to the general assembly and church of the Firstborn, which are written in heaven, and to God the judge of all, and to the spirits of just men made perfect, and to Jesus the Mediator of the new covenant, unless he becomes as a little child, and is taught by the Spirit of God. (Teachings of the Prophet Joseph Smith, p.12)

Joseph Fielding Smith

The Prophet says a man may enter into the terrestrial or the telestial kingdom who has not been baptized with water and who has not in this life received these ordinances, but he can never enter into the celestial kingdom without complying with these eternal laws. Each kingdom, of course, is governed by laws. **We have nothing to do with the laws of the telestial or terrestrial kingdoms, so far as the preaching of the gospel is concerned. Our mission is to preach the salvation of the kingdom of God, where he and Christ dwell, which is the celestial kingdom. And all of the principles of the gospel which have been given unto us pertain to the celestial kingdom.** (Doctrines of Salvation, 2:25-26)

No Revelation Concerning Ordinances For the Terrestrial and Telestial Kingdoms

Joseph Fielding Smith

• Will those who enter the terrestrial and telestial kingdoms have to have the ordinance of baptism? No! Baptism is the door into the celestial kingdom. The Lord made this clear to Nicodemus. We are not preaching a salvation for the inhabitants of the terrestrial or the telestial kingdoms. **All of the ordinances of the gospel pertain to the celestial kingdom**, and what the Lord will require by way of ordinances, if any, in the other kingdoms he has not revealed. (Doctrines of Salvation, 2:329)

• The First Presidency have said in answer to a similar question: **"We know of no ordinances pertaining to the terrestrial or the telestial kingdom. All of the ordinances of the gospel are given for the salvation of men in the celestial kingdom and pertain unto that kingdom."** (Doctrines of Salvation, 2:330)

Terrestrial Resurrection Limited in Powers and Progression

Joseph Fielding Smith

In both the terrestrial and the telestial glories the inhabitants thereof will be limited in their powers, opportunities, and progression, because, like the sons of perdition, "they were not willing to enjoy that which they might have received. (Doctrines of Salvation, 2:22

Shall Be Ministered to By Celestial and Shall Minister to the Telestial

Joseph Fielding Smith

Yet, through his abundant mercy, the Lord will do for all the best that can be done, and therefore he will give to all a place somewhere -- if not within the gates of the Holy City, then it must be on the outside -- where those who are not entitled to the fulness of blessings may be ministered to by those who have greater glory. For we read also here in this vision, where the glories are spoken of, **that those who dwell in the celestial kingdom shall minister unto those of the terrestrial kingdom; those in the terrestrial kingdom shall minister to those of the telestial kingdom.** The Son may go to the terrestrial, but they who enter into that kingdom shall not receive the fulness of the Father; they will not see the greatness of his glory. He withholds that from them. They never come back again into the fulness of his presence. Those who enter into the telestial kingdom will not receive the fulness of the Father or of the Son. They will not visit there but will send messengers to visit the inhabitants of that glory and instruct them.

Those in the terrestrial kingdom shall visit those in the telestial kingdom, and those of the celestial shall visit those in the terrestrial kingdom. Where the Father is these cannot come, for the Lord has said: *"Where God and Christ dwell they cannot come, worlds without end."* Yet in this very same section it is written that notwithstanding this fact, so great shall be the blessings that come to those who enter there that it is beyond our comprehension. Such is the great mercy of the Lord. **He will endeavor to save all his children and exalt as many as he possibly can.** (Doctrines of Salvation, 2:5)

Dallin H. Oaks

The next higher degree of glory, the terrestrial, *"excels in all things the glory of the telestial, even in glory, and in power, and in might, and in dominion"* (D&C 76:91). The terrestrial is the abode of those who were the *"honorable men of the earth"* (D&C 76:75). Its most distinguishing feature is that those who qualify for terrestrial glory *"receive of the presence of the Son"* (D&C 76:77). Concepts familiar to all Christians might liken this higher kingdom to heaven because it has the presence of the Son. ("Apostasy and Restoration,"Ensign, May 1995, p. 86)

ABOUT THE AUTHOR

Mike Stroud was born March 1944 to Walt and Eileen Stroud in Salt Lake City, Utah. He attended BYU and received a BA and MA degree.

He is trained in Outdoor Survival and Primitive Living, and has spent a lifetime in the outdoors as a hunter, tracker, and outdoorsman.

Mike enjoys training horses and has spent many years exploring wild places on horseback. He is a western history lover and re-enacts the mountain man era, and the old west.

He served a mission to Bavaria, Germany, and he and Margie have served missions together in Mongolia, Central Philippines, and in New Jersey.

Mike has spent his lifetime as a teacher, working 27 years in The Church of Jesus Christ of Latter-day Saints Church Education System. He retired from CES in 2006.

Mike and Margie reside in Eagar, Arizona. He is the father of 12 children, 29 grandchildren, and 7 great-grandchildren.

90826032R00162

Made in the USA
Lexington, KY
15 June 2018